W9-BFW-310

SCRIPTURE

SCRIPTURE

AN ECUMENICAL INTRODUCTION
TO THE BIBLE AND ITS INTERPRETATION

MICHAEL J. GORMAN, EDITOR

BS
475.3
S37
2005

© 2005 by Hendrickson Publishers, Inc.
P. O. Box 3473
Peabody, Massachusetts 01961-3473

ISBN 1-56563-927-8

All rights reserved. No part of this book may be reproduced or transmitted in any form or by any means, electronic or mechanical, including photocopying, recording, or by any information storage and retrieval system, without permission in writing from the publisher.

Printed in the United States of America

First Printing — August 2005

Except where otherwise noted, Scripture quotations are from the New Revised Standard Version of the Bible, copyright © 1989 by the Division of Christian Education of the National Council of the Churches of Christ in the United States of America, and are used by permission.

Cover Art: Donald J. Forsythe. "Fiery Furnace, 1994." Gouache monotype over unique paper pulp painting (29 inches in height by 21¾ inches in width). From the *Pilgrimage Series.* Courtesy of the collection of Dr. Crystal and Dr. David Downing. Photo Credit: Donald J. Forsythe. Used with permission.

The design for the first page of each chapter features a miniature image of the first page of Genesis from the Leningrad Codex, shown larger on page 106. (Photograph by Bruce and Kenneth Zuckerman, West Semitic Research with the collaboration of the Ancient Biblical Manuscript Center. Courtesy Russian National Museum [Saltykov-Shchedrin])

Library of Congress Cataloging-in-Publication Data

Scripture : an ecumenical introduction to the Bible and its interpretation /
    Michael J. Gorman, editor.
        p. cm.
    Includes bibliographical references and index.
    ISBN 1-56563-927-8 (alk. paper)
    1. Bible—Introductions. I. Gorman, Michael J., 1955–
    BS475.3.S37 2005
    220.6′1—dc22
                     2005010789

Contents

Introduction

MICHAEL J. GORMAN

This book would not have been possible to write or edit even fifty years ago. Today, despite their ongoing differences, Christians of different churches and traditions work, study, and pray together more than ever. The interpretation of the Bible, whether as a means of spiritual nourishment or as an exercise in professional academic scholarship (or both), is an ecumenical enterprise and a means of growth toward Christian unity. For this, we should all be grateful to God. The contributors hope that this book both reflects and extends those realities.

The idea for this book emerged from the experience of several professors in the Ecumenical Institute of Theology at St. Mary's Seminary and University in Baltimore. We had been teaching a new course, Orientation to Biblical Studies, and had never found quite the right introductory text to complement a text on methods of biblical analysis and interpretation (exegesis). "Why not write our own?" quickly became a kind of rhetorical question. This book, then, is the result: an attempt to introduce beginning theological students, and the interested general public, to the Bible. It has several unique features.

First, the contributors are current or former members of the faculty of St. Mary's Ecumenical Institute of Theology, known as the "E.I." The E.I. was founded in 1968 as a division of St. Mary's Seminary and University in order to offer accredited graduate-level theological education to people of all faith traditions. Currently there are some thirty Christian traditions represented within the student body of three hundred mostly part-time adult learners. This student body consists of people from Roman Catholic, Baptist, Presbyterian, Methodist, Episcopal, Lutheran, Orthodox, Mennonite, evangelical, nondenominational, and other churches. Approximately thirty-five percent of the students are African-American, largely from African Methodist Episcopal (A.M.E.), Baptist, and Pentecostal churches. The contributors have naturally had this kind of diverse audience in view in the process of writing the book. Like our students, our readers will no doubt be diverse, and we bring to the task of producing an introduction to the Bible a unique sensitivity to various ways of being Christian and of reading the Bible.

Second, as one might imagine, the Ecumenical Institute of Theology faculty is also diverse, representing an equally interesting array of churches and traditions. This book is one fruit of a collaborative effort among a truly ecumenical group of scholars who work together year in and year out to create a rich educational and theological experience highlighting both the diversities and the commonalities of the various Christian traditions. In addition, one member of our faculty (and of the contributors) is a Jewish rabbi with a PhD in early Christianity, representative of our commitment both to good scholarship and to Jewish-Christian relations.

Third, given the nature of their teaching experience at the Ecumenical Institute, the contributors understand the difficulties that face a student encountering the Bible in an academic setting for the first time. We have made every effort to walk students slowly and carefully through the major topics and issues in the study and interpretation of the Bible both as a collection of ancient writings and as a living word from God.

Having said all this, however, we cannot quite be "all things to all people." For example, there is no chapter on the interpretation of the Bible in Hispanic churches, largely because our own student body has few Hispanic students and our faculty currently has no Hispanic professors. Furthermore, there is no chapter on, say, specifically Lutheran or Presbyterian approaches to Scripture. We have had to be broader than that to keep the book focused and its length under control.

Some may wonder, therefore, why there is a separate chapter on the interpretation of the Bible in African-American churches when African-American Christians are Protestant, Catholic, or Orthodox, and there are chapters devoted to the interpretation of the Bible in these traditions. The answer to this is that besides reflecting the constituency of our institution, it reflects the reality that Scripture has had a distinctive role in African-American churches that transcends church and denominational lines.

The book is divided into two main parts, the first addressing the character, composition, and formation of the Bible itself in its historical context, and the second exploring the ways in which Christians have interpreted the Bible during the last two thousand years, with some attention to Jewish interpretation as well. Unless otherwise indicated, the Bible text used in this book is the New Revised Standard Version (NRSV).

In addition to the text of the sixteen chapters, each chapter concludes with a list of materials for further reading and study, and the entire book ends with a glossary and a subject index. (Glossary terms are set in boldface type the first time they appear in the book.) References within each chapter refer to books and articles in the bibliography for that chapter.

This book is intended as a companion to *Elements of Biblical Exegesis: A Basic Guide for Students and Ministers,* written by the editor of the present book and also published by Hendrickson Publishers. One helpful way to use the books together is to (1) study part one of the present book first to become acquainted with the Bible itself; (2) work carefully through *Elements of Exegesis* to learn the basics of careful biblical analysis; and then (3) read part two of this book to see how others have interpreted, and do interpret, the Bible.

The contributors owe an immense debt of gratitude to each and every person who read various versions of these chapters. In addition to our fellow contributors, we especially wish to thank all recent students in Orientation to Biblical Studies, especially Lyle Brecht, plus Fr. Gregory Matthewes-Green, Robert A. Kraft, Elizabeth Patterson, John Riches, Jane-Adair Seleski, and others.

The editor would like to thank four members of the Ecumenical Institute of Theology staff who assisted with proofreading and indexing, Judy Langmead, Patty Rath, Zenaida Bench, and Theresa Jesionowski, and one who helped with the selection of photos, Patty Rath. They are dear friends, too.

Contributors

Rev. Michael L. Barré, SS is Professor of Sacred Scripture at St. Mary's Seminary and University. A translator for the New American Bible and a former President of the Catholic Biblical Association, he has taught Hebrew and Old Testament at the Ecumenical Institute of Theology. He earned his PhD from The Johns Hopkins University.

Carole C. Burnett is Staff Editor of The Fathers of the Church series, published by The Catholic University of America. A Roman Catholic, she also teaches early and medieval church history at the Ecumenical Institute of Theology, and she has taught at Wesley Theological Seminary. Dr. Burnett's PhD is from The Catholic University of America, and her research and scholarly papers are in the field of patristics.

Rev. John R. Donahue, SJ was from 2001 to 2004 the first Raymond E. Brown Distinguished Professor of New Testament at St. Mary's Seminary and University (now Emeritus), after holding several previous major teaching posts. In addition to teaching courses in New Testament and ethics at the Ecumenical Institute of Theology, for three years (1999–2002) he wrote a regular commentary on the Sunday lectionary readings for *America* magazine. For many years he has conducted workshops in the United States and abroad on biblical topics such as social justice. Fr. Donahue is the author of many articles and several books, most recently (with Daniel Harrington) *The Gospel of Mark* in the Sacra Pagina commentary series and, earlier, *The Gospel in Parable: Metaphor, Narrative, and Theology in the Synoptic Gospels* and *What Does the Lord Require? A Bibliographical Essay on the Bible and Social Justice.* His PhD is from the University of Chicago.

Patricia D. Fosarelli is the pastoral associate at a Catholic parish in Baltimore and teaches spirituality and practical theology at the Ecumenical Institute of Theology, where she is also the Assistant Dean. She has published books and articles in the field of medicine as well as spirituality and ministry. Dr. Fosarelli earned her MD from the University of Maryland Medical School and her DMin from Wesley Theological Seminary.

Stephen Fowl is Professor of Theology and Chair of the Department of Theology at Loyola College in Maryland. An Episcopalian, he has taught courses in biblical studies at the Ecumenical Institute of Theology. Among his numerous publications are the book *Engaging Scripture* and forthcoming commentaries on both Philippians and Ephesians. He earned his PhD at the University of Sheffield in England.

Michael J. Gorman is Professor of New Testament at St. Mary's Seminary and University, where he is also Dean of the Ecumenical Institute of Theology. Among his books are *Elements of Biblical Exegesis* and two on the Apostle Paul. A United Methodist, he earned his PhD at Princeton Theological Seminary.

Edwin C. Hostetter teaches religious studies at several Baltimore-area colleges and Hebrew Bible at the Ecumenical Institute of Theology. A Methodist, he is the author of numerous encyclopedia articles and a textbook for biblical Hebrew. He received his PhD from The Johns Hopkins University.

Rev. C. Anthony Hunt was Executive Director of the Multi-Ethnic Center for Ministry of the Northeastern Jurisdiction of the United Methodist Church before becoming a District Superintendent in the Methodist Church. His publications include books on ministry in the African-American community and on Rev. Dr. Martin Luther King Jr. At the Ecumenical Institute of Theology, he teaches African-American studies and practical theology. His DMin is from Wesley Theological Seminary, and his PhD from the Graduate Theological Foundation.

Rev. Janyce C. Jorgensen is pastor of a congregation of the Evangelical Lutheran Church of America. She teaches Scripture, ecumenical relations, and religious education at the Ecumenical Institute of Theology. Her PhD is from the Catholic University of America.

Rabbi Shira Lander is the scholar-in-residence at the Beth Tfiloh Dahan Community High School in Baltimore. She teaches courses on early Christianity, Judaism, and Jewish-Christian relations at the University of Maryland Baltimore County and at the Ecumenical Institute of Theology. Her PhD is from the University of Pennsylvania.

Rev. David A. Leiter pastors a Church of the Brethren congregation in central Maryland. He teaches courses in the Hebrew Bible/Old Testament at the

Ecumenical Institute of Theology, and he has published articles in that field. He received his PhD from Drew University.

Karen J. Wenell earned her PhD in New Testament studies at the University of Glasgow in Scotland. An Anglican, she has taught New Testament at the Ecumenical Institute of Theology and at several institutions in Scotland. She has special research interests in the lands of the Bible.

Very Rev. Ronald D. Witherup, SS is the Provincial of the U.S. Province of the Society of St. Sulpice. He formerly taught New Testament at the Ecumenical Institute of Theology. A prolific writer, he has published books and articles on the Gospels, Paul, Catholic approaches to Scripture, and fundamentalism. Fr. Witherup earned his PhD at Union Theological Seminary in Richmond, Virginia.

Rev. Paul P. Zilonka, CP is Associate Professor of Biblical Studies at St. Mary's Seminary and University. He teaches courses in both Testaments at the Ecumenical Institute of Theology. His SSL is from the Pontifical Biblical Institute, and his doctorate is from the Gregorian University.

Abbreviations

GENERAL ABBREVIATIONS

AV	Authorized Version (King James Version)
B.C.E.	Before the Common Era (alternative to B.C.)
C.E.	Common Era (alternative to A.D.)
DSS	Dead Sea Scrolls
LXX	Septuagint (Greek translation of the Hebrew Bible/ Old Testament)
NAB	New American Bible
NIV	New International Version
NRSV	New Revised Standard Version
NT	New Testament
OT	Old Testament

BIBLICAL BOOKS

Hebrew Bible/Old Testament (excluding the Deuterocanonical/ Apocryphal books)

Gen	Genesis
Exod	Exodus
Lev	Leviticus
Num	Numbers
Deut	Deuteronomy
Josh	Joshua
Judg	Judges
Ruth	Ruth
1–2 Sam	1–2 Samuel

1–2 Kgdms	1–2 Kingdoms (LXX)
1–2 Kgs	1–2 Kings
3–4 Kgdms	3–4 Kingdoms (LXX)
1–2 Chr	1–2 Chronicles
Ezra	Ezra
Neh	Nehemiah
Esth	Esther
Job	Job
Ps/Pss	Psalms
Prov	Proverbs
Eccl (or Qoh)	Ecclesiastes (or Qoheleth)
Song (or Cant)	Song of Songs (Song of Solomon, or Canticles)
Isa	Isaiah
Jer	Jeremiah
Lam	Lamentations
Ezek	Ezekiel
Dan	Daniel
Hos	Hosea
Joel	Joel
Amos	Amos
Obad	Obadiah
Jonah	Jonah
Mic	Micah
Nah	Nahum
Hab	Habakkuk
Zeph	Zephaniah
Hag	Haggai
Zech	Zechariah
Mal	Malachi

Deuterocanonical books/Apocrypha and Septuagint

Add Dan	Additions to Daniel
Add Esth	Additions to Esther
Bar	Baruch
Bel	Bel and the Dragon
Ep Jer	Epistle of Jeremiah
1–2 Esd	1–2 Esdras
Jdt	Judith
1–4 Macc	1–4 Maccabees
Pr Azar	Prayer of Azariah

Pr Man	Prayer of Manasseh
Ps 151	Psalm 151
Sg Three	Song of the Three Young Men
Sir	Sirach/Ecclesiasticus
Sus	Susanna
Tob	Tobit
Wis	Wisdom of Solomon

New Testament

Matt	Matthew
Mark	Mark
Luke	Luke
John	John
Acts	Acts
Rom	Romans
1–2 Cor	1–2 Corinthians
Gal	Galatians
Eph	Ephesians
Phil	Philippians
Col	Colossians
1–2 Thess	1–2 Thessalonians
1–2 Tim	1–2 Timothy
Titus	Titus
Phlm	Philemon
Heb	Hebrews
Jas	James
1–2 Pet	1–2 Peter
1–2–3 John	1–2–3 John
Jude	Jude
Rev	Revelation

Part One

The Bible

Chapter 1

The Bible as Book and as Library

PAUL P. ZILONKA

The title of this book contains within it two ways of referring to its subject matter: **Scripture** and the **Bible.** The first, Scripture, sometimes used in the plural (the Scriptures), comes from the Latin for "writings" (*scriptura*); this in turn corresponds to a common way of referring to sacred writings in **Greek:** *hai graphai* ("the writings"). The second, Bible, comes from the Greek word for "book," *biblion.* What we are about to explore, then, is a book, or collection, of sacred writings. For this reason, people of faith sometimes call this book the "Sacred Scriptures" or the "Holy Bible."

Although many people use the terms "Bible" and "Scripture" interchangeably, as we will do, the two terms can suggest different nuances of meaning. For instance, many religious traditions have sacred texts, or "scriptures," but only Judaism and Christianity refer to their scriptures as "the Bible." Ironically, however, some people feel that the term "Bible" is more religiously neutral, and perhaps more academic, than the term "Scripture," with its connotation of holiness or divine inspiration.

In this and the following chapters, we will attempt to look at the Bible, or Scripture, from both an academic perspective and a faith perspective. That is to say, we want to understand it both as a human book and as a sacred text, emphasizing the former in part one, which focuses on the Bible itself, and the latter in part two, which is concerned with the Bible's interpretation, especially in the Christian churches. Our investigation begins with a consideration of the Bible as both book and library.

THE BIBLE AS BOOK

As we have just noted, the English word "Bible" originated from the Greek term for "book" (*biblion*), which is derived from the Greek word for the **papyrus** plant (*biblos*). Egyptian craftsmen produced an ancient version of paper by matting together strips of this marshland plant. The dried sheets of papyrus were then glued together in rolls to become a **scroll.** Jeremiah 36 gives a colorful example of how the invention of these materials contributed greatly to the development of the Bible:

> In the fourth year of King Jehoiakim, son of Josiah of Judah, this word came to Jeremiah from the Lord: Take a scroll [Greek *chartion bibliou*] and write on it all the words that I have spoken to you against Israel and Judah and all the nations, from the day I spoke to you, from the days of Josiah until today. (Jer 36:1–2)

Baruch, Jeremiah's secretary, refers to the process: "He dictated all these words to me and I wrote them with ink on the scroll [Greek *en bibliō*]" (v. 18). Even though the angry king burned the document "until the entire scroll was consumed in the fire" (v. 23), Jeremiah dictated another with "all the words of the scroll that King Jehoiakim of Judah had burned in the fire, and many similar words were added to them" (v. 32). From this biblical passage, it is relatively easy to understand the transition from writing on *papyrus* (Greek *biblos*) to naming the finished product a *book* (Greek *biblion*).

Ordinarily, only one side of a papyrus scroll contained writing. (The heavenly visions in Ezekiel and in Revelation specifically mention writing on both sides of the papyrus as a sign of an extraordinary, supernatural message: Ezek 2:10; Rev 5:1.) Scrolls were the ordinary instrument for preserving and reading the sacred texts in synagogues; locating a particular passage required some dexterity with large scrolls. The Gospel of Luke describes the scene in the Nazareth synagogue when "the scroll of the prophet Isaiah was given to [Jesus]. He unrolled the scroll and found the place where it was written: 'The Spirit of the Lord is upon me . . .' " (4:16–17).

Papyrus was not the only material on which ancient writers inscribed texts. After animal skins were thoroughly cleaned and stitched together, they served the same purpose as the more costly papyrus, which only grew in certain regions (e.g., Egypt, Galilee) and thus often had to be imported. The abundance of sheep and goats in Palestine provided a steady source of durable scrolls called **parchment** (Greek *membrana*). Scribes who produced the collection of Jewish manuscripts (from around the time of Jesus) that scholars today call the **Dead Sea Scrolls** (DSS) used these animal skins, which were durable enough to survive after more than 1,900 years in clay jars.

In Roman times, writing tablets with wax surfaces were framed and hinged together along one edge. Since the frames were made of wood (Latin *caudex*), the set of writing tablets was called a **codex.** This arrangement allowed for writing on both sides. (It was the precursor of the modern book.) Soon sheets of papyrus or parchment were sewn together at the "spine." By the second century

The first page of the Gospel of John from 𝔓66 (Papyrus Bodmer II), the earliest
relatively complete manuscript of that Gospel, dating from ca. 200 C.E.
(Courtesy Fondation Martin Bodmer, Cologny, Switzerland)

C.E.,[1] the books of the Christian Bible were recorded exclusively in this kind of
codex, while the Jewish community retained the scroll format. The practicality
and economy of a portable document with writing on both sides was eminently
suited to the rugged missionary lifestyle of Christian evangelists, and the codex
helped Christians to think of their various sacred texts as constituting one book.

THE BIBLE AS ONE BOOK

Most people come to the reading of the Scriptures with some preconcep-
tions about what they are. Since they are often described by one, singular title—
"the Bible"—and since, like most other books, the Bible has a front and back
cover, it is understandable that so many people think of the Bible simply as
one book. A quick glance at the titles in the Table of Contents might give the

---

[1] Abbreviation for "Common Era" (i.e., the shared Christian and Jewish era), a
scholarly alternative to "A.D."

impression that the Bible is one book with many chapters. Likewise, religious believers confidently speak of the whole Bible as the "word of God." This familiar heartfelt expression of faith significantly reinforces the idea that God is the one author of everything contained in its unified pages. And, to be sure, the Bible does tell one grand story of God's love for humankind, which theologians have tried to summarize in such biblical words as grace, salvation, the kingdom of God, or **covenant.**

However, even after spending only a little time paging through the dozens of individual sections of the Bible, we discover great diversity in writing style and content, suggesting many different human authors and objectives. In addition, the dates implied in these texts range from the beginning of the world to what seems like its end in the not-too-distant future. This variety of historical epochs suggests long periods of use and reinterpretation of earlier documents.

Honestly recognizing the complexity of the Bible as a diverse collection prepares us to experience both why it is a treasure of great spiritual value and why it also requires careful study. In fact, the Bible attests to its own diversity.

THE BIBLE AS MANY BOOKS

The Bible clearly indicates that it contains other books within itself. Frequently, the Bible refers to the "book of the law of Moses" (2 Kgs 14:6) or the "book of Moses" (Mark 12:26). Mention is also made of other specific documents, such as the "book of the words of the prophet Isaiah" (Luke 3:4; cf. 4:17), the "book of the prophets" (Acts 7:42), the book of "Hosea" (Rom 9:25) and the "book of Psalms" (Acts 1:20).[2]

The Gospel of John also refers to itself as a "book" (John 20:30; Greek *biblion*). Likewise, the author of the Acts of the Apostles tightly knits that document to the story about Jesus that the same person had presented "in the first book" (or "account"; Greek *logon*), namely the Gospel according to Luke (Acts 1:1; cf. Luke 1:1–4).

This little journey of discovery alerts us to the truth that the Bible is not really just one book. In fact, we can speak quite appropriately of it as a "library of books."

---

[2] The Bible also refers to other books that, though not included in the Bible itself, were apparently used as sources for the composition of some biblical texts. This phenomenon is mostly associated with descriptions of the deeds of the Israelite monarchy; for example, there is the "Book of the Acts of Solomon" (1 Kgs 11:41), as well as the "Books of the Annals of the Kings of Israel" (1 Kgs 14:19) and the "Book of the Annals of the Kings of Judah" (1 Kgs 14:29). There is a similar phenomenon in the NT. Luke 1:1–4 makes mention of more than one previous narrative of what Luke also intends to write as an "orderly account" (v. 3).

THE BIBLE AS A LIBRARY

In a library, individual books are usually organized according to particular topics. There are sections for science, philosophy, religion, history, art, music, biography, fiction, etc. An educated person has certain expectations about what information would be contained in the books grouped in these various sections of the library. Since library books are not generally organized by the dates they were written, two books by two authors who lived twenty centuries apart can stand side by side. For example, we might find a philosophical work by Plato (430–347 B.C.E.) on the same shelf as a commentary on that work by a modern philosopher and published just last year. Despite the vast difference of time, both books focus on the same literature of Plato. We benefit greatly when we read both works together, even though they were written more than two millennia apart.

In the Bible, individual books containing material spanning many decades (in the case of the **New Testament**) or even many centuries (in the case of the **Old Testament**) are joined together in collections. For example, the first five books in the Jewish collection (the Christian Old Testament) are usually associated with Moses, whose story links four of them (all but Genesis) together, yet the books were not written at the same time. Other books from different periods are grouped together because of their association with the ministry of individual Hebrew prophets. A smaller group of writings from various centuries concerns itself with provocative topics of a general nature, such as the challenge of belief in a God of love and justice while believers live in a world where innocent people suffer and their oppressors prosper. The book of Psalms gathers together 150 hymns written over many centuries. **Gospels** attributed to four different Christian authors stand side by side, even though many factors, including date of composition, distinguish them from one another. The same is true of letters by various Christian missionaries. The profound religious relationship among all of these writings from various time periods is not always immediately evident.

The diversity in the Bible with respect not only to date, but also to literary **genre** (type), is thus quite remarkable. As the previous paragraph suggests, the Bible contains historical works, prophetic books, quasi-philosophical writings, hymns, biographies (the Gospels[3]), and letters. There are also legal documents, short stories, collections of proverbs, sermons, records of visions, and other kinds of literature. Within each of these kinds of books, we find numerous additional literary forms, such as the well-known parables.

---

[3] The Gospels may be understood as ancient, not modern, biographies.

Having all the books of the Bible gathered together between two covers of one book makes them all available to us at the same time. Even though they have much in common with one another, we should never forget that each book has its own history of development and its own unique perspective. Despite some strong literary ties among them, most of the books in the Bible are quite independent of one another, just like the books in any other kind of library.

IN SEARCH OF A NAME

What's in a name? We are all sensitive to people who misspell or mispronounce our personal names. Thus, people of Jewish and Christian faith who cherish these collections of religious books are justifiably sensitive to the names other people use to designate their sacred writings. For example, **Jews** organize their 39 books into three collections that they call **Torah** ("tradition" or "law"), **Nevi'im** ("prophets") and **Kethuvim** ("writings"). The whole library of Jewish documents taken together is called **TaNaK, or Tanakh,** which simply vocalizes an acronym formed from the initial **Hebrew** letter of each collection: **T, N,** and **K.**[4] Jews may also call this collection simply "the Bible" or "the Scriptures." Christians usually refer to it as "the Old Testament" or "the Christian Old Testament" (see further discussion below). Some Christians and biblical scholars who prefer a more neutral term than "Old Testament" designate these same documents as the **Hebrew Bible,** since most of the collection was originally written in Hebrew, though there are several portions in **Aramaic,** the language that gradually replaced spoken Hebrew after the **Babylonian exile** (587–539 B.C.E.).[5]

The cessation of Hebrew as a spoken language and the rise of the empire under Alexander the Great (356–323 B.C.E.)—which spread Greek culture, religion, and language—threatened the religious and cultural heritage of Jews scattered around the Mediterranean and further East.[6] Under these circumstances, Jews had to find a way to preserve their sacred text for a new cultural and linguistic reality.

---

[4] Alternate transliterations for the second and third divisions are Nebi'im and both Ketuvim and Kethubim; for the whole, Tanak.

[5] Dan 2:4b–7: 28; Ezra 5:3–6:14; Jer 10:11. "B.C.E." means "Before the Common Era."

[6] While we today take for granted that the Bible should be translated into every language of the earth so that its message might be accessible to all, this was a new idea two millennia ago. Indeed, even today the Qur'an in its original Arabic is the sole norm for Muslim worship and scriptural study, no matter what the nationality or ethnic background of those who embrace Islam. Only recently has the Roman Catholic Church authorized its worship in vernacular languages after Latin prevailed generally for 1,500 years in the Latin Rite churches.

The Septuagint (LXX)

About 250 B.C.E., Greek-speaking Jewish inhabitants of Alexandria in Egypt took the bold step of translating their Hebrew scriptures into Greek. The *Letter of Aristeas* (written around 120 B.C.E.) offers a defense for the evolution of the Greek translation that came to be known as the **Septuagint** (a Latin expression for "seventy"). This name and its customary abbreviation, LXX (the Roman numerals for 70), stem from the sacred legend, recorded in the *Letter of Aristeas,*[7] that seventy Jewish scholars produced the translation independently of one another under the inspiration of God and without any error or confusion. Although scholars today provide a more nuanced theory for the growth of the Septuagint as a long-term process, the existence of this Greek translation facilitated the popular acceptance of other inspirational Jewish books written in Greek rather than in Hebrew. These include the Wisdom of Solomon, Judith, Baruch, the Letter of Jeremiah, 1–2 Maccabees, and some short Greek additions to Esther and Daniel. (Today, these books are included in some Christian Bibles, but not in the Jewish Bible; see the tables below and the discussion in chapters three and six.)

Jesus read from the Hebrew Scriptures in the synagogue of Nazareth, but soon after his death and resurrection disciples like Paul of Tarsus evangelized Jews, converts to Judaism ("proselytes"), and non-Jews in many Greek-speaking cities of the Mediterranean world. The Christian church was born with a "Bible" in its cradle, namely, the Greek Septuagint. The twenty-seven Christian documents that came out of that period of growth of the early church are treasured today as the New Testament. They were originally written in Greek, and when those documents quote from the Jewish Scriptures, they clearly demonstrate a preference for the LXX version rather than the original Hebrew text.

Old Testament, New Testament

The Christian Bible has two divisions, or **testaments.** As noted above, Christian tradition designates the books of Tanakh with the term "Old Testament" in light of the customary name of its own collection of twenty-seven documents as the "New Testament"—from a Latin word (*testamentum*) that can mean "covenant."[8] The literary and theological relationship between the Jewish

---

[7] A second-century B.C.E. Jewish document considered to be one of the OT pseudepigrapha (see chapter five).

[8] Henceforth in this book, Old Testament and New Testament are generally abbreviated OT and NT.

and Christian collections—the two parts of the Christian Bible—explains both the origin and the significance of these related titles.

"Covenant" (Hebrew *berît;* Greek *diathēkē*) is one of the most significant concepts in the experience of Jewish and Christian faith. This important term links together the salvation stories associated with Noah, Abraham, Moses, David, and Jesus. Indeed, the collections of Jewish and Christian writings arose over centuries as the respective communities described, commented upon, and propagated the realities of successive covenants. When Jer 31:31 speaks of God establishing a "new covenant with the house of Israel and the house of Judah," the foundation was laid in the minds of later generations for some new revelation that would add to what was not yet present in the former experiences of covenant. Thus, the Christian writings characteristically refer to the "Scripture(s)" (Tanakh) being "fulfilled," that is, brought to completion in some new way by a person or event in Christian experience (e.g., John 19:24, 36; cf. Luke 24:27, 44–45).

As if to echo the words of Jeremiah, in the Gospel tradition Jesus explicitly refers to the "new covenant in my blood" (Luke 22:20; cf. 1 Cor 11:25). Paul speaks of old and new covenants (2 Cor 3:6, 14). Even more explicitly alluding to Jer 31:31, the Letter to the Hebrews contrasts the former covenant with Israel with the Christian experience of Jesus as mediator of a "better" (7:22; 8:6), and "new" (9:15) covenant.

So as to address a perceived disparaging tone in the comparison of "old" and "new" covenants, academic scholars and Christians concerned about Jewish-Christian dialogue sometimes suggest more neutral terms such as Two Testaments, though this still involves speaking of the **First Testament** and the **Second Testament.** In reality, the Christian Bible "shares" the Tanakh with the continuing religious community of Judaism today as one of its two parts. Even Augustine's assertion, centuries ago, that the New Testament lies hidden in the Old and the Old is made manifest in the New, supports this "shared" understanding of the Hebrew Scriptures. One Christian scholar, Philip Cunningham, suggests rewording Augustine's formula in this way: "In the Shared Testament, the rabbinic texts and the Christian Testament find their perpetual foundations; in the Christian Testament, the Shared Testament is intensely read anew in Christ" (*Sharing the Scriptures,* p. 18).

Perhaps sensitivity is best exercised by taking into account the religious context of discussion. Differing Jewish and Christian titles such as Tanakh, Old Testament, and New Testament make eminent sense within their respective faith communities. These terms do have a biblical basis for their origin and usage. The use of these tradition-specific terms, even in scholarly discussion, acknowledges how the diverse faith groups have traditionally thought of their own documents.

CANONS

A collection of sacred texts forms a standard or norm for a particular religious community. The Jewish and Christian communities use the term **canon** (Greek *kanōn*) for their respective official lists of individual books they consider inspired and sacred. The root meaning of this term is "measuring stick"; hence, the canon is the standard that guides a tradition's belief and behavior. (Though a *canon* of biblical books is quite different from a *cannon* used in military combat, biblical canons have led to a lot of heated debate over the centuries.) As chapter six explains in some detail, each faith community had its own process and criteria for the inclusion or exclusion of individual books in their different lists.

Jewish practice since at least the rabbinic era includes twenty-four books in Tanakh (thirty-nine as counted in the Christian Bible), while Christian practice since the late fourth century includes twenty-seven books in the NT.[9] But Christian Bibles contain different numbers of books in their OTs. Students who come to the Bible for the first time often ask why the Protestant, Catholic, and Orthodox Bibles do not agree on the number of books in the OT. A glance at the various canons of Jewish writings in the list provided in the table clarifies the matter. While the Roman Catholic Church follows the (longer) Septuagint list as the basis for its OT, churches that follow the Reformation of the sixteenth century have opted to use the (shorter) Hebrew canon as the basis for their translations. They designate the additional Septuagint books written in Greek the (OT) **Apocrypha,** from the Greek word for "concealed" or "hidden." Catholics acknowledge the inspired status of these books but designate them the **deuterocanonical** ("secondarily canonized") books because they were not originally included in Jerome's Latin **Vulgate** translation of OT books that had been the official Bible of the church from the fourth to the sixteenth centuries. Many ecumenical editions of the Christian Bible contain the apocryphal/deuterocanonical books in recognition of their canonical status for Catholic and Orthodox Christians, and in order that others may consult them. The following tables exhibit the various canons of the OT/Hebrew Bible:

---

[9] There are minor exceptions. A small part of the Syrian Orthodox tradition (the Nestorian Church) has never accepted the books of 2 Peter, 2–3 John, Jude, and Revelation, and the Ethiopic Church's "broader" NT canon has 35 books (compared to its "narrower" 27–book canon).

The Jewish Scriptures (24 Books)		
Torah	**Prophets**	**Writings**
Genesis	Joshua	Psalms
Exodus	Judges	Proverbs
Leviticus	Samuel (1–2)	Job
Numbers	Kings (1–2)	Song of Songs (Song of Solomon)
Deuteronomy	Isaiah	Ruth
	Jeremiah	Lamentations
	Ezekiel	Ecclesiastes
	The Twelve	Esther
	Hosea	Daniel
	Joel	Ezra-Nehemiah
	Amos	Chronicles (1–2)
	Obadiah	
	Jonah	
	Micah	
	Nahum	
	Habakkuk	
	Zephaniah	
	Haggai	
	Zechariah	
	Malachi	

The Protestant Old Testament (= the Jewish Bible counted as 39 books)		
Pentateuch	**Historical and Poetic Books**	**Prophetic Books**
Genesis	Joshua	Isaiah
Exodus	Judges	Jeremiah
Leviticus	Ruth	Lamentations
Numbers	1–2 Samuel	Ezekiel
Deuteronomy	1–2 Kings	Daniel
	1–2 Chronicles	Hosea
	Ezra	Joel
	Nehemiah	Amos
	Esther	Obadiah
		Jonah
	Job	Micah
	Psalms	Nahum
	Proverbs	Habakkuk
	Ecclesiastes	Zephaniah
	Song of Songs (Song of Solomon)	Haggai
		Zechariah
		Malachi

The Orthodox Old Testament (= the Jewish Bible in the LXX + ca. 10 additional LXX books [in italics])		
Historical Books	**Poetic and Didactic Books**	**Prophetic Books**
Genesis	Psalms (incl. Ps. 151)	Hosea
Exodus	Job	Amos
Leviticus	Proverbs	Micah
Numbers	Ecclesiastes	Joel
Deuteronomy	Song of Songs (Song of Solomon)	Obadiah
Joshua	*Wisdom of Solomon*	Jonah
Judges	*(Wisdom of) Sirach*	Nahum
Ruth		Habakkuk
1–2 Kingdoms (1–2 Samuel)		Zephaniah
3–4 Kingdoms (1–2 Kings)		Haggai
1–2 Chronicles		Zechariah
1 Esdras		Malachi
2 Esdras (Ezra, sometimes also Nehemiah)		Isaiah
Nehemiah		Jeremiah
Esther (with the six additions)		*Baruch*
Judith		Lamentations
Tobit		*Letter of Jeremiah*
1–3 Maccabees		Ezekiel
		Daniel[10]
		Also:
		4 Maccabees, in an appendix
		Prayer of Manasseh, in an appendix
		3 Esdras in Slavonic Bibles of the Russian Orthodox Church, in an appendix

---

[10] Including the Prayer of Azariah and the Song of the Three Jews, Susanna, and Bel and the Dragon.

The Catholic Old Testament (= the Jewish Bible [plus minor additions] + 7 deuterocanonical books [in italics] = 46 books)		
Pentateuch	**Historical and Wisdom Books**	**Prophetic Books**
Genesis	Joshua	Isaiah
Exodus	Judges	Jeremiah
Leviticus	Ruth	Lamentations
Numbers	1–2 Samuel	*Baruch* (incl. *Letter of Jeremiah*)
Deuteronomy	1–2 Kings	Ezekiel
	1–2 Chronicles	Daniel[11]
	Ezra	Hosea
	Nehemiah	Joel
	Tobit	Amos
	Judith	Obadiah
	Esther (incl. the six additions)	Jonah
	1–2 Maccabees	Micah
		Nahum
	Job	Habakkuk
	Psalms	Zephaniah
	Proverbs	Haggai
	Ecclesiastes	Zechariah
	Song of Songs (Song of Solomon)	Malachi
	Wisdom of Solomon	
	Sirach (Ecclesiasticus)	

---

[11] Including the Prayer of Azariah and the Song of the Three Jews, Susanna, and Bel and the Dragon.

NAMES AND CONTENTS OF BOOKS

While most traditional names or titles of biblical books may offer some limited information about the contents of the book, many do not. The names arose in various ways.

Sometimes the titles of individual books of the Bible come from the first word of the book. For instance, the name of the first book in Tanakh is *Bereshith,* from the first word in Hebrew (meaning "in the beginning" of something). Christians usually refer to this same book with the Septuagint title "Genesis," which is not a translation of *Bereshith* but a reference to the initial story of the "*generations* of the heavens and earth when they were created" (Gen 2:4). The last book in the NT begins with the Greek word *apokalypsis,* giving rise to the naming of the book as **Apocalypse** when transliterated, or as "Revelation" when translated into English.

At other times, the title of a biblical book designates a collection of similar items, such as the book titled Psalms, which contains 150 examples of the same type of literature. While there is a variety of psalms (e.g., praise, lament, thanksgiving), they all follow the general format of a hymn written in poetic **parallelism,** or "thought rhyme."

Often, the name of a biblical book bears relation to the principal character in the book, such as Hosea or Amos, or to the alleged author of the work, such as Matthew, Mark, Luke, and John. However, a name does not immediately settle the question of authorship, or of content. Names can be misleading in a number of ways. For instance, the Acts of the Apostles is not really about the "twelve apostles." Rather, it focuses principally on Peter, one of the original Twelve, and Paul, the apostle to the Gentiles, who was not part of the original group of Twelve with Jesus.

The content of individual books ranges from the words and ministry of individual prophets, such as Jeremiah, to the grand panorama of Israelite history sketched in 1 and 2 Kings. The apostolic letters attributed to Paul, James, Peter, and John give insight into the early decades of the Christian community. On the other hand, Ecclesiastes deals with issues of good and evil that transcend any particular century of human history and even the limited boundaries of specific religious groups.

It is obvious that a book's title is not always the key to understanding the full scope of what may lie between its covers. For instance, the Song of Songs does not discuss music, nor is it a hymn itself (though it may have been composed from the lyrics of some local wedding songs). Rather, the repetition of the word "song" in the title expresses the superlative degree in Hebrew. A more accurate translation of the title would be "The Greatest Song."

The titles of groups of biblical books may also be somewhat misleading. For example, the first five books of the Hebrew Bible are grouped under the Hebrew term *torah,* which is best translated as "tradition." In Christian writings, under the influence of the LXX translation of *torah* into Greek as *nomos* ("law"), this same group of books is referred to as "law." We would expect a modern library with a section devoted to "law" to be stocked with materials on legal matters for the sake of lawyers, judges, and other interested persons. While at least four of the five books of the *torah* do contain some "laws," much more is present there, making it inaccurate to think of those books as if they were simply legal codes. Rather, "the law" begins by reflecting on the origins of the earth and the human family before extolling the family traditions of Israel's ancestors.

Finally, a word about the section "subheads" that appear in many Bibles within the text itself. Apart from the brief letter that Paul the apostle wrote to Philemon, and some of the other letters in the NT, most books in the Bible today cover many pages in length. We are accustomed to using the editorial headings that divide each book into smaller, more manageable portions to help us follow the development of the story, or to call our attention to significant topics, such as "The Ten Commandments" or "The Baptism of Jesus." However, these are not part of the biblical text, and it is important to realize that these good efforts to help readers may reflect modern concerns or the perceptions of translators and editors more than the intentions of the original authors.

Chapters and Verses

When we write a letter to a friend, we do not usually group the paragraphs into "chapters." Nor do we number the sentences as "verses." If we did so, people might think us a bit pretentious or odd. But that is precisely what we find when we open our Bible to read Paul's letters to the Romans or Galatians. Paul would most certainly have considered that behavior as unusual as we do today. He wrote in a straightforward fashion with passion and powerful rhetorical skill. But hundreds of years later, practically every sentence of his letters, and the rest of the Bible, had become so important in church debates that it became convenient to number them in order to keep straight which verse the debaters were talking about.

Historical Development

Divisions in biblical manuscripts had a rich history even before the rise of the current system that has held sway for the past five hundred years. Early Jewish and Christian religious leaders and scholars divided the books of the Bible into sections according to various methods. Our modern system of chapter divisions dates back to the Middle Ages and Stephen Langton (d. 1228), a lecturer at the University of Paris working with the Latin Bible, or Vulgate. His system was diffused more widely through a **concordance** (alphabetical index) to the Latin Vulgate that was produced by Cardinal Hugo of St. Cher (d. 1263). Gradually, the same system was used with Bibles in other languages.

But it would be another two hundred years before the further subdivision of the text into verses started appearing in various ways. In 1440, Rabbi Isaac Nathan numbered verses in the Hebrew Bible for his Hebrew concordance. However, Robert Stephanus (Estienne) was the first person to issue the whole Bible (including the Apocrypha) with the current system of verses in his edition of the Latin Vulgate at Geneva in 1555.

The use of punctuation to separate chapters and verses in biblical references has varied over time and still varies around the world. The standard form in the United States now is to divide chapter and verse by means of a colon (e.g., Gen 1:1, referring to the first verse of the first chapter of Genesis [Genesis 1]), though occasionally a period is used (e.g., Gen 1.1). It is also standard practice to indicate a continuous passage (set of verses) with a hyphen (e.g., Gen 1:1–3, referring to the first three verses of Gen 1) and to separate a list of noncontinuous verses with commas (e.g., Gen 1:1, 3, 5, referring to verses 1, 3, and 5 of Gen 1).[12]

Modern Uses and Cautions

Some people familiar with the Bible can quote "chapter and verse." This is an advantage for locating a familiar or beloved text quickly, such as Psalm 23, which begins, "The Lord is my shepherd." In the case of a psalm, dividing a short section of Scripture into verses is not a great problem because a psalm is generally a short unit unto itself with a clear beginning and ending. The parallelism, or "thought rhyme," characteristic of Hebrew poetry often quite naturally divides the thoughts from one another. But when a letter of Paul with a complicated theological discussion (such as Rom 9–11 or 1 Cor 12–14) is chopped into chapters and verses, the modern divisions often do not respect Paul's original line of thought. (See, for example, 1 Cor 11:1, which is actually the conclusion to chapters 8–10!) Such inappropriate divisions of the text may significantly interfere with our correct comprehension and interpretation of a biblical text.

The medieval chapter divisions occasionally correspond appropriately to movement within the biblical text, such as Matt 5:1, when Jesus goes up the mountain to teach. But the subsequent division of this "Sermon on the Mount"

---

[12] There is also a variety of abbreviations for the biblical books; U.S. scholarly standards are provided in the front of this book.

into chapters two more times (as Matt 6 and 7) makes it clear that the traditional system is primarily of utilitarian value and should not dissuade us from searching out the more intrinsic points of division within each biblical document in the course of our study.

Modern attention to the narrative and rhetorical quality of biblical documents enhances our appreciation of the literary skill of the original authors. The study of the narrative character of biblical documents gives attention to the natural progression of the story line in the document and may clearly indicate divisions in the text that do not coincide with traditional chapter and verse divisions. Modern commentators emphasize literary elements within the text, such as movement from place to place, repetition of the same idea at a later time, and shifts in content and tone. Consequently, outlines in modern commentaries (and even in study Bibles) regularly disagree with traditional chapter and verse divisions.[13]

Conclusion: "We Are Here to Serve You"

Libraries are so vast and specialized that we would be foolish to think we could navigate a new one easily. That is why we often need the assistance of a librarian to locate quickly the information we are seeking.

What is the role of the contributors to this book? We are like librarians who have some familiarity with what you can discover in the Bible. Our goal is to help you find your own way. You may have many questions as you begin your biblical study, and we will provide answers to some of them. But, like any library, the Bible contains answers to many questions you have not yet imagined. We hope to point you in the direction of some of those interesting questions and answers.

One cannot judge a book by its cover, nor understand its contents solely by looking at its title. One must be ready to sit down with it for a while before being able to understand what importance it might hold. This ecumenical introduction to the Bible will help you find your way around the library of the Bible. A good study Bible prepared by a team of scholars—such as *The HarperCollins Study Bible, The Catholic Study Bible,* or *The New Interpreter's Study Bible*—is also a helpful resource. But when all is said and done, you can only know the breadth and depth of Sacred Scripture by taking the time to read through its many books reflectively.

---

[13] Readers who have a computer version of the Bible may wish to test their own ability in analyzing the structure of biblical texts. They can print out a few chapters of Exodus or Romans or Matthew, deleting the customary chapter and verse numbers. They can then set about trying to discover the inner dynamic of the biblical passages without the distraction of the later editorial divisions. This little experiment often gives new insight into familiar passages, as well as others that are less widely known.

For Further Reading and Study

Aageson, James W. *In the Beginning: Critical Concepts for the Study of the Bible.* Boulder, Colo.: Westview, 2000. A collection of sixteen short essays introducing critical thinking about the Bible, the interpretation of biblical texts, and the role of the Bible in religious communities.

Barrera, Julio Trebolle. *The Jewish Bible and the Christian Bible: An Introduction to the History of the Bible.* Translated by Wilfred G. E. Watson. Leiden: Brill/ Grand Rapids: Eerdmans, 1998. An interdisciplinary discussion of the formation of the Hebrew Bible and of the authoritative Christian and Jewish texts it generated.

Brown, Michael Joseph. *What They Don't Tell You: A Survivor's Guide to Biblical Studies.* Louisville: Westminster John Knox, 2000. A popular introduction to the academic approach to Scripture and to the integration of that approach with the Christian faith.

Coote, Robert B., and Mary P. Coote. *Power, Politics and the Making of the Bible: An Introduction.* Minneapolis: Fortress, 1990. A study of the Bible in its relation to the larger history of the biblical and early Christian period from 1250 B.C.E. to 550 C.E.

Cunningham, Philip. *Sharing the Scriptures.* A Stimulus Book, vol. 1. Mahwah, N.J.: Paulist, 2003. A booklet on the role of the Bible in Jewish-Catholic relations.

Metzger, Bruce, and Michael Coogan, eds. *The Oxford Companion to the Bible.* New York: Oxford University Press, 1993. A useful, encyclopedia-like, one-volume reference work with articles on such topics as books and bookmaking in antiquity, chapter and verse divisions, the canon, covenant, and much more.

Riches, John. *The Bible: A Very Short Introduction.* Oxford: Oxford University Press, 2000. A brief, popular account of the formation of the Bible as canonical literature with particular emphasis on the history of interpretation over the past 2,000 years.

Rogerson, John. *An Introduction to the Bible.* New York: Penguin, 1999. A survey of the history and composition of the books of the OT and the NT, including contemporary issues of the Bible's relationship to matters such as science, the life of Jesus, and fundamentalism.

————, ed. *The Oxford Illustrated History of the Bible.* Oxford: Oxford University Press, 2001. A beautifully crafted history of the composition and interpretation of the Bible.

SOME RECOMMENDED STUDY BIBLES

The Catholic Study Bible, edited by Donald Senior et al. New York: Oxford University Press, 1990.

The HarperCollins Study Bible, edited by Wayne A. Meeks et al. New York: Oxford, 1993.

The Jewish Study Bible, edited by Adele Berlin and Mark Zvi Brettler. New York: Oxford University Press, 2004.

The New Interpreter's Study Bible, edited by Walter Harrelson. Nashville: Abingdon, 2003.

Chapter 2

The Geography, History, and Archaeology of the Bible

KAREN J. WENELL

This chapter deals not so much with biblical texts and their *content*, but rather with their *context*, the world in which they may be situated. The biblical texts we now have were written over the course of hundreds of years and come from a certain part of the world—the **Ancient Near East** and the **Mediterranean Basin.** Our goal in this chapter will be to introduce the relationship between the texts of the OT and NT and the contexts of the biblical world to which they belong. The focus will be on **Palestine,** since that is the locus of almost all events associated with the OT and the NT Gospels. We will also briefly consider areas west of Palestine (Asia Minor, Greece, and Italy) to which early Christianity spread.

One way to illustrate the connections between geography, history, and archaeology is to propose *land* as an important element for all. That is, geography deals with how *land* may be mapped, noting different regions, topography, and climate. In terms of history, *land* may be designated as the particular area where certain events are known to have taken place. Archaeology entails excavating the *land* itself in order to find traces of past societies—material culture—showing how different peoples lived in the past. In terms of biblical texts, when God first promises a *land* to the descendants of Abram (Gen 12:7), this is not a "scientific" description (verifiable in light of geographical, historical, or archaeological evidence) but rather symbolizes the beginning of a relationship of God-people-land. Here, *land* is a "promised land" and part of a covenant.

The example of the "promised land" reminds us that the Bible is full of symbolic meanings and descriptions even though it is also concerned with Israel's (and the Christian church's) past. It is perhaps best to think of an ongoing dialogue among the disciplines of geography, history, archaeology, and biblical studies. In different ways, these fields inform one another as scholars from each discipline gather new information, increasing their knowledge of the ancient world in which the biblical texts are situated and in which the biblical authors accomplished their—primarily religious—purposes.

A NOTE ON TERMINOLOGY: LAND AND PEOPLE THEN AND NOW

There is some potential confusion when it comes to distinguishing the ancient world from modern entities (such as Israel and Palestine). Related to this is the question of how to refer to the people who belong to that part of the world, both then and now. The following definitions correspond to their use in this chapter and throughout the book:

- *The Ancient Near East*—Mesopotamia (the land between the Tigris and Euphrates Rivers), Egypt, and Israel of the ancient world. The kingdom of Assyria was located in the north of Mesopotamia, Babylonia in the south.

- *Mediterranean Basin*—The lands surrounding the Mediterranean Sea—Asia, Africa, and Europe—where Greco-Roman cultures thrived in antiquity.

- *Roman Empire*—The military, political, and legislative entity that grew out of the Roman Republic (governed by an oligarchy, the Senate) and began with the establishment of the first emperor, Octavian, in twenty-seven B.C.E.

- *Asia Minor*—The peninsula (roughly equivalent to modern Turkey) that has as its northern border the Black Sea, on its western side the Aegean Sea, and to the south the Mediterranean Sea.

- *Palestine*—The name of the territory from the Mediterranean Sea to the Jordan Valley and from Galilee in the north to the Negev (or Negeb) in the south; it is derived from the Hebrew word for "land of the Philistines" and dates from the fifth century B.C.E. Generally, this is the preferred scholarly designation as it encompasses a broad definition.

- *Israel*—The "promised land" of the Hebrew Bible; the name refers in biblical texts both to a geographical region (the extent and meaning of which varies from era to era) and to the nation/people residing there.

- *Hebrews*—The ancestors of the Israelite nation (Abraham and Sarah to Moses).

- *Israelites*—The people of God from Moses to the exile.

- *Jews*—The descendants of the Israelites after the exile; derived from the Hebrew term for Judeans

- *Israelis/Palestinians*—Modern peoples living within the region of ancient Palestine.[1]

MAP AND GEOGRAPHY OF THE ANCIENT NEAR EAST AND THE MEDITERRANEAN BASIN

There are many maps we could draw to illustrate the lands that relate to the Bible. For instance, within Palestine itself we could show a map of the twelve tribes, David's kingdom, the divided kingdom (Israel and Judah), the Hasmonean conquests, or political boundaries (e.g., Judea, Samaria, Galilee) at the time of Jesus. In addition to this, we could depict the areas of Egypt, the Sinai Peninsula, and Babylonia, which relate to Israel's exodus and exile, or of Asia Minor and Europe, which relate to the missionary journeys of Paul. Each of these would relate to a different historical era and to different biblical texts. The list could go on, suggesting maps for different areas and different eras of history, such as may be found in a Bible atlas. For purposes of simplification, we will include on pages 26–27 just one map that shows some of the places relevant to the Bible across historical eras. Places change, as do their names, but the purpose of the conglomerate map is to give a relative picture of certain places in relationship to the wider geographical region (which has even different names today).

Palestine

Ancient Palestine is located within the Fertile Crescent, the area of arable land stretching from the Nile Valley at the southeast coast of the Mediterranean Sea to the Persian Gulf, making a curved or crescent shape around the Syrian desert along the way. Within Palestine itself, there are five main geographical regions[2]: the coastal plain, the central hills, the Jordan Valley, the plateau of Jordan, and the deserts. The Sea of Galilee and the Dead Sea are the major bodies of water within Palestine. Starting just north of Lake Huleh (itself just north of the Sea of Galilee),

---

[1] Adapted in part from Bandstra, *Reading the Old Testament.*

[2] Five regions will be discussed, though it should be noted that another region is also discernible: the Shephelah (Hebrew for "lowlands"). This is a small area separating the coastal plain and the central hills in the southern region of Palestine. Lachish is the major city of the Shephelah region (see map and table of major events).

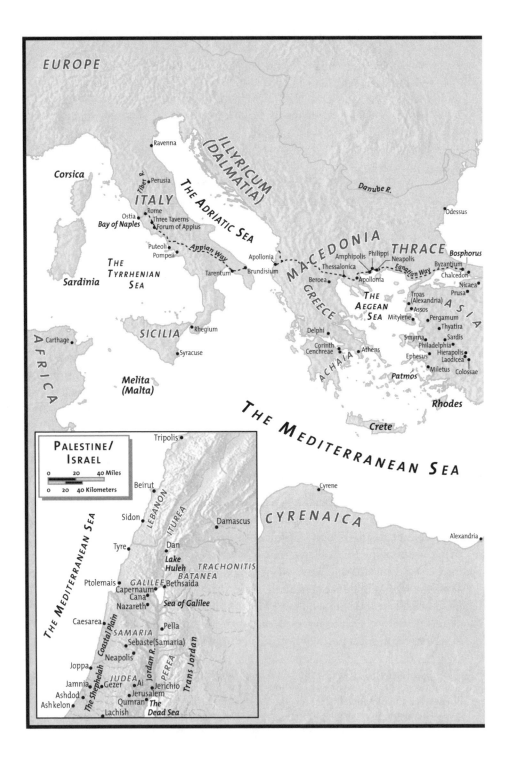

THE ANCIENT NEAR EAST
&
THE MEDITERRANEAN BASIN

- • City
- ----- Roman road
- ----- King's Highway

0   100   200 Miles

0   100   200 Kilometers

THE BLACK SEA

THE CASPIAN SEA

Cyrus R.

Lake Seyan
•Artaxata

Araxes R.

Lake Van

Lake Urmia

BITHYNIA & PONTUS

ASIA MINOR
(ANATOLIA)

GALATIA

•Ancyra

Halys R.

CAPPADOCIA

Antioch in Pisidia•

PISIDIA •Iconium

Lystra•

PAMPHYLIA •Derbe
•Perga   Tarsus•   Issus•
Attalia•

Seleucia•   CILICIA

•Edessa
•Carrhae (Harran)

Europus (Carchemish)

Euphrates R.

Nineveh•

ASSYRIA
MESOPOTAMIA

Tigris R.

BABYLONIA

PERSIA

CYPRUS •Salamis

Paphos•

SYRIA

Tripolis•

Syrian Desert

•Dura-Europos

Syrian Antioch•

PHOENICIA

Sidon•
Dan•   •Damascus
Tyre• •Caesarea Philippi
Ptolemais•
ISRAEL •Tiberias
Caesarea Maritima• •Scythopolis
Sebaste•
Joppa• JUDAH
Gaza• •Jerusalem
•Masada
Negev •Dead Sea
IDUMEA 'EDOM
Pelusium•   •Petra

Seleucia•
•Babylon

THE PERSIAN GULF

FOR DETAIL
SEE INSET

Jordan R.

King's Highway

•Memphis

Elath•

EGYPT
•Oxyrhynchus

Sinai Peninsula

Gulf of Suez

Aqabah Gulf

ARABIA

Nile R.

THE RED SEA

N

©2005 CHK AMERICA WWW.MAPSUSA.COM

the Jordan River winds southward between the two seas. There are other rivers in Palestine, many of which are seasonal, existing only when there is sufficient rain or melting of snow. As our aim is to discuss both text and context, we will include some relevant biblical examples as we describe each region.

The Coastal Plain

The coastal plain includes an ancient international highway known as the *Via Maris* ("way of the sea"). This road extended from Egypt through Palestine along the Mediterranean Sea all the way around the Fertile Crescent to Mesopotamia. Isa 9:1 mentions the Via Maris and the time when it will be made "glorious." The Coastal Plain in Palestine extends 125 miles from Gaza in the south to Lebanon in the north. The Philistines, who were enemies of the Israelites, were located in the southern part of the Coastal Plain area, in the Negev (a semidesert region) on the southern border.

The Central Hills

This area is probably the most important geographic region of Palestine. Generally speaking, it is located to the east of the Coastal Plain and runs about 180 miles from Galilee in the north to Sinai in the south. It includes highlands (in Judea, Samaria, and Galilee), valleys, and plains. In Galilee, for instance, a valley (east-west) divides Lower Galilee from Upper Galilee, whose elevations differ by approximately one thousand feet. Locations in Lower Galilee are mentioned frequently in the Gospels (e.g., Nazareth, Capernaum, Cana). After the second Jewish revolt (132–135 C.E.), the areas of both Upper and Lower Galilee were important for both Jews (the rabbis) and the early Christians. Also within this region, about 20 miles west of the northernmost tip of the Dead Sea, is the city of Jerusalem, in which the temple was located.

The Jordan (or Rift) Valley

As we move east again from the Central Hills, there is a dividing feature of the landscape—a depression in the land that runs for about 260 miles between Dan in the north and Elath in the south. Between Lake Huleh (now drained) and the Dead Sea, the Jordan River flows along the Rift Valley. At 1,300 feet below sea level, the point where the Jordan River ends at the Dead Sea is the lowest place on earth. In the NT, John's ministry and baptism of forgiveness took place in and around the Jordan River in Judea (see, e.g., Matt 3:5–6).

The Plateau of Jordan

To the east of the Jordan River, a level plateau running north-south from Damascus to the Aqabah Gulf is appropriately termed the Jordan Plateau. Another major international route called the King's Highway passes through the Plateau of Jordan. In Num 20:17 the King's Highway is mentioned in a message from Moses to the king of Edom. In the story of Joshua's division of the land (Josh 13), the land east of the Jordan River (the Transjordan, or area east of the Jordan River and west of the Syrian Desert) features in the tribal divisions.

Desert

The most easterly region is that of the Syrian desert, which borders on the Plateau of Jordan and reaches north toward Syria as well as eastward into present-day Saudi Arabia. This mostly uninhabited region shapes the arc of the Fertile Crescent to the north and forms a natural barrier, since the desert was not suitable to be traversed by traders or armies.

As we are able to see, the geography of Palestine is highly diverse, so it makes sense that the climate will also vary from region to region. For instance, Jerusalem in the Central Hills region gets approximately twenty-five inches of rain per year, while the Dead Sea in the Jordan Valley gets only about four inches of rainfall. Generally speaking, there are only two seasons in Palestine. Summer lasts from May to October, while winter falls between October and April. The first-century C.E. Jewish historian Josephus notes (*Against Apion* 1.60) that agriculture was the basis of the economy of Palestine in ancient times. This was also true for many surrounding regions.

Asia Minor, Greece, and Italy

Moving westward, we will give a brief overview of some of the areas of the Roman Empire most important to the biblical (NT) context: Asia Minor/ Anatolia (modern Turkey), Greece, and Italy. These regions were part of the Mediterranean Basin, which was divided into provinces during the Roman period. One such province, Galatia, is familiar from Paul's letter to the Galatians. Networks of well-built paved roads made it possible to move throughout the Empire, whether for military or trading purposes. The sea itself may also be considered a "highway" of sorts, and transport by ship would at times have been cheaper than travel by land. As was the case in Palestine, the climate of the Mediterranean Basin has two seasons—summer and winter—and agriculture was central to its economy.

Asia Minor

The peninsula of Asia Minor (roughly equivalent to modern Turkey), also known as Anatolia ("land of the East"), has as its northern border the Black Sea, on its western side the Aegean Sea, and to the South the Mediterranean Sea. It is about 720 miles in length. Some of the provinces of Asia Minor mentioned in the NT (e.g., Acts 2:9; 1 Pet 1:1) are Cappadocia, Bithynia, Pontus, and Asia (the westernmost Roman province of Asia Minor, not to be confused with the continent of Asia). Galatia is also one of the provinces of Asia Minor, located roughly at the center of the peninsula and containing mountainous regions (in the southern part of the province). The well-known city of Ephesus, a port on the Aegean Sea, was the capital of the Roman province of Asia and also the first of the seven cities (all located in Asia) mentioned in the book of Revelation (chs. 1–3).

Greece

The famous Egnatian Way (*Via Egnatia*) was a major Roman road linking Italy to Asia. It extended from the western coast of Greece (Adriatic Sea) to the Byzantium straits in the east. In Macedonia, a key province in northern Greece, the Egnatian Way passed through the cities of Thessalonica and Philippi. Paul would have traveled along this road on his second missionary journey (Acts 15–18). The cities of Athens and Corinth, both visited by Paul, were located in the province of Achaia, in southern Greece.

Italy

The city of Rome, founded in 753 B.C.E. (traditional dating), became the capital of the Roman Empire and a major center for its administration. Most of the land of Italy is peninsular (separated from mainland Europe in the north by the Alps), and therefore the seas were essential for transportation to and from Italy during the period of Roman rule. On land, the Appian Way (*Via Appia*) extended across Italy from the Bay of Naples to the Adriatic Sea. It is likely that Paul would have traveled along the Appian Way on his journey to Rome (Acts 28:11–15).

MAJOR BIBLICAL EVENTS FROM CA. 1800 B.C.E.
TO CA. 100 C.E.

We will not be able to go into any great detail in describing almost two thousand years of history, but it is nonetheless possible to give a broad overview, taking into account major occurrences that are essential to understanding the world of the Bible—its context. We will proceed in summary fashion, following the table of major periods and biblical events found at the end of this chapter and including references to some of the important archaeological discoveries relating to each period of history.

A portion of the archaeological excavations of Jericho, revealing remains of the famous Canaanite walls that surrounded the city. (Todd Bolen/BiblePlaces.com)

The Ancestral Period, the Exodus, and the Settlement of Palestine (ca. 2200–1000 B.C.E.)

Genesis 1–11 contains fascinating accounts of the origins of the world from creation to the spread of people and language over the earth in the story of the Tower of Babel. The rest of Genesis (chapters 12–50) focuses on Abraham and Sarah and their descendants—the ancestors of the Israelite nation. Because there is no evidence outside the Bible to aid scholars in dating the **Ancestral Period**[3] (the time period from Abraham and Sarah to Moses), there has been much debate over historical placement. For many scholars, finding the best fit between the Genesis narratives and what is known historically means placing the time of the **Hebrews** in the Middle Bronze Age (2200–1550 B.C.E.). Notably, writing was developed in the Ancient Near East during the Middle Bronze Age. The famous Law Code of Hammurabi, which dates to the eighteenth century B.C.E., when Hammurabi was king of Babylonia, has parallels with the laws contained in the Pentateuch.

The next phase of biblical history includes the **exodus** from Egypt and **Conquest,** or **Settlement,** in Israel. This corresponds to the Late Bronze Age through the beginning of the Iron Age (1550–1000 B.C.E.). The earliest mention of Israel

---

[3] It is common to refer to this period as the Patriarchal Period, but the more inclusive term "Ancestral Period" takes into account not only Abraham, Isaac, Jacob, and his twelve sons, but also the important matriarchal figures: Sarah, Rebekah, Rachel, and Leah.

from any material source occurs in the Merneptah stele—a ten-foot-tall black stone slab with an inscribed surface—dating to 1209 B.C.E. This granite stele, found in western Thebes among the remains of the pharaoh Merneptah's funerary temple, is an account of some of the military victories of his rule, which lasted from approximately 1213 to 1203 B.C.E. It is interesting that among defeated Canaanite peoples such as those of Ashkelon and Gezer, which are designated as city-states by an Egyptian hieroglyph on the stele, "Israel" is written along with the hieroglyph used for nomadic peoples. If the end of the thirteenth century B.C.E. were to be fixed as the beginning of Israelite presence in Palestine, this would date the exodus to sometime around the middle of that century, perhaps 1250–1240 B.C.E. However, there are many scholarly debates over the historicity and date of the exodus.

Related to this issue is the dating and history of Israelite settlement in Palestine. Basically, there are two biblical portrayals of the settlement—one in Joshua and one in Judges—and several scholarly theories that attempt to reconcile the portrayals with historical and archaeological evidence. The traditional theory about the settlement follows the accounts in Joshua and argues for decisive military campaigns against various cities and peoples within Palestine. There are, however, difficulties when it comes to correlating this with nonbiblical archaeological evidence. For instance, extensive excavations at Jericho and Ai have not revealed evidence of destruction and occupation to corroborate the biblical accounts. Alternative theories have been offered to explain Israel's origins in Palestine, including the "peaceful infiltration" model, which holds that nomadic peoples gradually settled within the land, and the "peasant revolt" model, which posits that social unrest led to a revolution that promoted "Yahwism" (the worship of **Yahweh/YHWH**).

Regardless of the manner in which the entity "Israel" came to exist in Palestine, the end result was that a tribal people accepted the leadership of various dynamic figures—the "judges"—and gradually moved toward centralization. Archaeological evidence indicates that the population of Palestine increased at the beginning of the Iron Age. Excavations have uncovered houses that had two to four rooms on their lower levels (referred to as "the four-room house"). These served as home to nuclear families and were sometimes arranged in clusters or villages.

The Monarchy, Exile, and Return (ca. 1020–333 B.C.E.)

During the period of the Monarchy (1020–587 B.C.E.), centralization of the tribal people was brought about through the institution of kingship. The stories of Saul (the first king), David, and then Solomon are found in 1–2 Samuel,

1 Kings, and 1–2 Chronicles. Under the leadership of these three important fig-ures, Israelites from north and south were joined together under a **United Mon-archy** (ca. 1020–922 B.C.E.). It was during this time that Jerusalem came to be an important city, both religiously and politically. It became the capital of the king-dom under David and the center of Israelite worship when David's son Solomon built the temple there. The temple housed the formerly mobile entity, the ark of the covenant, the locus of Yahweh's presence with the people. Solomon also or-ganized the construction of a large and lavish palace complex adjacent to the temple site. Unfortunately, because Israel's conquerors later destroyed the temple and other public buildings in the city, there are very few remains that can be positively identified with the Jerusalem of the time of the Early Monarchy.

After the demise of Solomon, Israel and Judah continued as separate entities with their own kings. This period is therefore known as the **Divided Monarchy** (922–721 B.C.E.). By the eighth century B.C.E., Israel in the north was the weaker of the two kingdoms and was defeated when Samaria (which belonged to the northern kingdom) fell to the Assyrian king Sargon II in 721 B.C.E. (2 Kgs 18–25). Some of the inhabitants of the fallen kingdom of Israel migrated to Judah, and the population of Jerusalem expanded at this time. Hezekiah, who was king of Judah from 715–687 B.C.E., took measures to reform cultic practice, the result of which was the bolstering of public worship in Jerusalem.

Archaeology confirms some of the biblical history of this period, particu-larly references to places and topography. To give one example, 2 Chr 32:9 men-tions that forces of the Assyrian king Sennacherib were at Lachish during the time of Hezekiah. The Lachish Reliefs from Sennacherib's palace in Nineveh confirm an Assyrian victory at Lachish in 701 B.C.E. and depict Israelite prisoners being led away from the battle.

In 612 B.C.E. the Babylonians defeated the Assyrians and took over the for-mer kingdom of Israel. The relatively small kingdom of Judah was in a precari-ous position between Egypt and Babylonia and was attacked by Babylonian forces. The last Israelite king to rule Judah was Zedekiah, who came into conflict with Nebuchadnezzar, king of Babylon. Nebuchadnezzar's defeat of Judah is mentioned on a tablet called the Babylonian Chronicle as occurring in the sev-enth year of his reign. Jerusalem and the temple were destroyed during this at-tack. Zedekiah and many of the inhabitants of Judah were deported to Babylon in two phases, marking the beginning of the Babylonian exile in 587 B.C.E.

Exile and Return

The Babylonian exile (586–539 B.C.E.) was a major catastrophe in Israelite/ Jewish history, and the resulting sense of loss is reflected in many biblical texts, particularly Psalms and Lamentations. Nonetheless, a number of the inhabitants of Judah appear to have remained in their land and were not sent into exile in Babylon. Among those Jews who were exiled, many were afforded economic opportunities, and it is likely that many of them prospered. The prophets of the exile (e.g., Jeremiah, Ezekiel, Second Isaiah [see discussion in chapter three]) issued warnings of judgment but also proclaimed a message of hope for God's people.

The period of the exile came to an end in 539 B.C.E. when the Persian king Cyrus defeated the Babylonians and issued a decree freeing the Jews from their captivity. The Cyrus Cylinder—a nine-inch cylinder inscribed in Babylonian cuneiform and made of baked clay—is an account of military ventures of the Persian king in Babylonia. Though it does not mention Judea in particular, it shows Cyrus's general policy of restoring the religious practices of conquered people and allowing them to return to their homelands. Thus, as described in Ezra 6, Cyrus allowed the Jews to return to Judea and to rebuild their temple, granting them considerable autonomy under his rule.

The temple built in Jerusalem after the return from exile is referred to as the Second Temple because it was constructed on the foundations of the first—or Solomon's—temple (Ezra 5:15; 6:7). The beliefs and practices of Jews ("Judahites") during the period of the Second Temple (including Herod the Great's reconstruction of that temple) came to be known as **Judaism.** During this time, called **Second Temple Judaism** (and sometimes **early Judaism**), the temple was of central significance for Jews in Palestine as well as for Jews of the **Diaspora,** or "dispersion."[4] This period of Judaism, which extends into the Hellenistic and Roman periods (see below), was characterized by diversity, as evidenced by the appearance of groups such as Pharisees, Sadducees, Essenes, and Zealots. Its end may be marked by the destruction of the temple in 70 C.E. and the subsequent emergence of rabbinic Judaism.

The Hellenistic and Roman Periods
(ca. 333 B.C.E.–100 C.E.)

Yet another change for land and people in Palestine occurred in 333 B.C.E. when Alexander the Great defeated the Persians at the battle of Issus (in southeastern Asia Minor) and marched in to take control of the Near East. This marks the beginning of Greek rule and the influence of **Hellenism,** or Greek culture, in Palestine. An example of this influence is the building of the Xystos center in Jerusalem. This structure, known from archaeology, was the site of a famous Hellenistic gymnasium (a center for education and physical activity). Another

---

[4] Because of their distance from the temple, their attachment to it would have been different from that of their counterparts in Palestine.

example is the translation of the Hebrew Bible into **Greek** (the Septuagint), begun around 250 B.C.E.

After Alexander's death in 323 B.C.E., this **Hellenistic Period** continued under his generals Ptolemy (who ruled Egypt, Phoenicia, and Palestine from 323 to 282 B.C.E.) and Seleucus (who ruled Syria and Mesopotamia from 312 to 281 B.C.E.). The dynastic successors of Ptolemy and Seleucus fought over Palestine, which bordered their territories. The Seleucid empire gained the upper hand in 198 B.C.E. when Antiochus III Epiphanes (223–187 B.C.E.) took control of Palestine from Ptolemy V (successor to Ptolemy I). His infamous son, Antiochus IV Epiphanes, ruled from 175 to 164 B.C.E. and was called "an evil root" (author's translation) in the book of 1 Maccabees (1 Macc 1:10) because he forbade Jewish religious practices and defiled the Jerusalem temple by sacrificing a pig (an offence to biblical law) and building an altar to Zeus. These actions of Antiochus sparked the **Hasmonean** revolt in which Judas Maccabeus ("the hammerer") liberated Jerusalem in 164 B.C.E. and rededicated the temple.[5]

The Hasmonean and Herodian Periods

The Hasmonean family become a dynasty, expanding their kingdom and establishing Jewish dominance throughout Palestine. The Hasmonean period lasted from 152 to 37 B.C.E. Among other Hasmonean leaders, Aristobulus (104–103 B.C.E.) and Alexander Janneus (103–76 B.C.E.) extended Jewish rule to the boundaries of the Davidic kingdom, once more including Galilee. This period of independence and expansion constituted a remarkable achievement in light of the foregoing history of domination of the land by foreign empires, though it was not without conflict and pressures—both internal and external.

It was during the Hasmonean era that the Pharisees and Sadducees emerged as two groups concerned with interpretation of the law. Recent archaeological excavations in Galilee, Samaria, and Judea have uncovered structures called *miqvaot*, which were ritual baths used to maintain purity, an important issue for Pharisees and Sadducees as well as the Jewish population in general. Stone vessels (which could not contract impurity) and ossuraries—stone boxes for burial of bones—are also important archaeological discoveries relating to this time period. Yet another set of very significant discoveries from this era are the remains of the community at Qumran, established on the upper western shore of the Dead Sea between 166 and 159 B.C.E. and continuing in use until its destruction in 68 C.E. The most important of these remains are the famous Dead Sea Scrolls (discussed in chapter five).

---

[5] The feast of Hanukkah derives from this event.

The nearly eighty years of Jewish independence ended when the Roman general Pompey conquered Judea in 63 B.C.E., making it part of the Roman province of Syria. The territories won by the Hasmoneans now all paid tribute to Rome. Rome's expansive power, known to much of the Mediterranean basin already during the latter part of the Roman Republic (509–27 B.C.E.), grew still further in the imperial era. Augustus, the grandnephew and adopted son of Julius Caesar and the first Roman emperor, reigned 27 B.C.E.–14 C.E. and extended the empire to include additional regions of Europe and Asia Minor, as well as Egypt. Thus began the so-called "Pax Romana"—a period of relative peace and stability throughout the conquered lands that lasted until the early fifth century C.E..

The **Herodian period** (37 B.C.E.–66 C.E.) is a kind of "sub-era" of the Roman period in Palestine. All of the Herodian rulers from Herod the Great to his great-grandson (Herod) Agrippa II owed their political power to Rome. Herod the Great, famous from the opening of Matthew's gospel (Matt 2), ruled Judea, Idumea (south of Judea), Perea (east of the Jordan), Samaria, and Galilee from 37 B.C.E. to his death in 4 B.C.E. He is known for his many building projects, most notably the re-construction of the Jerusalem temple in Hellenistic style. This magnificent building project begun by Herod and completed by Agrippa II in 64 C.E. was admired widely in the Greco-Roman world. Some of Herod the Great's other building projects included fortresses, palaces, and a city named in honor of the Emperor—Caesarea.[6]

The "New Testament Period"

The "New Testament period" is also a sort of sub-era of the Roman period (though not technically an historical period defined by rulers or other normal markers). It may be said to begin around the time of Herod's death in 4 B.C.E. (Scholars estimate that Jesus was born in approximately 6 B.C.E.) In his will, Herod indicated a three-way split of his kingdom among his sons Archelaus, Antipas, and Philip.[7] The reign of Archelaus over Judea, Idumea, and Samaria was very brief, lasting only from 4 B.C.E. to 6 C.E. Thereafter, Rome ruled Judea directly by prefects (or procurators) who lived in Caesarea on the coast; Pilate, who is portrayed in the Gospels, held this title from 26 to 36 C.E. In Galilee, Herodian rule lasted longer than it did in Judea. Herod Antipas, who is simply called "Herod" in the NT, ruled over Galilee from 4 B.C.E. to 39 C.E. He is the

---

[6] Located 25 miles north of modern Tel Aviv, on the Mediterranean, the city is also known as Caesarea Maritima, distinguishing it from the inland city of Caesarea Philippi.

[7] Archelaus (named ethnarch of Judea, Idumea, and Samaria, ruling 4 B.C.E.–6 C.E.), Antipas (tetrarch of Galilee and Perea 4 B.C.E.–39 C.E.), and Philip (tetrarch of Batanea, Trachonitis, and Iturea, 6–41 C.E.).

Herodian ruler most frequently referred to in the NT (see, e.g., Luke 3:1 as well as Matt 14, Mark 6, Luke 23, and Acts 12).

After the crucifixion of Jesus in about 30 C.E. the message of his life, death, and resurrection—the gospel, or good news—spread from Jerusalem (the location of the Pentecost experience described in Acts 2) into the surrounding Greco-Roman world. The writings of Paul, the "apostle to the Gentiles" (Rom 11:13), are dated to the 50s of the first century C.E. and give insight into some of the places or communities where Christianity was gaining acceptance in the Gentile world.

When Paul wrote his letters, he was sometimes in prison or perhaps under house arrest. Suffering was a reality for early Christians (see chapter four). Paul himself had been a persecutor of the church prior to his conversion (Phil 3:6). The last Herodian rulers, Agrippa I (41–44 C.E.) and Agrippa II (48–66), probably persecuted Christians (Acts 12:1–2), and the NT tells us that communities in provinces and cities outside Palestine, such as Galatia, Asia (e.g., Pergamum), and Macedonia (e.g., Thessalonica, Philippi) were also under persecution.[8]

Tensions rising over Roman rule in Judea and Galilee led to the start of the First Jewish Revolt, which began in 66 C.E. and ended with the fall of Masada in 73–74 C.E. The devastating final blow to this uprising was the destruction by the Romans of the Jerusalem temple in 70 C.E. (The Western or Wailing Wall of today's Jerusalem is part of the remains of the great Herodian temple, completed only six years before its destruction.) In about 90 C.E. the heirs of the Pharisees, the Rabbis, formed a council at Jamnia, or Yavneh, where there was a rabbinic school. From Jamnia and other locations, they worked to develop their traditions—the "oral law." The realm of the rabbis was the synagogue, and many of the first Christians were Jews who participated in synagogue worship. Over time tensions arose in synagogues in which Christians (or Jewish-Christians) and Jews were both active (as can be seen in the Gospel of John, also dated to around 90–95 C.E.; e.g., John 9:22). By the end of the first century C.E., Judaism and Christianity had begun a gradual process of separating into distinct entities.

The most important evidence we have for the spread and development of early Christianity in the first century C.E. is found within the NT itself, but these texts are subject to various interpretations (e.g., regarding the controversies at churches mentioned or alluded to in Paul's letters). Among the sparse external evidence is an inscription that helps to date some of the work of Paul and his colleagues. This inscription was found at Delphi in Greece and dates to ca. 52 C.E. It mentions Gallio, who held the title of proconsul of the Roman province of

---

[8] See, e.g., Acts 16:16–24; 17:1–15; Phil 1:29; 1 Thess 1:6; 2:2, 14–16; 1 Pet 1:1–9; and Rev. 3:12–13. It should be noted that this persecution was not systematic but sporadic and was often instigated by mobs rather than Roman officials.

The ruins of the agora (forum) and temple of Apollo in Corinth, one of the most important crossroads of the Roman Empire and a focal point of the Pauline mission. (M. Gorman)

Achaia (southern Greece), of which Corinth was the capital. Acts 18:12–17 also refers to Gallio, allowing scholars to place Paul's stay at Corinth during his second missionary journey (Acts 18:11) in the early 50s C.E.

Jews living in communities outside Palestine—the Jewish Diaspora—at this time actually outnumbered those living within the land of Israel. An inscription (partially deteriorated) found at Corinth that reads "Synagogue of the Hebrews" provides evidence of a Jewish community located there. Movement throughout the empire was vitally important to the spread of the Christian gospel and the formation of Christian communities. Paul and his co-workers would have traveled along sea routes and imperial roads to visit cities where there were Diaspora communities. In this way their message gained acceptance among Jews and Gentiles (non-Jews), especially in Asia Minor and Greece. Key centers of early Christianity outside Palestine included Syrian Antioch (north of Palestine), Ephesus, Corinth, and of course Rome.

Archaeologists and historians have learned much about the social world of the NT, including its customs and moral attitudes, that illuminates the NT texts themselves. But there is relatively little material evidence that sheds light on the early Christian communities. For example, in many of the areas where Christianity was spreading throughout the first century, groups of Christians are believed to have met in homes, or "house churches." Since no early examples of these meeting places have yet been found by archaeologists, we must study various kinds of actual houses that have been excavated so as to learn something about house churches. We may also observe the development of the "house church" in later examples such as a third-century C.E. chapel within a domestic residence excavated at Dura-Europos on the Euphrates River. The only other significant archaeological evidence regarding the presence and beliefs of Christians around this time (third and fourth centuries C.E.) is the remaining Christian graffiti, which includes signs such as crosses and the "*chi rho*" (the first two letters of the word "Christ," *christos,* in Greek, written together). The NT remains the largest deposit of evidence for the development of Christianity in the first century.

TEXTS IN CONTEXTS: FINAL REMARKS

In the space of a brief discussion of the geography, history, and archaeology of the Bible, we have not achieved the goals some people may have in pursuing these fields: we have not "proven" that the Bible is true or even that it is necessarily accurate. Rather, we have explored some of the different contexts in which biblical texts are situated. For any detailed and serious study of the Bible, it is important to have an awareness of the physical setting, significant events, and material culture relating to the world of the texts. This knowledge is invaluable as it allows us to gain insights into the way that biblical texts emerged out of particular historical situations and were shaped by them. Even so, we must always keep in mind the purpose of the texts as mentioned at the beginning of the chapter. That is, they are primarily written not to inform us of history but to show history in terms of the relationship between God and humanity. Nonetheless, they contain messages and meanings that still speak to the unique contexts of readers and hearers today.

Table of Major Periods and Biblical Events			
Archaeological Periods and Finds		**Major Events and Associated Biblical Books[9]**	**Years**
Middle Bronze Age	*Hammurabi's laws (1792 B.C.E.)*	Ancestral Period (Abraham and Sarah)	*Genesis (12–50)*	ca. 2200–1550 B.C.E.
Late Bronze Age I & II	*Merneptah Stele— first mention of Israel (1230 B.C.E.)*	Egypt and exodus (Moses)	*Exodus, Leviticus, Numbers, Deuteronomy*	ca. 1550–1200 B.C.E.
Iron Age I	*The "Four-Room House"*	Conquest / Settlement (to 1020 B.C.E.)	*Joshua, Judges, 1 Samuel*	ca. 1200–1000 B.C.E.
Iron Age II	*Sennacherib (Assyrian king)* *Reliefs showing Israelite prisoners captured at Lachish (701 B.C.E.)* *Babylonian Chronicle*	Unified Kingdom (1020–922 B.C.E.) Israel and Judah (922–721 B.C.E.) Judah alone (721–587 B.C.E.) Death of Josiah, king of Judah (609 B.C.E.) Destruction of Jerusalem (587 B.C.E.)	*1–2 Samuel, 1–2 Kings, 1–2 Chronicles, First Isaiah (Isa 1–39), Jeremiah, Hosea, Amos, Micah, Nahum, Habakkuk, Zephaniah*	ca. 1020–587 B.C.E.
Babylonian and Persian Periods	*Cyrus Cylinder* *Darius I Inscription*	Babylonian exile (586–539 B.C.E.) Return and restoration (539–333 B.C.E.) Battle of Issus (333 B.C.E.) Conquest of Palestine by Alexander the Great (333–332 B.C.E.)	*1–2 Chronicles, Ezra, Nehemiah, Esther, Second and Third Isaiah (Isa 40–66), Jeremiah, Lamentations, Ezekiel, Joel, Obadiah, Haggai, Zechariah*	586–332 B.C.E.

---

[9] The inclusion of a biblical book in the "Major Events and Associated Biblical Books" column indicates that the particular book has some relevance to that period, not that its authorship dates to that era, though it may be noted that all of the books of the NT were written during the Roman Period. For the dating of OT writings, see chapter three.

Table of Major Periods and Biblical Events			
Archaeological Periods and Finds		**Major Events and Associated Biblical Books**	**Years**
Hellenistic Period I	*Hellenistic Gymnasia* *Xystos in Jerusalem* *Qumran Caves*	Septuagint begun (ca. 250 B.C.E.) Profanation of the temple by Antiochus Epiphanes (167 B.C.E.) Maccabean revolt (167–142 B.C.E.) Liberation of the temple (164 B.C.E.) Foundation of the community at Qumran (ca. 166–150 B.C.E.)	*Daniel, Ecclesiastes, Sirach, 1–2 Maccabees* 333–152 B.C.E.
Hellenistic Period II (Hasmonean)	Miqvaot *Ossuaries* *Stone Vessels* *Jerusalem Temple*	Galilee added to the Jewish kingdom under Aristobulus (103 B.C.E.) Pompey conquers Judea, makes it part of the Roman province of Syria (63 B.C.E.)	*1–4 Maccabees* 152–37 B.C.E.
Roman Period	*Synagogues* *House Churches* *Early Christian Symbols*	Herod the Great rules under Roman authority (37–4 B.C.E.) Jesus born (ca. 6 B.C.E.) Jesus crucified (ca. 30 C.E.) Letters of Paul (50s C.E.) Destruction of Jerusalem (70 C.E.) Fall of Masada (73–74 C.E.) Jamnia Council (ca. 90 C.E.)	*New Testament* 37 B.C.E.–ca. 100 C.E. (last NT writings)[10]

---

[10] The actual end of the Roman empire, and therefore the Roman period, is variously dated to the fourth or (more often) fifth century.

FOR FURTHER READING AND STUDY

Bandstra, Barry L. *Reading the Old Testament: An Introduction to the Hebrew Bible*. 2d ed. Belmont, Calif.: Wadsworth, 1999. A thorough introductory text containing numerous maps, tables, time lines, charts, and pictures, plus a CD-ROM.

Barclay, John M. G., *Jews in the Mediterranean Diaspora: From Alexander to Trajan (323 B.C.E. – 117 C.E.)*. Berkley, Calif.: University of California Press, 1996. A detailed description and evaluation of Diaspora Judaism in the Hellenistic-Roman period in Egypt, Syria, Cyrenaica, and Rome.

Bartlett, John R., ed. *Archaeology and Biblical Interpretation*. London: Routledge, 1997. A collection of seven essays on topics that explore the ways that biblical texts (OT and NT) and archaeological discoveries may illuminate each other.

Coogan, Michael D., ed. *The Oxford History of the Biblical World*. New York: Oxford University Press, 1998. An invaluable reference work for biblical history (and archaeology), with chapters relating to historical eras from the ancestral period to the spread of Christianity in the Roman world.

Crossan, John Dominic, and Jonathan L. Reed. *Excavating Jesus: Beneath the Stones, Behind the Texts*. San Francisco: HarperSanFrancisco, 2001. The collaborative effort of historical Jesus scholar John Dominic Crossan and Galilean archaeologist Jonathan Reed to elucidate the life and social world of Jesus.

Ehrman, Bart D. *The New Testament: A Historical Introduction to the Early Christian Writings*. 3d ed. New York: Oxford University Press, 2003. A textbook introduction to the NT that is historical in orientation and contains numerous pictures and useful supplementary material in boxes.

Fant, Clyde E., and Mitchell G. Reddish. *A Guide to Biblical Sites in Greece and Turkey*. Oxford: Oxford University Press, 2003. A reference guidebook that presents accessible information on significant sites in Greece and Turkey relating to the Bible (mostly NT, but some OT places as well).

Gordon, Cyrus H., and Gary A. Rendsburg. *The Bible and the Ancient Near East*. Rev. ed. New York: W. W. Norton, 1997. A reconstruction of the history relating to the Hebrew Bible (through the Hellenistic Age), utilizing both archaeological evidence and literary parallels.

Hayes, John H., and Sara R. Mandell. *The Jewish People in Classical Antiquity: From Alexander to Bar Kochba*. Louisville: Westminster John Knox, 1998. A treatment of Jewish history in Judea and Jerusalem from 333 B.C.E. to 135 C.E.

Hayes, John H., and J. Maxwell Miller, eds. *Israelite and Judaean History*. Philadelphia: Westminster, 1977; Philadelphia: Trinity Press International, 1990.

A reprint of a classic volume containing chapters on periods of history up to the Roman era, including discussion of archaeological and written sources as well as the state of scholarly discussion.

Laughlin, John C. H. *Archaeology and the Bible*. London: Routledge, 2000. A detailed discussion of the archaeology of the Ancient Near East from the Early Bronze Age to Iron Age II.

Mitchell, T. C. *Biblical Archaeology: Documents from the British Museum*. Cambridge: Cambridge University Press, 1988. Descriptions of the extraordinarily rich collection of antiquities held by the British Museum relating to biblical archaeology.

Pritchard, James B., ed. *The Harper Concise Atlas of the Bible*. San Francisco: HarperCollins, 1991. A manageable atlas with text providing historical, archaeological, and literary background as well as helpful charts and tables.

Riches, John. *The World of Jesus: First Century Judaism in Crisis*. Cambridge: Cambridge University Press, 1991. A concise, readable introduction, setting the NT teachings of Jesus within the socio-historical context of first-century Judaism.

Rogerson, John, and Philip R. Davies. *The Old Testament World*. Sheffield: Sheffield Academic Press, 1989. An introduction to the background of the OT, focusing on setting, history, religious beliefs, types of literature, and the formation of the OT.

Sanders, E. P. *Judaism: Practice and Belief, 63 B.C.E.–66 C.E.* London: SCM Press, 1992; Philadelphia: Trinity Press International, 1994. An influential study of Judaism in the years prior to the first Jewish revolt that highlights the importance of distinguishing "common Judaism" or the religious practices of most Jews who were not part of any special group.

Chapter 3

The Character and Composition of the Books of the Old Testament

DAVID A. LEITER

The Old Testament is a collection of faith-oriented writings from ancient Israel that carry authoritative status for Christianity, Judaism, and (to some degree) Islam.[1] Although the importance of this literature varies among these three major religions and also within each one, the OT is a remarkable collection of texts that portray the presence and acts of God within the history of ancient Israel.

The OT's literary materials are eclectic in nature, as a wide variety of literary genres makes up the collection. These genres include narratives, prophetic speeches, psalms, legal collections, and wisdom literature. Although this list of literary types is merely illustrative and not exhaustive, it demonstrates the complex nature of the OT and allows us to appreciate the magnificence of its range and depth.

The story line of the OT covers more than one thousand years of the social, religious, and political history of ancient Israel and its neighbors. The subject matter begins with Abraham of the ancestral (or patriarchal) period and moves onward to Ezra of the postexilic era and to the figures of the Maccabean period for the deuterocanonical, or apocryphal, books. Although the OT recounts historical events, it is a book that intertwines the history and faith story of ancient

---

[1] The body of literature considered in this chapter has numerous designations, such as Old Testament, Hebrew Scriptures, Hebrew Bible, First Testament, and Tanakh. Each designation has its advantages and disadvantages. For example, while the designation *Hebrew Bible* does not have the pejorative connotations of *Old Testament,* the deuterocanonical books are not written in Hebrew, so this label is problematic for the entire body of literature. For the sake of simplicity and tradition, the term "Old Testament" (abbreviated OT) will be used on a consistent basis in this chapter.

Israel as opposed to a book that simply contains historical and literal facts. What we have, more or less, is a collection of faith documents that have historical value and import.

Not only does the OT cover a wide time span, but also its contents stem from various communities within ancient Israel and the ancient Near East. No single individual or group of persons in ancient Israel can be considered the author of its contents. In fact, the authorship of most of the OT is anonymous. Many of the literary materials originated in oral form and were passed on from community to community and from generation to generation. This includes various narratives and sagas as well as specific psalms and wisdom sayings. Primarily for the purposes of preservation, these materials were gradually transmitted into written form and then gathered into larger collections.

The OT has been organized in various ways down through the ages, with such arrangements based primarily upon manuscript traditions. Most Jewish and Protestant Bibles follow the Hebrew manuscript tradition and contain what is sometimes called the **protocanonical** ("first canon") material. The Roman Catholic and Orthodox Bibles are based upon the Greek Septuagint (LXX) and Latin manuscript traditions; in addition to containing the protocanonical writings, they also include deuterocanonical literature, or the Apocrypha. (For the various canons, see chapter one.)

The discussion of the OT in this chapter will follow the Hebrew manuscript tradition primarily because the organization of this tradition illustrates how the OT was ultimately put together. This tradition is comprised of three major sections: the Torah/**Pentateuch,** the **Prophets,** and the **Writings.**[2] It is commonly believed that the Torah/Pentateuch was the first section to attain completion. The next collection that came to be assembled was the Prophets. The primary core of this tradition includes the writing prophets: Isaiah, Jeremiah, Ezekiel, and the Book of the Twelve, also known as the **Minor Prophets.** An historical narrative running from Joshua to 2 Kings precedes this core. This narrative has traditionally been labeled the **Former Prophets,** while the writing prophets are known as the **Latter Prophets.**

The remaining documents of the OT were then brought together to form the last section, known as the Writings. This section includes the book of Psalms; wisdom writings such as Proverbs and Job; the Five Scrolls, including Ruth, Song of Songs, Ecclesiastes, Lamentations, and Esther; the book of Daniel; and the

---

[2] As noted in chapter one, in the Jewish tradition, these three sections are labeled Torah (law/tradition), Nevi'im (prophets) and Kethuvim (writings). The first letter of each label is taken to form the acronym TaNaK or Tanakh. Based on the three major divisions, this acronym is often used by Jews to refer to the Jewish Scriptures. For various views on how the three parts came together as one canon, see chapter six.

historical books of Chronicles, Ezra, and Nehemiah. The Hebrew manuscript tradition does not include the deuterocanonical/apocryphal books; most of those works will be discussed along with the Writings because their formation and dating correspond to that section of the OT.

THE TORAH/PENTATEUCH

The first five books of the OT are often called "Torah" or "law."[3] These five books are also designated as the Pentateuch ("Five Scrolls"). The thematic content of the Pentateuch covers topics such as creation, God's promises to Abraham and the ancestors, the exodus out of Egypt, the covenant at Mount Sinai, and the wandering in the wilderness.[4]

Literary Features

It has already been mentioned that from a literary perspective the OT contains a rich variety of genres. The Pentateuch is no exception. The book of Genesis consists primarily of narrative. The range of narratives in this book, however, is striking. The first creation narrative in Gen 1 exhibits elements of ritual and has formulaic plot lines common in nonbiblical narrative of the time, while the second creation narrative in Gen 2 reads more like a story that contains the standard elements of narrative plot such as exposition, conflict or complication, and resolution. One also finds longer narratives such as the flood story in Gen 6–9. Such narratives then give way to the central narrative feature in Genesis, namely, the **saga.** A saga, as depicted in the book of Genesis, is a lengthy narrative that is made up of shorter episodic stories centering on specific themes or characters. The Abraham saga, for example, runs from Gen 12 to 26. Nestled in the midst of

---

[3] Although this Hebrew term is frequently translated as "law," it is also used in a general sense to refer to an authoritative canonical collection such as the first five books or simply the entire OT.

[4] In addition to the designation "Pentateuch" for the first five books, other proposals have been suggested. If Deuteronomy is the last book of the Pentateuch, then the first section of the OT ends with the ancient Israelites still in the wilderness and with God's promises unfulfilled. Identifying the opening section as a **Hexateuch** allows us to add a sixth book, the book of Joshua, thus bringing to conclusion many of the themes, promises, and stories discussed in the previous five books. On the other hand, the book of Deuteronomy can be seen as an introduction to the longer narrative that follows, namely Joshua–2 Kings. If one considers Deuteronomy to be the beginning of this section, then the introductory section of the OT is a **Tetrateuch,** consisting of Genesis, Exodus, Leviticus, and Numbers. Of these three major designations, the Pentateuch is favored by scholarly consensus and follows the traditional view that these five books were initially a separate collection.

The traditional site of Mount Sinai (*Jebel Musa* in Arabic), overlooking Saint Catherine's Monastery, where the important fourth-century C.E. biblical Codex Sinaiticus was found in the nineteenth century (see chapter seven). (Todd Bolen/BiblePlaces.com)

the ongoing narratives are also literary gems such as **etiologies** (narratives explaining the origin of something) and genealogies. The books of Exodus and Numbers also contain substantial narratives that exhibit legendary qualities.

Another primary literary feature in the Pentateuch is the presence of legal collections. There are two primary versions of the **Decalogue** (the Ten Commandments) found in Exod 20 and Deut 5, and there are longer legal collections in Exod 20–23 (the Covenant Code), Lev 17–26 (the Holiness Code), and Deut 12–26 (the Deuteronomic Code). In addition to legal collections, the Pentateuch also contains literature that emerges out of a worship or liturgical context, such as blessings (e.g., Num 6:22–26 and Deut 33), rituals that describe the importance of ceremonial offerings (Deut 26:1–11), and prescriptions for sacrifices (Lev 1–7).

Archaeological discoveries of ancient Near Eastern cultures during the last 100 years or so have uncovered stories of creation, a great flood, and nomadic heroes who travel to distant lands to settle down. Such stories, as well as legal collections originating in these ancient cultures, bear a resemblance to quite a few of the genres found in the Pentateuch. Although further study and analysis are required to make a tight connection between the literary genres of other ancient Near Eastern cultures and those of ancient Israel, one can at least recognize that the literary forms found in the Pentateuch are also found in other ancient cultures.

Authorship, Sources, and Traditions

Biblical and church traditions attribute authorship of the Pentateuch to Moses. Passages from some of the later books of the OT and the deutero-canonical literature (such as 2 Chr 23:18 and Sir 24:23) refer to the Pentateuch as the "law," or "book," of Moses. The assumption that Moses wrote the Penta-teuch derives especially from Moses' substantial role in Exodus to Deuteronomy. However, a close reading and examination of the material calls this assumption into question. First, there is the problem of anachronistic references in the Pen-tateuch. If Moses indeed is the author of the first five books of the Bible, then why does he write about his own death in Deut 34? Other passages indicate that the author was writing much later than the historical period reflected in the Pen-tateuch.[5] Second, there are numerous stories or accounts that are repeated throughout the Pentateuch. The story of Moses drawing water from a rock for a thirsty and complaining people occurs in Exod 17:1–7 and Num 20:2–13. And of course there is the previously mentioned repetition of the Ten Commandments in both Exod 20 and Deut 5.

Once we recognize the repetition of certain material in the Pentateuch, then we are able to comprehend the various inconsistencies that exist as well. In some places the mountain where God makes a covenant with Moses and the people is called "Sinai," while in other places the mountain goes by the name "Horeb." There is a similar issue with God's name in the Pentateuch. The nar-rative account in Exod 3–6 suggests that God's name, YHWH ("Yahweh"), was unknown until the time of Moses. However, the name occurs repeatedly in the book of Genesis.

Numerous scholars have struggled with the blatant differences in literary style, duplication of material, anachronisms, and inconsistencies within the Pentateuch. Perhaps the most enduring challenge to Mosaic authorship of the Pentateuch, as well as an attempt to explain the diverse literary styles and fea-tures, is what is most commonly referred to as the **Documentary Hypothesis.** In the late 1800s, the German scholar Julius Wellhausen (1844–1918) developed this thesis in an effort to challenge the notion that the Pentateuch was a unified work written by a single author. Wellhausen proposed that the Pentateuch was

---

[5] For example, in Gen 36:31 the writer refers to the Israelite monarchy in such a way that presupposes its existence long before it was a reality. There is also mention of the Philistines in Exod 13:17, even though this group of peoples was unknown during the time of Moses.

made up of four literary sources, abbreviated **J, E, D,** and **P,** each having its own literary style and distinctive use of Hebrew vocabulary. Each source, he argued, stemmed from a different period in ancient Israelite history, and its contents reflect that time period from which it arose.

According to Wellhausen, the Yahwist source (commonly called J from the German word "Jahwist") was written during the early period of the ancient Israelite monarchy, perhaps sometime during the tenth or ninth century B.C.E. It consistently used the name "YHWH" ("Yahweh") when referring to God. The material in the Elohist source (E) reflected a time period somewhere around the eighth century B.C.E. when the monarchy was well established in ancient Israel but after the united kingdom had been divided into the north (Israel) and south (Judah). The label "Elohist" derives from this source's consistent use of the name "Elohim" when referring to God. The book of Deuteronomy (D) makes up the third source, representing the style and theology that existed during the reign and reform of King Josiah during the latter part of the seventh century B.C.E. The Priestly source (P) was considered to be the latest strand of the Pentateuch, reflecting a postexilic period in the fifth century or later, attentive to priestly matters such as liturgy, ritual, and sacrifice.

Wellhausen's thesis of four written documents that were eventually combined during the postexilic period was merely a starting point for understanding the complex nature of the Pentateuch, and it has been significantly modified during the last century. Instead of assuming that the four Pentateuchal documents originated in written form, scholars have recently paid attention to the oral history lying behind many of the biblical texts. Currently, most scholars view the Pentateuch as comprised of different *traditions* rather than literary *documents*. These traditions demonstrate a rich heritage of both oral and written sources that eventually led to the canonical material we now call the Torah or the Pentateuch.

An Example: Two Creation Accounts

A brief comparison of the two creation stories in Genesis aptly illustrates the claim that the Pentateuch is comprised of various traditions containing different literary styles and features. The first creation story, Gen. 1:1–2:4a, is prose but exhibits a strong poetical flavor. There are many refrains, such as "Let there be _____," "And God saw that it was good," "And it was so," and "And there was evening and there was morning, the [X] day." God's role is somewhat distant; God creates by speaking and does not actively engage the creation. The liturgical features of this account reflect the concerns of the Priestly tradition, suggesting that it arose in a worship **Sitz im Leben** (German for "life setting").

The second creation account, Gen. 2:4b–25, is a story with no repetitive poetic refrains or formulas. The first human has a more substantive role in this account than in the previous one, and God also assumes a less distant and more active role. God is intimately involved with the creation and takes on anthropomorphic (human) features: God walks, works, breathes, and creates by stooping, molding, and planting. Unlike the first account that is neatly mapped out in seven days, the time frame of the second account is less definite. This account is attributed to the Yahwist tradition because of its consistent use of the word "YHWH" for God and its narrative features. The difference in style between the two creation accounts is striking, and although someone or a group of editors ultimately decided to include both stories at the beginning of Genesis, it is virtually impossible to deny that these two accounts, summarized in the following chart, stem from two very different and distinct traditions.

The Genesis Creation Accounts		
Narrative Features	**Gen. 1:1–2:4a**	**Gen. 2:4b–25**
Literary expression	Prose with poetic refrains and formulas	Prose with no poetic refrains and formulas
God's role	Distant and remote	Involved in an anthropomorphic manner
Mode of creation	God creates by speaking	God creates by molding, forming, and planting
Time frame	Seven days	Less definite

The Pentateuch as an Entity

A discussion of sources and traditions in the Pentateuch, however, can only take us so far, helping us understand how the text came to be in its present form. What concerns us most today is the final form of the text. The Pentateuch tells the beginning story of ancient Israel. The kernel of this story is the covenant that God makes with Moses and the people on Mount Sinai (Horeb). This kernel encompasses the books of Exodus and Leviticus as well as the first ten chapters of Numbers. Preceding the drama and detail of the encounter on Mount Sinai (Horeb), are stories of the creation of the universe to the Tower of Babel (Gen 1–11). This section is often called the Primeval History of ancient Israel. Following this series of stories is a collection of sagas regarding the ancestors (Gen 12–50).

The overall narrative continues with the equally dramatic and detailed encounter between Moses and Aaron, who are the divinely appointed leaders of the people, and the pharaoh of Egypt. Finally, the exodus event takes the people to the foot of the mountain. The people then leave Mount Sinai after receiving God's covenant, and they travel in the wilderness toward the promised land (narrated in the remainder of Numbers). Deuteronomy sets the stage for the entry into the land as Moses commands the people to obey God during and following the takeover of the land.

The Pentateuch provides the backdrop for life in the land of Israel. The remaining two sections of the OT, the Prophets and the Writings, pick up the story and describe how this life plays out from the united kingdom to a time in which the monarchy fades into the sunset in the postexilic period. The story of ancient Israel, as recounted in the pages of the OT, has a beginning and an end. As the beginning of this story, the Pentateuch—in addition to its elaboration of the promises and covenant between God and the people—puts the reader into position to encounter and embrace the highlights and downfalls of life in ancient Israel with YHWH as the Israelites' God.

THE PROPHETS

The second major division of the OT is the Prophets. The first part of this division, the Former Prophets (Joshua–2 Kings), primarily sketches the story of ancient Israel from the settlement period to the fall of the monarchy. The Latter Prophets contains material that is more characteristic of prophetic literature. Its major works are those of the writing prophets Isaiah, Jeremiah, and Ezekiel, plus the Book of the Twelve, or the twelve "minor" prophets.

The Former Prophets

The Former Prophets form a narrative block consisting of the books of Joshua, Judges, 1 and 2 Samuel, and 1 and 2 Kings. Most modern Bibles follow the Greek manuscript tradition of the Septuagint, by including Ruth, 1 and 2 Chronicles, Ezra, Nehemiah, and Esther (as well as the deuterocanonical books of Tobit, Judith and 1 and 2 Maccabees, if included) with the Former Prophets, primarily because of their historical character. As noted earlier, this chapter will follow the Hebrew manuscript tradition and discuss these books with the writings because most of them were added to the OT canon at a much later date than the Former Prophets.

Survey

The book of Joshua provides an account of the people, under the leadership of Joshua, entering into the promised land and conquering various cities throughout Palestine. The rest of the book deals with how the land is to be divided among the tribes of Israel. The book of Judges begins with a lengthy introduction that revisits the entry into Canaan discussed in Joshua, but from a different perspective. Instead of the sort of massive military invasion described in Joshua, the entry into and takeover of the land depicted in Judges is a more gradual and less violent one. The remainder of the book uses a flexibly designed literary device to tell the story of the judges. This literary device takes the form of a pattern, or cycle, that involves idolatry, judgment (by means of an external enemy), repentance, and deliverance through a "judge" or military leader. The land rests and is at peace for a period of time until the pattern begins again. People who play a central role as judges include Othniel, Ehud, Deborah, Gideon, Jephthah, and Samson.

First Samuel tells about the establishment of the monarchy in ancient Israel and the rise and fall of Israel's first king, Saul. The last part of the book brings David into the picture and weaves together many stories about the tension between David and Saul. For the most part, 2 Samuel is devoted to the kingship of David. It traces his successes as a political leader and also recounts his internal struggles within the kingdom, especially the rebellion of David's son Absalom. First Kings begins with David's death and the coronation of Solomon as king. Solomon is pictured as a wise leader who accumulates wealth and establishes international trade. After Solomon's death, however, there is strife within the united kingdom, and it is divided into two parts, the north (Israel) led by Jeroboam and the south (Judah) led by Solomon's son Rehoboam. The book ends with a series of stories about the prophet Elijah.

The book of 2 Kings records Elijah's death and his succession by Elisha. It continues with a series of stories about Elisha and northern kings such as Omri and Ahab. These stories are followed by an account of the fall of the northern kingdom to Assyria in 721 B.C.E. The remainder of 2 Kings focuses upon the kingdom of Judah. After the reigns of Hezekiah and Josiah, the narrative takes the reader through the turmoil that leads to the fall of Judah to Babylon (587/586 B.C.E.) and the eventual collapse of the ancient Israelite monarchy.

The Deuteronomistic History

The Former Prophets are commonly referred to in academic circles as the **Deuteronomistic History.** This characterization stems mainly from the appearance of several key themes from Deuteronomy in these books. These themes include the importance of the law and the covenant between God and the people; a broad sense of retributive justice, where disobedience to the law and the covenant brings about calamity and God's curse, while obedience leads to God's blessing; and the increasing importance of a single sanctuary in

Jerusalem for Israel's worship (as opposed to various local sanctuaries spread throughout the land).

Several scholarly proposals have surfaced regarding how the Former Prophets or the Deuteronomistic History came to be a separate unit in the OT canon. One suggestion is that this narrative block is the work of a single writer, the **Deuteronomist Historian,** dating from about 550 B.C.E. during the exilic period. The primary purpose of this writer would have been to explain the history of Israel and Judah by way of the theological concepts established in the book of Deuteronomy.

A second proposal sees the Deuteronomistic History going through at least two editions before reaching its final completion. According to this theory, the first edition was composed in the late seventh century and contained two major contrasting themes: the sin of Jeroboam that led to the destruction of the northern kingdom, and the faithfulness of David. The second edition was created by a writer in the exilic period who completed the story of Judah by reporting on its destruction and the deportation of its leaders to Babylon.

No matter how one explains the formation of the Deuteronomistic History, it is important to note that this work is not simply a reporting of national and international events. Rather, it is a description of the way that the history of ancient Israel plays out in direct response to Israel's obedience or disobedience to God's covenant and law.

The Latter Prophets: Prophecy and Prophetic Literature

The Latter Prophets are typically divided into the Major Prophets—Isaiah, Jeremiah, and Ezekiel—and the Minor Prophets, or the Book of the Twelve. Because of the diverse nature of the individual prophets in the OT and of the materials that we classify as prophetic literature, it is difficult to develop simple definitions of "prophet" and "prophecy." One thing is clear, however: the prophets did not simply predict the *future* (though sometimes they did), but primarily they attempted to communicate God's message to the people and the leaders in the *present* circumstances. The prophet was an intermediary between God and the people; the prophetic message directed toward the people often began with the messenger formula, "thus says the Lord." Along with communicating God's message to the community came the role of challenging the established social order by reminding those in power of their obligation to keep the covenant and to execute justice for the people (on this subject, see chapter fifteen).

Although the focus of most discussions of OT prophecy is on the "classical" or writing prophets, the substantive role of the early prophets narrated in the Deuteronomistic History cannot be ignored. Prophets encountered in the Former Prophets such as Samuel, Micaiah, Elijah, and Elisha helped set the stage for the better-known Latter Prophets. A characteristic that is often attributed to the early prophets is ecstasy, an intense personal experience with God. Although there continues to be considerable debate regarding the extent to which the ecstatic experience persisted among the Latter Prophets, at least some subsequent prophets (such as Ezekiel) received numerous prophetic messages from God by way of ecstatic experiences.

The phenomenon of prophecy was not unique to ancient Israel. Archaeological records and documents from other ancient Near Eastern civilizations demonstrate that various sorts of communication with the divine were believed to be carried out by religious leaders. Such records are prominent from the ancient Mesopotamian, Egyptian, and Canaanite cultures.

A primary literary feature of OT prophetic literature is poetry. In fact, some modern writers have classified the prophet as poet and claimed that one cannot fully understand prophecy without considering its poetic context. That said, it must be noted that positing too tight a connection between prophetic literature and poetry downplays the importance that prose accounts have in the prophets' writings. One way to classify the diverse literary forms found in the prophets is through the three categories of *reports* (e.g., vision accounts, call narratives, and historical narratives); *speeches* (e.g., prophecies of disaster and/or salvation, oracles of woe, trial speeches, and disputation speeches); and *prayers* (e.g., praise, lament, and intercession). Knowing about this wide range of literary genres helps the reader appreciate the complexity, depth, and richness of the prophetic literature in the OT.[6]

The Major Prophets

Isaiah

The book of Isaiah is sixty-six chapters in length. Although it is clearly a self-contained entity, there are indications within the book strongly suggesting that it was not composed in one historical context. The first thirty-nine chapters, commonly known as **First Isaiah,** describe historical events (such as the war between Judah and Israel and Syria) that occurred in the eighth century B.C.E. When the reader comes to chapter 40, however, the historical context is vastly different. References to historical figures such as Cyrus, the king of Persia, and to Judean exiles in Babylon suggest an exilic setting in the sixth century B.C.E. Chapters 40–55,

---

[6] Most Bibles include the book of Daniel among the Latter Prophets, and the Roman Catholic translations also include the book of Baruch and the Letter of Jeremiah after Lamentations (see table in chapter one). The Hebrew manuscript tradition included Daniel among the writings because of its late date and its lack of traditional prophetic material. We will discuss these three books with the Writings because of their late date and their literary differences from the traditional prophetic books.

Jerusalem (seen here from the Mount of Olives), the city of God's past, present, and/or future kingship, according to many of Israel's prophetic and poetic writings. (M. Gorman)

reflecting this situation, are commonly called **Second** (or **Deutero-**) **Isaiah.** There also appears to be a third historical context assumed at the end of the book, consisting of chapters 56–66, known as **Third** (or **Trito-**) **Isaiah.** Although the distinction between Second Isaiah and Third Isaiah is not as sharp and obvious as the one between First Isaiah and Second Isaiah, Isa 40–55 does appear to be addressed to exiles in Babylon, whereas Isa 56–66 suggests a later, postexilic date in which the addressees are (once again) living in Judah.

Although recent discussions about the book of Isaiah have stressed the unity of the book as a whole, the thematic and theological content of the book also seems to support the threefold division of Isaiah. In Isa 1–39 judgment is the dominant theme, with Isaiah's announcing the imminent destruction of Israel and Judah due to societal injustices and the corruption of worship. The importance of Jerusalem (Zion) and the Davidic covenant is highlighted in these chapters.

The prophecies in Second Isaiah tell a different story. The writer of this section looks ahead to the restoration and renewal of the Judean community. Second Isaiah calls the exilic community in Babylon to look forward to a new exodus out of Babylon and back to Judah. The writer thus draws upon the important exodus motif embedded in the Torah and reshapes it to address the exilic context. Other theological elements appear in Second Isaiah, such as the mission of a servant devoted to God (e.g., Isa 53) and the superiority of Israel's God to the Babylonian gods.

When we move into Third Isaiah, we notice various hints that these prophecies are spoken to those who have returned to or who remained in the promised land. However, the return that did take place did not turn out to be the dramatic and glorious event envisioned in Second Isaiah. The social and economic conditions were not the best. The destruction of Judah not only left the country in economic and political ruins, but it also opened the door for exploitation of the less fortunate by the more prominent members of society. The message of Third Isaiah is one of salvation, providing hope for those attempting to transform the economic hardship and political instability that exists in postexilic Judah.

In spite of the three divisions of Isaiah, a compiler (or a group of compilers) saw fit to bring the three bodies of literature together to form a whole. Even with the mixture of various social locations and time periods, when read as a single work the book of Isaiah provides an extraordinary balance of doom and hope that offers a unique understanding of the wrath and mercy of God.

Major Divisions of Isaiah		
Division	**Date**	**Themes**
First Isaiah (chs. 1–39)	Eighth Century B.C.E.	Judgment, destruction, societal injustices, and corruption of worship
Second Isaiah (chs. 40–55)	Early–Mid Sixth Century B.C.E.	Restoration, renewal, and a new exodus
Third Isaiah (chs. 56–66)	Late Sixth Century B.C.E.	Salvation, hope in the midst of economic and political instability

Jeremiah

The book of Jeremiah consists of prophetic oracles from the late seventh century to the early sixth century B.C.E. Jer 1–25 consists mainly of poetry and contains prophecies against the people of Judah for failing to keep the Mosaic covenant with God. This section includes the well-known "Confessions of Jeremiah" (throughout chs. 11–20), which primarily have the literary form of the lament. They indicate Jeremiah's internal struggles as one of God's prophetic spokespersons to an unrepentant people.

Jeremiah 26–45 consists primarily of biographical narratives (many of them attributed by scholars to Jeremiah's scribe, Baruch) about Jeremiah's ministry and the opposition and persecution that he encountered. Also contained in this section is the Book of Consolation or Comfort, which includes the well-known text promising a new covenant that will be written on the hearts of the people rather than on stone tablets (31:31–34). Jeremiah 46–52 contains prophecies against other nations (such as Egypt, Philistia, Babylon, etc.) that add an international flavor to the book and demonstrate that Jeremiah's prophetic activity was not restricted to Judah.

Instead of drawing upon Zion traditions (like First Isaiah), the book of Jeremiah focuses upon the exodus and Mosaic covenant traditions. Jeremiah preached loyalty and obedience so that the Mosaic covenant could be fulfilled. Like many other prophets, Jeremiah confronted the powers of the social order because of the rampant social injustice. He complained that while there was trust in religious institutions, there was distrust and oppression among the people. Jeremiah also had confrontations with other prophets and protested that they preached a false hope when destruction—due to the people's sins and their refusal to repent—was just around the corner. Although such destruction was inevitable, Jeremiah was a prophet of hope as he envisioned a new people, a new age, and a new covenant (Jer 30–33). The books of Jeremiah and Isaiah are very different in structure and character, but one can find a similar balance between judgment and hope.

Ezekiel

The setting of the book of Ezekiel is the Judean exilic community in Babylon at the settlement of Tel Abib. Ezekiel was taken off to Babylon during the first deportation in 597 B.C.E., where he prophesied while awaiting the impending destruction of Judah and Jerusalem. The first twenty-four chapters of the book contain powerful visions, allegories, and symbolic acts that prophesy the doom and judgment against Judah and Jerusalem that would occur in 587/586 B.C.E. Ezek 25–32 consists of diatribes and oracles against other nations. Chapter 33 is a transitional chapter to the latter, more hopeful, part of the book (chs. 34–48). Chapters 34 to 39 contain passages of restoration, including the well-known "dry bones" passage (Ezek 37). Ezek 40–48 consists of an elaborate vision of the New Jerusalem and the future temple. God is to be a temple in the midst of the people, worship will be rejuvenated, and a life-giving river will flow forth from the temple.

Primarily because of his priestly lineage, Ezekiel confronted the sins of the people in matters of worship and the temple. One of his visions portrays the abominations being practiced at the temple and the resulting departure of God (Ezek 8–11). Although Ezekiel viewed Judah's coming destruction to be inevitable and sanctioned by God, he also saw hope and restoration on the other side of that destruction, as seen in the above-mentioned passages. Once again we have a prophetic book that balances the themes of judgment and hope.

The Book of the Twelve/The Minor Prophets

Rounding out the Latter Prophets is a collection of twelve prophetic books that range in length from several verses (Obadiah) to over a dozen chapters

(Hosea, Zechariah). Although there is no scholarly consensus as to how these twelve prophetic books were formed into a single collection, references from other sources lead us to believe that it became a collection no later than 200 B.C.E. (Sir 49:10). The "Minor Prophets" are not listed in chronological order, and a close assessment reveals that they span more than four hundred years (approximately 750 to 350 B.C.E.).

Three of the Minor Prophets stem from the eighth century B.C.E. Amos and Hosea directed their prophecies to the northern kingdom, while Micah prophesied to the southern kingdom. Amos severely criticized the oppressive sociopolitical system in the north: "Let justice roll down like waters," he famously wrote (Amos 5:24). Hosea focused upon Israel's idolatrous unfaithfulness to God, comparing it to having relations with a prostitute. Micah contrasted oracles of judgment and hope, and he viewed Jerusalem as Israel's holy center and a place where nations would come together.

Three prophets in the Book of the Twelve emerged during the late seventh century B.C.E. The book of Zephaniah is basically a small collection of sayings that includes diatribes against Judah and other nations. The book of Nahum centers its prophecy on the Assyrian city of Nineveh. Nahum recorded words of judgment for the Assyrian Empire, which had oppressed Judah for centuries but was now in decline and moving toward destruction. Habakkuk emerges soon after the death of Josiah, king of Judah, in about 609 B.C.E. He uses the literary device of a dialogue between himself and God to portray the despair that exists when wicked persons in society seem to triumph while the innocent suffer.

The only Minor Prophet dating specifically from the exilic period is Obadiah. The book of Obadiah consists mainly of a vision regarding Edom, Judah's southeastern neighbor. The vision begins with a call to rise up against Edom and then goes on to announce Edom's destruction.

Several of the Minor Prophets lift up their voices during the postexilic period of ancient Israel. Haggai and Zechariah are among the exiles who returned from Babylon, and they call upon both the leaders and the people to engage in the restoration of the temple in Jerusalem. The enigmatic book of Joel combines elements of preexilic prophecy with elements of postexilic prophecy. Joel uses powerful imagery (e.g., a swarm of locusts) to express the wrath of God, but at the same time he expresses a degree of hope that God will reach out to the people of postexilic Judah and hear their prayers.

Malachi uses the literary device of question and answer to challenge the people and call them to accountability. Although specific issues such as divorce, corrupt worship, and tithing are addressed, the book's primary theme is the importance of faithfulness to God's covenant with the people.

The first verse of the book of Jonah identifies Jonah in a prophetic role, but from a literary standpoint, the book itself does not resemble prophetic literature.

Instead of containing prophetic oracles, Jonah is a narrative about the prophet that is interrupted in chapter two with a psalm of thanksgiving. As the plot unfolds and Jonah's character is developed, the book teaches the reader about various aspects of the prophetic vocation and the nature of God.

THE WRITINGS

The last division of the OT includes a miscellaneous collection of diverse literary materials such as psalms, wisdom books, historical materials, and short stories. Since the Writings was the last division of the OT to come into formation, most of the books in this division are relatively late and can be dated to the postexilic period. Most of the deuterocanonical books stem from this period as well, so it is best to discuss them here, too.

The Psalms

The book of Psalms (sometimes called the Psalter) is a collection of 150 prayers and hymns that stem from various worship experiences of ancient Israel. These psalms are arranged into five smaller collections (1–41, 42–72, 73–89, 90–106, and 107–150), but there is no systematic arrangement to these collections. The book of Psalms did not begin as a deliberate collection of 150 texts. Individual psalms were written, and then small collections were formed, which were made into larger collections until the entire book was completed.

By and large, the individual psalms are anonymous. Although seventy-three psalms are ascribed to David, this does not necessarily mean that David composed them. It is more probable that they were attributed to the name and honor of David because of his place in ancient Israelite history. Many of the psalms have titles or superscriptions that were added by later hands to give the psalms historical relevance, and to connect these psalms to specific individuals, groups, or events in Israel's history.

The psalms are clearly written as poetry. Some of the poems are simple and brief, but others are lengthy, elaborate literary masterpieces. For example, Ps 117 is a brief hymn comprising only two verses, while Ps 119 is an acrostic[7] poem of 176 verses. The three primary literary categories of the psalms are hymns of praise, laments, and psalms of thanksgiving.

---

[7] The first eight verses of this psalm begin with the first letter of the Hebrew alphabet, the second eight verses begin with the second letter of the Hebrew alphabet, and so on.

Major Types of Psalms

A *hymn of praise* (e.g., Pss 29; 100; 146; and 150) lifts up the glory and great-ness of God while centering upon God's activity in the ancient Israelite commu-nity. Most hymns of praise are not prayers to God per se but texts *about* God that stress the importance of praising God. They are diverse in nature and structure, but they generally begin with a call to praise and then recount great things God has done that are worthy of praise.

Nearly one-half of the psalms in the Psalter are examples of the *lament* (e.g., Pss 5; 13; 22; and 88). While hymns of praise express joy and exultation, laments express a sense of sorrow and distress that exists in individual or community life. One often finds deep emotions expressed in the lament psalms, such as grief, agony, defeat, despair, sorrow, and/or feelings of abandonment or betrayal. Sometimes these emotions are directed toward an enemy or a difficult general situation in life, while at other times they are directed specifically toward God. The internal structure of the basic lament usually includes several elements: (a) the complaint; (b) confession of trust; (c) petition for divine intervention; and, sometimes, (d) praise or a vow of praise. However, not all psalms of lament fol-low this structure rigidly.

Another major category of the psalms is the *psalm of thanksgiving* (e.g., Pss 30; 34; 107; and 116). The notion of thanksgiving here is not general gratitude. Rather, the psalm of thanksgiving takes the reader through a recent experience in which God has delivered the psalmist from a situation of distress and for which the psalmist give thanks. (It is very important to note that the psalmist is on the other side of the distress and that deliverance has indeed taken place. This is in contrast to the lament psalms, where the psalmist is still in the midst of the distress.) The psalm of thanksgiving is about transformation: from despair to joy, from darkness to light, from near death to new life. As in the case of the la-ment psalm, there is a basic structure to the psalm of thanksgiving: (a) introduc-tion; (b) account of the distress, petition, and divine deliverance; and (c) statement of thanks or praise.

In addition to these three primary types of psalms, there are other types that add to the richness and the diversity of the Psalter. These include psalms of trust (Pss 23 and 121), creation psalms (Ps 8), enthronement psalms (Pss 95–99, fo-cusing on God as ruler and king), royal psalms (Ps 2, focusing on the human king), hymns of Zion (Ps 84), Torah psalms (Ps 119), wisdom psalms (Ps 1), and storytelling psalms (Pss 105 and 106).[8] Because of this diverse nature of the Psal-ter, there is a lack of continuity that might bring the psalms together in a tight and connected fashion. Therefore, one of the best ways to study the psalms is to

---

[8] The parenthetical examples are illustrative, not exhaustive.

examine each psalm on its own merits. On the other hand, one paramount theme in the psalms is the significance, for both the individual and the community, of developing and maintaining a relationship with God.

Wisdom Literature

The protocanonical books of Proverbs, Job, and Ecclesiastes, as well as the deuterocanonical books of Sirach and the Wisdom of Solomon, have come to be known as wisdom books. These five books differ in style and material content, but there are several qualities that distinguish them from other canonical books. In wisdom literature, the writers reflect about the issues and problems of life. Such reflection often leads the reader on a quest to discern how suffering and justice relate to each other and to attempt to discover what universal truths do indeed exist in this world. There is also a concern for identifying the basic rules by which people are to live by reflecting upon life experiences. Additionally, wisdom teachings focus on the world order by discerning how this creation is ruled by God. Such teachings view the recognition of God as creator as a central point for genuine wisdom and understanding.

Proverbs

The book of Proverbs is primarily a collection of short two-line statements, dating from a preexilic context, that impart practical wisdom. These brief statements comprise the bulk of the book in chapters 10–29. These chapters are preceded and followed by longer wisdom poems in Prov 1–9 and 30–31, respectively. Underlying Proverbs is a conventional wisdom that encourages people how to live and outlines a clear understanding of the difference between right and wrong. This pragmatic and optimistic understanding postulates that the wise people in society are known by their righteous behavior, and that God grants them happiness and the good things of life. Foolish persons, on the other hand, are known by their wicked behavior; as a result, they are destined to misery and suffering as punishment from God.

Job

The book of Job moves away from the practical and optimistic wisdom of Proverbs and adopts a more reflective and skeptical position. In fact, interpreters of biblical wisdom literature have viewed Job as a rebuttal to, or protest against, the conventional wisdom found in Proverbs. Scholars have dated this work from as early as sometime in the preexilic period to as late as the postexilic period.

One can scarcely understand the book of Job without noting that the book is comprised of both prose and poetry. The beginning two chapters and the last eleven verses (42:7–17) are in narrative form; they frame the poetry found in Job 3:1–42:6. The narrative concerns a prosperous man named Job who loses his family and possessions as a result of a wager between God and "the Satan."[9] In this story, Job accepts his suffering by rationalizing that just as God gives prosperity and blessing, God can also take it away. The tale ends on an upbeat note, when—without warning or explanation—Job is blessed a second time with material possessions and additional family.

The character of Job in the poetry contrasts sharply with the Job depicted in the narrative section. In the former, Job challenges God and demands his day in court. Through a cycle of speeches between Job and his friends Eliphaz, Bildad, and Zophar, Job argues that he has done nothing deserving of his suffering, while his friends conclude that because Job has experienced this immense suffering he must have sinned against God. After this series of speeches, Job takes his case directly to God, and at the end of the poetry section God offers a response. The response does not explain Job's innocent suffering, as Job requests, but rather focuses on God's omnipotence. By challenging the conventional wisdom represented by Proverbs, the book of Job identifies the existence of innocent suffering and also questions what role God plays in the midst of it. Although the book does not offer simple answers, it explores how faithful individuals struggle to understand their relationship with God as they encounter problematic and distressful experiences.

Ecclesiastes

The book of Ecclesiastes, dating from about 300 B.C.E., is similar to the book of Job in the way it challenges the optimistic wisdom tradition of Proverbs. The basic thinking of the writer, often referred to as Qoheleth or Koheleth (meaning "preacher/teacher," which is how the author is identified in the Hebrew text of 1:1), can be summed up in the phrase that begins and ends the book: "Vanity of vanities! All is vanity" (1:2; 12:8). Embarking on a quest to discover the meaning of life, the author shares various observations and reflections. Qoheleth concludes that injustice prevails as the righteous perish and the wicked flourish. Therefore, the neat notion of retributive justice outlined in Proverbs does not play out in life, according to Qoheleth's experience. Because the wise and the foolish endure the same fate in the end, namely death, Qoheleth laments that there is a strong sense of futility that pervades life.

---

[9] In the OT the Hebrew word for Satan does not designate a demonic figure or the devil but rather a member of God's heavenly entourage who assumes an adversarial role. In fact, in Num 22:22 "the Satan" is actually an angel of God who takes on an adversarial role against Balaam.

Because of this it may not come as a surprise that the addition of Ecclesiastes to the OT canon was disputed. Despite its pessimism, however, the writer asserts that there is a God, that life is worth living, and that people should live joyously and in the best way they can until death comes. They should do so without trying to change the unchangeable and without expecting rewards or punishments. Along with its pessimism, then, Ecclesiastes does stress the importance of faith in God even when God's ways elude human understanding.

Sirach and the Book of Wisdom

The two deuterocanonical books that fall under the rubric of wisdom literature are Sirach and the Book of Wisdom (Wisdom of Solomon). Although Sirach was originally written in Hebrew in about 180 B.C.E., modern versions of both books are based on Greek translations of the Hebrew. Sirach revisits the theme of the fear of God as pointing one to wisdom and leaves the heavy existential questioning of Job and Ecclesiastes behind. The writer of Sirach picks up on the doctrine of retributive justice present in Proverbs, while also recognizing that there are ambiguities in life and various limitations to human knowledge. The last chapters of the book, Sir 44–50, consist of one long hymn praising renowned figures in ancient Israel's history. Sirach praises the ancestors for the ways in which they exemplified cultural values that are important to the wisdom tradition.

The Book of Wisdom, or the Wisdom of Solomon, was most likely written sometime during the first century B.C.E. The book spoke to ancient Israelites who found themselves in the Greek culture of Alexandria in Egypt. The writer was influenced by this Greek culture; traces of philosophical Stoicism and Platonic idealism can be found in the book. Instead of confining the notion of retributive justice to this world, where the righteous either receive just rewards (Proverbs) or are punished unfairly (Job and Ecclesiastes), the Book of Wisdom introduces the theme of immortality to demonstrate that the righteous may not be rewarded in this life but will receive grace and mercy in the life to come. The writer also recontextualizes the story of the exodus to show that God protected the people and rules the world by wisdom. Perhaps the Book of Wisdom's primary task was to preserve the heritage of ancient Israelite faith within the midst of Greek and Roman influences in an effort to encourage Jews in a foreign land to proclaim their faith in God.

The Scrolls

The book of Ruth, the Song of Songs, Ecclesiastes, Lamentations, and Esther have been combined in the Hebrew manuscript tradition to form a collection called the scrolls or **Megilloth.** These five books have been grouped together because they are each associated with a specific Jewish festival, as shown in the table below.

The books of Ruth and Esther are narratives that resemble the short story. Ruth deals with issues regarding loyalty and family; it addresses the social questions of foreigners functioning in the land of Israel and the plight of widowed women in a patrilineal culture. The book of Esther, on the other hand, takes up the issue of certain Israelites living in a foreign land. This was of grave importance during the postexilic period since not all exiles chose to return, or were permitted to return, to Judah. The deuterocanonical version of Esther includes additions that are basically a dream, plus prayers by Mordecai (Esther's cousin who encourages Esther to persuade King Ahasuerus in order to prevent the annihilation of her people).

The Song of Songs[10] is a collection of love poems that exalt the unending love between two people. By focusing upon the wonders of the natural world and the beauty of the human body, these poems underscore the fact that love, sexuality, and creation are blessings from God that should be cherished. In contrast, the book of Lamentations is a collection of five poems that take the form of laments and dirges. These poems lament and ponder the destruction of Jerusalem, with hope that God will restore the people and the land.

The Five Scrolls (Megilloth) and Their Associated Festivals	
Scroll	**Ancient Israelite Festival**
Ruth	Festival of Weeks
Song of Songs	Passover
Ecclesiastes	Festival of Tabernacles
Lamentations	Ninth of Ab[11]
Esther	Purim

Historical Books

There are several books in the Writings that focus on various aspects of ancient Israel's history. In many ways the Books of 1 and 2 Chronicles tell much of the story recounted in 1 and 2 Samuel and 1 and 2 Kings. However, the

---

[10] Also known as Canticle of Canticles (abbreviated Canticles) and the Song of Solomon.

[11] The date on which the temple was destroyed.

Chronicler writes during the (postexilic) Persian period and has a different agenda than the Deuteronomist Historian. Although the Deuteronomist Historian looks upon David in a favorable manner, the Chronicler paints an even more positive picture of David. The Chronicler views David as the one who set the building of the temple in motion (even though it was actually built under Solomon's reign). Narratives that portray the negative side of David's character, such as the story of David and Bathsheba, are either downplayed or omitted altogether. The Chronicler also stresses the importance of the temple because the monarchy had come and gone, and the restoration of the temple was a matter of crucial importance during postexilic times.

The books of Ezra and Nehemiah were originally one work that was subsequently divided into two separate books. The two books contain narratives about Judean life in the latter part of the sixth century and the beginning of the fifth century B.C.E. Ezra is known for coming to Jerusalem and calling the people to return to the religious and social standards set forth in the law. Nehemiah is known for initiating the project of rebuilding the temple. Both books identify problematic issues in postexilic Judah, such as intermarriage, economic disparity, disregard for ordinances pertaining to sacrifices, worship, and special ancient Israelite customs. The necessary reforms spelled out in each book illustrate how these two leaders helped Judah regain a sense of religious identity by reclaiming the power and authority of the law.

The deuterocanonical books 1 and 2 Maccabees take the history of Judah into the second century B.C.E. at a time when the Hellenistic Seleucid Empire (centered in Syria) gained control of Palestine under the reign of Antiochus IV, known as Antiochus Epiphanes. Antiochus Epiphanes attacked Jerusalem and desecrated the temple. Judas Maccabeus, son of Mattathias, led a revolt that resulted in a brief period of independence for Judah. First Maccabees provides an historical account of the events, while 2 Maccabees is a collection of dramatic stories that focus on the heroes of this historic era.

Additional Writings

The book of Daniel neatly divides into two distinctive parts. The first six chapters emerged sometime in the Persian period, anytime between 538 and 333 B.C.E., and consist of stories about Daniel and his colleagues. Daniel 7–12 was probably completed around 165 B.C.E.; it is a series of **apocalyptic** visions and their subsequent interpretations. (The deuterocanonical version inserts the Prayer of Azariah between Dan 3:23 and 3:24 and tacks on to the end of the book the stories of Susanna [chapter 13] and Bel and the Dragon [chapter 14].)

Although Daniel finds its place among the Prophets in most Protestant Bibles, the book is not prophetic literature. Many interpreters classify the latter half of Daniel as apocalyptic literature because of the nature of the visions, which contain symbolic and obscure terminology. God is in control of the world events but enters into conflict with evil forces, manifesting a type of dualism that is characteristic of apocalyptic literature. In the end, God triumphs and a new age is ushered in. It is often believed that the events depicted in the latter half of Daniel reflect the time of the Maccabean crisis (second century B.C.E.) between the ancient Israelites and Antiochus Epiphanes. Although the Israelites held off the Seleucid emperor, they endured much suffering and persecution before they gained victory. Such circumstances provide the setting for apocalyptic literature.

Like the books of Esther and Ruth, the deuterocanonical books of Tobit and Judith are short stories. The story of Tobit focuses upon two characters who have been afflicted. Tobit suddenly loses his sight, and his future daughter-in-law Sarah is possessed with a demon. With the intervention of God's angel, Raphael, Tobit regains his sight, Sarah's demon is driven out, and Sarah marries Tobit's son Tobias. The story of Judith is about a widow who uses cunning and deception to defeat the Assyrian army, which is on the verge of destroying her people and land. The ostensible historical setting of Tobit is the Assyrian exile, while the setting of Judith is the Babylonian exile (though the book itself includes historical inaccuracies as it postulates that Nebuchadnezzar was king of the Assyrian Empire). Both books, however, contain numerous hints that suggest a later time period sometime in the postexilic era but prior to the rise of Hellenistic domination.

In the deuterocanonical tradition, the book of Baruch concludes with the Letter of Jeremiah. The book contains confessions, a wisdom poem, and prophetic oracles of hope purportedly written by Jeremiah's scribe Baruch. Although most Bibles include Baruch among the Prophets (following Jeremiah and Lamentations), we include it in this section because of its probable later dating. Similar to the books of Tobit and Judith, Baruch demonstrates limited knowledge of the exilic era and is considered to be written at a much later time during the postexilic period.

The deuterocanonical books we have discussed to this point are recognized by both the Roman Catholic Church and the Orthodox Churches. But the Eastern Orthodox canon also includes 1 and 2 Esdras, the Prayer of Manasseh (in an appendix), Psalm 151 and 3 Maccabees. First Esdras and 3 Maccabees are historical writings. First Esdras begins with the reign of Josiah and recounts the subsequent fall of Jerusalem. The book then moves into the Persian period by including virtually all of the book of Ezra and a few verses from the book of Nehemiah. The historical setting of 3 Maccabees is a time when the Ptolemaic Empire controlled Palestine prior to the Maccabean era discussed in 1 and 2 Maccabees. The book

reports an unsuccessful attempt by the Ptolemaic emperor to enter and thus dese-
crate the sanctuary of the temple of Jerusalem, as well as his subsequent wrath
upon the Israelites in Egypt once he returns.

The Prayer of Manasseh is a short penitential prayer calling for God's mercy
and forgiveness by King Manasseh, who is pictured by the Deuteronomist Historian as one of the more evil kings in ancient Israelite history. Psalm 151 is a brief
poem that recounts God's choosing of David to become king and his exuberant
triumph over Goliath. Second Esdras, like the book of Daniel, is commonly classified as apocalyptic literature. It consists primarily of a series of seven visions
that denounce the Roman Empire and deal with the issue of God's goodness and
power in the midst of the evil of the world. It is the only OT book written after
the birth of Jesus, sometime toward the end of the first century C.E.

CONCLUSION

It is an impossible task to do justice to the OT in one chapter of an introduction to the Bible. In fact, entire textbooks have often fallen short of capturing the
full beauty and richness of the character and composition of the OT. This chapter
has attempted to cover some basics of OT literature and introduce the most significant aspects of this massive document. We have shied away from lengthy and
technical discussions since more detailed discussions on some of the more de-
batable and problematic issues can be found in the basic OT textbooks, specific
monographs, and commentaries. Although this chapter could have been organized in numerous ways, by following the Hebrew manuscript tradition and introducing the deuterocanonical material at appropriate points, we hope that
readers will not only gain an appreciation for the OT's rich diversity, but also understand that the individual books relate to one another by the way in which
they were put together to form one document. Furthermore, it is important to
note that the Bible itself is one document, and many messages and theological
themes developed in the OT are addressed and reshaped by the NT writers. Such
themes include creation, covenant, sin, redemption, justice, peace, and salvation. The presence of such themes in the NT demonstrates the importance of the
OT Scriptures to later writers and allows for continuance of and elaboration
upon the biblical story.

FOR FURTHER READING AND STUDY

Anderson, Bernhard W., and Katheryn Pfisterer Darr. *Understanding the Old
Testament.* 4th ed., abridged and updated. Englewood Cliffs, N.J.: Prentice

Hall, 1997. A solid introduction that addresses the basic historical and literary aspects of the OT with adequate attention to the archaeology of ancient Israel.

Birch, Bruce C., Walter Brueggemann, Terrence E. Fretheim, and David L. Petersen. *A Theological Introduction to the Old Testament.* Nashville: Abingdon, 1999. A text that focuses on the theological impact of the OT material while addressing basic historical, literary, and sociological issues.

Boadt, Lawrence. *Reading the Old Testament: An Introduction.* New York: Paulist, 1985. A standard introduction with special attention to the deuterocanonical books.

Brueggemann, Walter. *Theology of the Old Testament: Testimony, Dispute, Advocacy.* Minneapolis: Fortress, 1997. An in-depth treatment of OT theology by perhaps the leading American OT theologian in recent decades.

Childs, Brevard S. *Introduction to the Old Testament as Scripture.* Philadelphia: Fortress, 1979. An introduction written from a canonical-critical approach.

Gottwald, Norman K. *The Hebrew Bible Today: A Socio-Literary Introduction.* Philadelphia: Fortress, 1985. A comprehensive, intermediate introduction emphasizing the sociological and literary contexts of the OT, with many helpful maps, tables, and charts.

Harrington, Daniel J. *Invitation to the Apocrypha.* Grand Rapids: Eerdmans, 1999. A basic introduction to the OT Apocrypha.

LaSor, William, David Allan Hubbard, Frederic William Bush, and Leslie C. Allen. *Old Testament Survey: The Message, Form, and Background of the Old Testament.* 2d ed. Grand Rapids: Eerdmans, 1996. A standard introduction with an evangelical flavor.

McKenzie, Steven L., and M. Patrick Graham, eds. *The Hebrew Bible Today: An Introduction to Critical Issues.* Louisville: Westminster John Knox, 1998. An excellent text that examines the critical issues of academic scholarship in the OT with special attention to scholarly consensus and dissension.

Soggin, Alberto J. *Introduction to the Old Testament: From Its Origins to the Closing of the Alexandrian Canon.* 3d ed. Louisville: Presbyterian Publishing Company, 1989. A technical introduction that aptly addresses the German contributions to OT studies.

Chapter 4

The Character and Composition of the Books of the New Testament

MICHAEL J. GORMAN

Like their counterparts in the Old Testament, the writings of the New Testament constitute a small library of sorts. Yet just as the OT is unified in its affirmation of the one God who has chosen to be in covenant relationship with Israel, there is also a unity to the NT. Its diverse documents all bear witness to Jesus of Nazareth, known by experience to be the resurrected Lord, as the one sent by the same God to be Israel's Messiah and Savior of all. In this chapter we briefly consider the nature of the books that make up the NT, and how they came into being.

AN OVERVIEW

The twenty-seven NT writings—the same twenty-seven for Catholics, Protestants, and Orthodox[1]—represent four basic genres, grouped together according to their type:

- *Gospels* (4)—The Gospels of (or according to) Matthew, Mark, Luke, and John, comprising about half of the NT text

- *Acts* (1)—The Acts of the Apostles

- *Letters* (21)—thirteen attributed to Paul (Romans through Philemon) and eight attributed to other writers or anonymous (Hebrews through Jude), comprising about one-third of the NT text

---

[1] Actually, as noted in chapter one, there are minor exceptions: a small part of the Syriac church has a twenty-two-book NT canon, and the Ethiopic church's "broader" NT canon contains thirty-five books.

- *Apocalypse,* or *Revelation* (1)—The Revelation to John

Each of these types of literature has much in common with similar kinds of Jewish and non-Jewish writings of the first century. At the same time, by virtue of the unusual subject matter and purpose of these writings, each genre is unique and is, in some sense, a new literary type. For example, it is sometimes said that Paul created the "pastoral letter," while someone (probably Mark) fashioned a new entity that told the story of the central figure in the Christian good news (Greek *euangelion*), or **gospel,** Middle English for "good news."

Like the OT, the NT includes writings from various times and places. While the chronological span is shorter than that of the OT, the geographical breadth is wider. The earliest NT writing (either 1 Thessalonians or Galatians) dates from about 50 C.E., nearly two decades after the death of Jesus (ca. 30–33 C.E.). The date of the latest books is more disputed (ca. 95 to ca. 150 C.E.), but the span is only about fifty years for the majority, if not all, of the documents. Yet these documents were written by and for people not only in Palestine and Syria, but also in other parts of the Roman Empire, including Asia Minor (modern Turkey) and Europe (modern Greece and Italy). Since the *lingua franca* ("common tongue") of the Roman Empire was Greek, all of the NT documents were written in Greek, not Hebrew, Aramaic, or Latin, though some of the sources for the Gospels may have been in Aramaic.

In many respects, the NT is an extended commentary on the OT in light of Jesus Christ (i.e., the Jewish Messiah). The NT contains more than three hundred direct OT quotations and probably several thousand additional allusions to the OT. Of particular importance to the NT writers are Genesis, Exodus, Deuteronomy, Psalms, Isaiah, Jeremiah, and Daniel. Commonly heard OT texts range from legal-ethical material (e.g., Lev 19:18: "love your neighbor as yourself") to royal-messianic poetry (e.g., Ps 2:7: "You are my son; today I have begotten you") to prophetic-apocalyptic promises and visions (e.g., Jer 31:31–34: the "new covenant"). Such texts reverberate throughout all NT genres and writings.

We consider now each of the four NT genres in turn. As we do so, we must keep in mind that biblical scholarship is constantly evolving, and that the "majority opinions" of today are not the "final answer."

THE GOSPELS

Scholars have scoured antiquity for genres, such as ancient biographies or "lives" of the famous or holy, into which they might place the four canonical Gospels. While comparing the Gospels to other ancient texts is useful, there is a uniqueness to these four writings that calls for a discrete classification. Our working definition of a gospel will be as follows: *an interpretive narrative of the appearance, ministry, death, and resurrection of Jesus and of the significance of that story for those who hear or read it.* Each gospel has its own literary and theological character, owing to the varied authors, communities, and circumstances that helped produce them. Most recent scholars have believed that each gospel was also written to address the needs of a particular community. But a growing number of experts think that the Gospels were designed for more universal Christian usage.

None of the gospels bears the name of an author (the "titles" having been added later), and early-church traditions associating each gospel with a particular apostle or his associate are probably oversimplifications of the actual situations. The gospels are not merely the records of eyewitnesses. Instead, a complex process of transmission seems to have occurred (see Luke 1:1–4) in several "stages," of which all but the first are overlapping:

- *The words and deeds of Jesus (late 20s? to early 30s)*—These were observed, remembered, and passed on, especially by Jesus' closest disciples. His oral Jewish culture encouraged both the careful preservation and the interpretation of these memories.

- *Oral transmission (30s to 60s and beyond)*—After their experience of Jesus' death and resurrection, the disciples and others increased the volume of oral recitation (and interpretation) of Jesus' words and deeds as they proclaimed Jesus to prospective and recent converts.[2] This process, of course, continued even after written sources emerged.

- *Early written sources (40s? and beyond)*—The gospels seem to incorporate earlier written documents, such as short collections of miracle stories or parables. An early written account of Jesus' passion may also have existed. Most importantly, many scholars believe that a significant collection of Jesus' teachings (in the form of sayings or discourses) was produced in the 50s and was used by both Matthew and Luke. It is designated **Q** as an abbreviation for *Quelle*, the German word for "source" (see further below).

- *The canonical gospels themselves (late 60s? to 90s?)*—Beginning just before or after the destruction of the Jewish temple in 70 C.E., the four canonical gospels (and probably others) were produced. Most scholars date Mark

---

[2] Some scholars believe that teachings and stories were not only *adapted,* but also regularly *invented*—and attributed to Jesus—during this period. But this view, especially in its most radical (and sometimes vocal) forms, is not the position of most NT scholars.

to the 60s or early 70s, Matthew and Luke to the 70s or 80s, and John to
the 90s. (A few scholars date Matthew and Luke before 70, and some put
John earlier than the 90s.) The individual responsible for a written gospel
is called an **evangelist.**

Scholars refer to the Gospels of Matthew, Mark, and Luke as the **Synoptic**
("seeing together") **Gospels,** or simply "the Synoptics," since they tell their story
of Jesus in a similar way, whereas John is quite different. Scholars have tried
to explain the similarities and differences among the synoptics (the so-called
Synoptic Problem). Especially striking are two phenomena: (1) the teachings
of Jesus common to Matthew and Luke but absent from Mark (designated
"Q") and (2) the similarities and differences in wording and arrangement
among all three.

The current majority opinion is that Mark is the earliest gospel (called
"Markan priority") and that Matthew and Luke each used and adapted both
Mark and the source Q. This is referred to as the **Two-Source Theory.** Most
scholars also believe that Matthew and Luke each added his own special material, abbreviated "M" and "L" respectively. Thus this hypothesis is also sometimes called the **Four-Source Theory** or (less accurately) the Four-Document
Theory and can be illustrated as follows[3]:

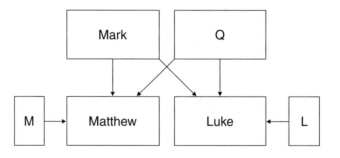

A growing number of scholars question whether the document Q ever existed,
mainly arguing that Matthew used Mark and was then used by Luke. A smaller
number believe that Matthew is the earliest synoptic gospel, used by both Mark
and Luke. Whatever their convictions about gospel origins, most scholars today
are committed to the interpretation of the final form of the text (the gospel itself).

---

[3] The abbreviations "M" and "L" should be used to refer to the unique Matthean and
Lukan material, regardless of whether that material is from written and/or oral sources.

Mark

According to most scholars, the Gospel of Mark is the earliest of the four gospels and dates from just before or after 70. It is the shortest, lacking much of the teaching material found in the other gospels, and it contains no birth or postresurrection appearance narratives. Rather, Mark is an action-packed story about the advent of the kingdom (or reign) of God that falls into two main sections. The first part reveals the *power* of Jesus in bringing the kingdom as healer and exorcist, while the second part (beginning at 8:27–30, Peter's confession of Jesus as Messiah at Caesarea Philippi) paradoxically stresses the *death* of Jesus, who takes on the role of Suffering Servant, as the ultimate purpose of his own coming, the paradigm of discipleship, and the manifestation of ultimate divine power.

Mark's audience should therefore expect to suffer like Jesus and to serve others, including the marginalized (such as children). It must reject the imperial values of power and domination. In addition, those who encounter this Gospel will likely find themselves mirrored in the descriptions of the disciples, who constantly do not "get it," for a suffering Messiah and costly discipleship are not easily accepted. Nevertheless, the disciples are explicitly commissioned early in the Gospel to share Jesus' mission, and they are encouraged to persevere. Moreover, when the Gospel ends surprisingly without any public testimony to Jesus' resurrection, the readers/hearers are implicitly invited to bear that testimony themselves.[4]

Traditional identifications of "Mark" as the John Mark of Acts (and a few Pauline letters) who was Peter's interpreter are disputed today. Most scholars, however, find credible the traditional association of this Gospel with Rome, though some argue for Galilee or Syria.

Matthew

The Gospel of Matthew appears to have been written in the 70s or 80s, though perhaps earlier, primarily for a Jewish-Christian audience. Many scholars believe the Gospel originated in Syria. Its principal theme is that Jesus fulfills the Scriptures of Israel. Jesus is, in fact, "Emmanuel," or "God with us" (1:23, citing Isa 7:14; cf. 28:20).

---

[4] The best manuscripts of the Gospel of Mark end this way at 16:8. The longer endings printed in some Bibles come from inferior manuscripts and were almost certainly added to the text of the Gospel to supplement the unusual ending (whether deliberate or accidental) at 16:8.

Part of the northern tip of the Sea of Galilee, looking from the "Mount of the Beatitudes," where tradition says Jesus delivered the Sermon on the Mount (Matt 5–7). (M. Gorman)

Matthew's probable use of several sources (Mark, Q, and M) does not produce a hodge-podge of material but an artfully designed literary whole. Unlike Mark, Matthew begins the story of Jesus with a birth narrative and concludes with resurrection appearances. The main part of the Gospel is structured in two parts (see 4:17 and 16:21), the first focusing on Jesus' preaching and healing, the second on his suffering and death. It also contains five distinct blocks of teaching material (like the so-called "Sermon on the Mount," chs. 5–7)—parallel to the five books of Moses—that alternate with miracle stories and other narratives. The evangelist thereby asserts that Jesus is now the Teacher for both Jews and Gentiles to follow.

To follow this Teacher is to pursue a "greater righteousness": to take up the yoke of a new Law of compassion and mercy rather than sacrifice. It is also, as in Mark, to expect suffering and to attend to the needs of the marginalized, such as the hungry and those in prison. Furthermore, it is explicitly to make disciples of all nations (28:16–20).

Luke

The Gospel of Luke is volume one of a two-volume (Luke-Acts) narrative of God bringing salvation to the whole world through the ministry of God's Son Jesus and his followers, empowered by the Spirit. The salvation and "peace on earth" (2:14) offered by God surpass the salvation and the *pax Romana* ("Roman peace") offered by the Emperor.

In addition to its emphasis on the Spirit and on universal salvation, Luke's Gospel highlights Jesus' ministry to the poor and oppressed, the role of women, and prayer. The special "L" material includes some of the synoptics' best-known texts, such as the parables of the Good Samaritan (10:25–37) and of the Prodigal Son (15:11–32). Like the other synoptics, Luke also assumes that Jesus' followers, who must share his mission of compassion and liberation (4:16–30), will be persecuted, and it encourages faithful witness in spite of such suffering.

The authorship and provenance of this Gospel cannot be ascertained with surety. The audience is almost certainly Gentile and probably urban; the evangelist may have been Paul's traveling companion, but many scholars question that traditional identification. Luke's Gospel is usually dated to the 70s or 80s, though it may be earlier.

John

Known for centuries as the "spiritual" gospel, the Fourth Gospel—the Gospel of John—is decidedly different from the synoptics. Nonetheless, it is of the same genre. It narrates the story of Jesus as the "incarnation" ("en-fleshment") of the divine Word.

In John, Jesus delivers long discourses, not short parables. Rather than healing multitudes and exorcising demons, he performs seven "signs" (none of which involves demons), many interpreted by a discourse. "I am" statements (e.g., "I am the bread of life") tersely summarize these discourses in OT-rich symbolic language. Rather than speaking only implicitly, at most, about his divinity, Jesus repeatedly affirms his unity with the Father. The Johannine Jesus does not speak about the kingdom of God, and his own style of speaking is remarkably similar to that of the narrator of the Gospel and even to that of 1 John. And in this Gospel, Jesus dies, not on Passover itself (as in the synoptics), but on the Day of Preparation, just as the Passover lambs are being slain.

The origins of the fourth gospel are disputed, but its current form—perhaps the last of several redactions, or editions—probably emerged in Ephesus (a chief city of the province of Asia, in the western part of modern Turkey), perhaps from within a community that originated in Palestine. There are hints in the Gospel that the community was persecuted and had been excluded or expelled from a synagogue. Most scholars believe that John is the latest canonical gospel (ca. 95), and yet that it is not literarily dependent on the earlier Synoptic Gospels—though it is possible that parts of one or more synoptics (or traditions behind them) served as sources.

To be sure, there are basic, reliable traditions about Jesus' ministry at the root of the discourses and signs of the Fourth Gospel. Some of these are clearly similar to the stream of oral traditions that fed the Synoptic Gospels, while others seem very different indeed. But there is little doubt that the discourses and accounts of signs have evolved over time. Some have suggested that this development is the creative or inspired work of the evangelist or of prophets in his community. The Gospel's narratives and discourses may well have been shaped to reflect the community's experiences, both good and bad. The evangelist would undoubtedly attribute this activity to the promised work of the Paraclete, or Spirit (14:26).

John's Gospel is usually divided into four parts: a prologue (1:1–18: "In the beginning was the Word. . . . "); the Book of Signs (through ch. 12); the Book of Glory (chs. 13–20); and an epilogue (ch. 21). Jesus has "descended" from God to bring true life to humanity, as the signs indicate, and will return to God. Jesus' death is interpreted as his glorification and as the means of healing and salvation for the world. Knowing Jesus means being attached to him as branches to a vine, and imitating the humble, loving service seen in his washing of the disciples' feet, itself a foreshadowing of his death.

ACTS

Together with Luke's Gospel, what we now call the Acts of the Apostles constitutes a history of the origins of the Christian faith. The narrative begins in Jerusalem, with the ascension of Jesus and the coming of the Spirit at Pentecost, and it ends in Rome, with Paul preaching there. There are literally dozens of stops in between, some briefly noted and others extensively chronicled.

Acts (like the Gospel of Luke) is a *theological* history in which God, especially the Spirit of God, is a primary actor. The movements and miracles of human actors, and thus the spread of the gospel, are explicitly attributed to divine activity. Acts is also a *selective* history. Despite its canonical title, it does not recount the deeds of all the apostles. Early on, Peter (plus James and a few others) is the focus of attention, while Saul/Paul, the apostle to the Gentiles, dominates the second half of the book. Nevertheless, the self-conscious agenda of the narrator is not early Christian missionary-heroes but the Spirit-empowered spread of the gospel from Jerusalem to Judea, Samaria, and the ends of the earth (1:8).

Traditionally, Luke was thought to be Paul's traveling companion who composed the so-called "we-sections" of Acts.[5] Much twentieth-century critical scholarship questioned the authenticity of these passages and the historical reli-

---

[5] Acts 16:10–17; 20:5–8, 13–15; 21:1–18; and 27:1–28:16, in which the text is narrated in the first-person plural ("we").

ability of Luke's other accounts, such as the many speeches he reports and the additional apostolic activity he recounts. Emphasis was placed on the evangelist's theological agenda and literary artistry, and "Luke" was not equated with the companion of Paul. Recently, however, there has been renewed interest in the historical value of Acts in its first-century context without discounting Luke's theological interests.

THE LETTERS

The twenty-one NT documents called "letters" (sometimes "epistles"[6]) can be divided into two main categories, the thirteen attributed to Paul and the eight others attributed to others or to no one (in the case of Hebrews). All twenty-one (except perhaps 1 John), by various writers, are examples of actual letters to real people. There are various kinds of letters, but for the most part they follow the basic, standard format of an ancient letter:

- Salutation ("Writer to Recipient")

- Greeting

- Prayer/wish

- Body of the letter

- Closing exhortations

- Greetings

- Final prayer/wish

The letters are also specimens of ancient **rhetoric;** that is, they resemble speeches or discourses—intended to appeal to the mind, will, and emotions of the hearers/readers—that have been put into written form. The combined epistolary and rhetorical aspects of these letters were experienced by most of the original audiences, who heard the letters read aloud (and probably interpreted) in the early Christian assemblies gathered for worship and instruction.

---

[6] Scholars used to distinguish between a more personal "letter" and a more formal and more literary "epistle," debating into which category certain NT documents fall. It appears that most NT letters/epistles are both "personal" and rhetorically structured, though some may have also been written as a kind of "official" correspondence. Today the terms "letter" and "epistle" are more or less interchangeable, though certain conventions remain (e.g., 1–2 Timothy and Titus are usually called the "Pastoral Epistles," not the "Pastoral Letters").

The question of the dating and authorship of the letters is a difficult one, for we have few pieces of hard evidence. Although many of the letters bear the names of apostles or were associated with apostles, scholars must study the evidence they can muster to determine whether the person to whom a letter is attributed is genuinely the author, or whether a later "disciple" or admirer wrote in the apostle's name. The phenomenon of such **pseudonymous** writings appears to have been accepted in Judaism and elsewhere as a way not of being dishonest but of honoring a teacher and continuing his tradition after his death. Though many scholars think that more than half of the NT letters are pseudonymous, there are still debates about the issue and about specific letters.

The Pauline Letters

Paul, the onetime persecutor turned apostle, dominates the pages of the NT once we move past the gospels. Sometimes with the assistance of companions and secretaries, he was apparently earliest Christianity's most prolific pastoral-letter writer. Drawing on the Scriptures, early Christian traditions, the teachings of Jesus, Jewish and non-Jewish wisdom of his day, and his own experience of the risen Lord, he corresponded with churches and individuals.

Of the thirteen letters attributed to Paul, the first nine in the canon are written to churches, the last four to individuals, with each group ordered (more or less) from longest to shortest. There is no serious dispute about the authorship of seven of the thirteen letters, known as the "undisputed letters": Romans, 1–2 Corinthians, Galatians, Philippians, 1 Thessalonians, and Philemon. The remaining six—2 Thessalonians, Ephesians, Colossians, 1–2 Timothy, and Titus—are called the "disputed letters." Their authorship is contested on the basis of three main criteria: their style (vocabulary, sentence construction, etc.); their theology, ethics, and ecclesiology (perspectives on Christ and salvation, behavior, and church life); and the historical situations reflected within them.

The undisputed letters—despite certain differences among them—appear to reveal the mind of one man writing in the 50s. The others vary sufficiently in style, content, and possible historical circumstances to make many scholars think that disciples or admirers of Paul, who adapted his gospel for a later generation, actually wrote them. (Those who are convinced of these letters' pseudonymity call them "inauthentic" [with respect to authorship] and give them the label the **deuteropauline letters,** or "the deuteropaulines.") If some or all of these letters are pseudonymous, they were written at various times after Paul's death in the 60s, but probably none later than about 100 C.E.

The following table shows two (of several) ways to group the thirteen Pauline letters:

Ways of Grouping the Thirteen Pauline Letters	
Canonical Order	**Authorship**
Letters to Churches	*Undisputed*
Romans 1 Corinthians 2 Corinthians Galatians Ephesians Philippians Colossians 1 Thessalonians 2 Thessalonians	Romans 1 Corinthians 2 Corinthians Galatians Philippians 1 Thessalonians Philemon
Letters to Individuals	*Disputed*
1 Timothy 2 Timothy Titus Philemon	1 Timothy 2 Timothy Titus Ephesians Colossians 2 Thessalonians

The Undisputed Letters

Romans and 1–2 Corinthians

Romans, Paul's longest letter and the most influential on Christian theology, has often been understood as a kind of miniature textbook on doctrine, a "compendium of the Christian religion," as Martin Luther's assistant Melanchthon called it. More popularly, it has often been read as a guide to how an individual can find salvation in Christ. Recent studies of Romans, however, have stressed that the document is truly a letter, not a systematic theology, and that its chief theological theme is not the salvation of individuals but the gospel of God's faithfulness and impartiality in justifying, or reconciling, both Jews and Gentiles in Christ.

Written in the mid- to late fifties from Corinth, Romans has a systematic feel to it because Paul is explaining his gospel in full, to a church he had not founded or visited, in order to win support for himself and his mission endeavors, and in order to help the multi-ethnic Roman church(es) live a harmonious, Christ-like life together.

According to Romans, both Jews and Gentiles need the gospel because both groups are under the power of Sin, which rules them like a master. Only God's faithfulness to Israel and to all, manifested in the faithful, self-giving death of Jesus and accepted by people in faith, can liberate and redeem enslaved humanity. Although most who have responded to Paul's gospel are Gentiles, and Paul is distressed that most of his fellow Jews have not believed, he stresses that God's covenant with Israel cannot be broken and that all Israel will be saved. In anticipation of that time, the church must be a hospitable place for both Jewish and Gentile believers in the gospel, in all their cultural diversity.

First and Second Corinthians, unlike Romans, are addressed to a church that Paul had founded—in the capital of the province of Achaia (southern Greece)—but where his gospel was somewhat misunderstood and his apostleship frequently questioned. Both letters (2 Corinthians may actually be a compilation of two or more letters) were written in the mid-fifties, before Romans.

In 1 Corinthians, a rhetorically skillful discourse, Paul seeks to unify a fractious and chaotic church by urging them to embody the gospel in purity and especially in Christ-like, selfless love. Some of Paul's most well-known texts appear in this letter as part of his response, including his discussion of sex and marriage (chs. 5–7), the Lord's supper (11:17–34), the church as the body of Christ (ch. 12), love that is patient and kind (ch. 13), and the final resurrection of the dead and destruction of death (ch. 15).

In 2 Corinthians we see Paul explaining and defending his apostleship. He has committed some *faux pas* in his relationship with the Corinthians, which he seeks to rectify early in the letter. He uses this as a bridge to explain the reconciling work of God in Christ, which yields one of his most succinct and profound expositions of what would later be called the incarnation and atonement (5:11–21). In rebutting his critics and those he labels "false" and "super-" apostles (chs. 10–13), Paul asserts that the true mark of an apostle is Christ-like suffering and weakness, for that is the way of the cross.

Galatians, Philippians, 1 Thessalonians, and Philemon

Sometimes called the Christian's "Magna Carta," Galatians is, for many, Paul's exposition of the doctrine of "justification by faith." It has often been interpreted as Paul's rejection of keeping the Jewish law, or performing any good deeds, in order to merit salvation; all that is needed is "faith." While there is some truth in this view, Paul's argument is subtler, and the traditional view can be misinterpreted to make Paul less Jewish and less concerned about "good works"—what he calls the "law of Christ" and the "fruit of the Spirit"—than he really is.

The relatively short letter, which could have been written in the forties or (more likely) the fifties, but before Romans, is addressed to some of the churches of ancient Galatia, in central Turkey. Paul wishes to convince his readers that Gentile believers do not need to be circumcised in order to be full members of

God's covenant community, as some interlopers have been telling the Galatians. Rather, their response of faith to Paul's gospel—that is, their identification ("co-crucifixion," 2:19–20) with Christ's faithful and loving, self-giving death—has brought them the gift of the Spirit and thus made them all (Jew and Gentile, slave and free, male and female) children of Abraham.

Philippians, written some time in the mid- to late fifties while Paul was imprisoned, is a short but rhetorically powerful letter to a church in the Roman colony of Philippi. The letter is an expression of friendship and thanks to a community in Macedonia (northern Greece) that has generously supported Paul. It also seeks to inspire unity in the midst of persecution from external opponents as well as certain tensions within the community.

Paul accomplishes this through an extended exposition of the central and most famous text in the letter, Phil 2:6–11, which is about Christ's self-emptying incarnation and death, and which many scholars believe to be an early Christian hymn that Paul cites, perhaps supplements, and interprets. The theme of the hymn becomes the theme of the letter and the pattern of Christian humility and love. The church is portrayed in political language as a kind of alternative to the Roman colony, with its own "lord" and "savior" (Jesus, not the Emperor).

First Thessalonians, probably Paul's earliest surviving letter (ca. 51), expresses Paul's thanksgiving that the tiny, beleaguered church in Macedonia has survived persecution. Paul first rehearses his own parent-like apostolic ministry with the believers there. He then encourages them to live together in holiness, faith, love, and hope in anticipation of the *Parousia* (appearance, second coming) of Jesus and their reunion with deceased fellow-believers, possibly martyrs.

Paul's short but powerful letter to Philemon concerns their relationship to Philemon's slave Onesimus. Onesimus had somehow wronged his master but then became a Christian through the ministry of Paul—who was also responsible for Philemon's conversion. Paul urges Philemon to recognize Onesimus as his brother, forgive his "debt," and (possibly) release Philemon.

The Disputed Letters

2 Thessalonians, Colossians, and Ephesians

Second Thessalonians is a brief letter with verbal similarities to, but also theological differences from, 1 Thessalonians. This combination divides scholars about evenly on the issue of Pauline authorship. The letter addresses a situation in which certain teachers are announcing that the "day of the Lord" has already arrived. The response—a rehearsal of events that must precede that day—is thought by some to contradict Paul's alleged belief in an imminent *Parousia* as expressed in 1 Thessalonians. The differences, however, may be generated by differing pastoral needs and may in fact be mutually compatible.

The letters to the Colossians and to the Ephesians are similar to each other in style and theology. Most scholars believe that Ephesians is a deuteropauline letter (perhaps from the 80s) that actually borrows from Colossians, whose Pauline authorship is more often (though not universally) accepted. Both letters present a cosmic Christ, who is the head of the church, seated in the heavenly places above the cosmic powers he has defeated. Believers are already seated with him in some sense even as they are required to live lives of love and purity here on earth. Both letters also contain texts known as "household codes," or "household tables," directions for relationships between Christian husbands and wives, fathers and children, and slaves and masters.

There are also differences between the letters. Colossians clearly addresses a concrete situation that has arisen in the church at Colossae (not far from the more important city of Ephesus). It seeks to warn its audience against a movement combining Jewish asceticism and mysticism with interest in angels and other cosmic powers (often called the "Colossian heresy" or the "Colossian error") by stressing the supremacy and sufficiency of the cosmic crucified Christ. Ephesians, on the other hand, addresses no obvious burning issue and appears to many scholars to be more of a general or circular letter about life in the church, which is made up of Gentiles and Jews reconciled in Christ.[7] Its rich ecclesiology and ethics have been very important throughout the centuries.

1–2 Timothy, Titus

Paul's first and second letters to Timothy and his letter to Titus have been collectively known as the **Pastoral Epistles** for several hundred years. They are addressed to two of Paul's colleagues in their capacity as church leaders, or pastors, continuing the Pauline tradition.

The three writings share a common, distinctive vocabulary and style that differ from the undisputed letters. Nevertheless, scholars today increasingly insist that 2 Timothy, which has the form of a testament (as Paul prepares to die) and is intensely personal, be distinguished from the other two. First Timothy and Titus focus on the ordering of church life and the responsibilities of various kinds of ministers (bishops/overseers, deacons, elders, and perhaps widows).

Almost all scholars consider the Pastoral Epistles to be pseudonymous and date them to the late first (or even early second) century, when the churches were developing more standardized forms of ministry and creed to combat **heresy** or **heterodoxy.** However, a growing number of scholars question this late date, especially for 2 Timothy, and a case can still be made for Pauline authorship.

---

[7] The general or circular character of Ephesians is further suggested by the absence of the phrase "in Ephesus" from the opening of the letter in the best manuscripts.

The majestic theater at Ephesus (see Acts 19), the prominent city of western Asia Minor (modern Turkey) that served as an important base for Paul and a center of early Christianity. (M. Gorman)

The Catholic (General) Epistles

The eight non-Pauline letters of the NT are usually referred to as the **Catholic Letters** or **Catholic Epistles,** or the **General Epistles.** However, although the intended recipients of these letters are sometimes unnamed in the text of the letter, or spread throughout a wide geographical area, it is doubtful that any NT letter was written for all the churches of its time. The Catholic Epistles as a part of the canon originally numbered seven, in part because that was an appropriate number and in part because Hebrews was thought to be Pauline. Today we may group Hebrews with the catholic letters. In general, these letters appear to be later than the (undisputed) Pauline writings.

Hebrews and James

The anonymous "letter" to (the) "Hebrews" calls itself a "word of exhortation" (13:22)—what we would call a **homily** or sermon. It does not begin like a letter, though it ends like one, suggesting perhaps that final exhortations and greetings were added to a homily and then sent off to a church. Although Hebrews has some similarities to the Pauline epistles, its style and method of argumentation differ markedly from the Pauline letters. Thus it is likely that the judgment of the third-century theologian Origen is correct: only God knows who wrote Hebrews.

Hebrews focuses on the superiority of Jesus (as Son of God and great High Priest), his sacrificial death, and the covenant it inaugurates, on the one hand, to Moses, the high priest/sacrificial system, and the covenant associated with them, on the other. This theme is presented as an argument *against* turning away from the new faith (apostasy) in the face of pressure and persecution, and *for* covenant faithfulness. It is joined with several strong warnings about the consequences of abandoning the faith as well as promises of reward for the faithful.

Both the content and the rhetorical style of Hebrews reveal a blend of typical Jewish biblical interpretation and a bit of Platonic philosophy. Some critics have found in Hebrews an anti-Jewish attitude, but that judgment may be both anachronistic and inappropriate, since the author is likely Jewish. (Nonetheless, Christians must be careful not to misuse Hebrews for anti-Jewish purposes.) One conspicuous feature of the argument is the absence of a reference to the temple; scholars debate whether that provides a hint to the date of Hebrews (before or after the destruction of the temple in 70 C.E.), but there is no consensus. Hebrews may have appeared as early as the 60s or as late as the 80s.

"A right strawy letter" is what Martin Luther called the Letter of James, because it supposedly contradicted Paul's teaching on justification and did not preach Christ or the gospel. In recent years, however, the epistle of straw has been rehabilitated as a major part of the NT's social conscience. This brief specimen of Jewish-Christian wisdom literature offers moral counsel in the tradition of the prophets and Jesus, as well as the wisdom writers. Topics treated include God-given wisdom, the necessity of "works" as a demonstration of faith, the dangers of wealth and the need for practical concern for the poor, and control of the tongue. Addressed to "the twelve tribes in the Dispersion [Diaspora]" (believers not living at home, probably meaning Jerusalem), the letter suggests an audience of poor and mistreated people located in more than one place. As to authorship and date, there are several possibilities: James the (step-?) brother of Jesus or James the son of Alphaeus, each of whom would have written in the 40s or 50s; or an unknown writer, probably decades later, creating a pseudonymous letter. Scholars are divided on these issues.

1–2 Peter and 1–3 John

Addressees similar in description to those of James—"exiles of the Dispersion"—are named in 1 Peter, indicating a significant aspect of early Christian self-understanding. This audience, however, is a group of Gentile churches located throughout the provinces of central and western Asia Minor, and they are suffering various forms of (probably non-state-sponsored) persecution. Although Peter is the named author, possibly located in Rome ("Babylon"—5:13), from what we know from other sources, the concerns of the book are more

Pauline than Petrine. If Peter is the author, it probably dates from the 60s, but if it is pseudonymous, as most scholars think, it is likely from the last quarter of the first century.

Using the language of the Scriptures, early Christian confessions of Jesus, and possibly an early baptismal liturgy or set of instructions for converts, the author of 1 Peter urges his audience to remain God's holy people in a pagan context; to imitate Jesus in innocent, non-retaliatory suffering; and to give outsiders no reason to mistreat them.

The short letter called 2 Peter is thought by most scholars to be pseudonymous, and perhaps the latest NT writing, though both issues are debated. It is generally characterized as a testament (or farewell address) in letter form, the purpose of which is the correction of misunderstandings of Christian **eschatology.** Many think it is a revision of the very brief letter of Jude (brother of James and of Jesus), which was written to discourage apostasy and is similarly debated with respect to its authorship and date.

Of the three Johannine letters (1–3 John), the second and third have the standard letter format, while 1 John lacks it, perhaps because of its broad theological and ethical appeal. First John deals with two basic problems related to the community to which it is addressed: the failure of some to live in imitation of the love of God/Christ, and the denial by others (who have left the church and whom the letter calls "antichrists") of the reality of Christ's incarnation and death. It eloquently presents a series of basic tests of authentic Christianity in response to these issues. Second and Third John, probably by the same author, continue some of 1 John's themes and concerns.

THE APOCALYPSE/REVELATION

The inspiration for woodcuts by Albrecht Dürer, colorful paintings by William Blake, and countless other works of art, the book of Revelation, or the Apocalypse, is the only example of a full-length apocalyptic work in the NT.[8] It has been the subject of immense debate almost since its revelations to John were first recorded. Some have accused the author of the book's fantastic images of being insane or on drugs, while countless literal-minded believers, especially in recent Western Christianity (witness the *Left Behind* series of books) have become obsessed by those images and the future realities they are believed to reveal. Scholars today insist that it is best to read the images, symbols, numbers,

---

[8] As noted in the previous chapter, Daniel 7–12 and 2 Esdras (in the Orthodox canon) are also apocalyptic works. Apocalyptic material may also be found in portions of the prophetic books, the Gospels, and various NT letters.

and so forth, not as if they were literal reports, but as dimensions of visionary, symbolic literature similar to political cartoons, with culturally understood symbols and codes, exaggerated features, and the like.

As with other apocalypses, the NT apocalypse communicates revelations about the unseen world of heaven and about future eschatological events in order to depict the cosmic struggle between God and God's enemies. This apocalypse, however, also begins and ends as a letter, even as it contains seven messages to specific churches in Western Asia Minor within it (chs. 2–3). Thus, it has a pastoral function like other NT letters; the burden of Revelation is not really the future but the present. The churches are being persecuted in various ways and are tempted therefore to accommodate to the Roman political, religious, and cultural system (represented by the infamous beasts of ch. 13). Drawing on Jewish apocalyptic and early Christian traditions, and alluding to the OT hundreds of times (without directly quoting it), John writes about the present and future reign of God and "the Lamb who was slain" (Christ) in order to strengthen, challenge, and reassure the churches in this situation.

Revelation begins with a graphic vision of the exalted Jesus, which leads to the collection of letters to the seven churches. These are followed by a long series of visions culminating in the fall of Babylon (Rome and, by extension, all powers opposed to God) and the descent of the new Jerusalem to earth.

Scholars are divided over the identity of John (a common name in early Christianity) and the date of his writing. His style differs markedly from that of the fourth evangelist, but he is clearly a respected church leader whose ministry in and around Ephesus has resulted in his exile to the nearby island of Patmos. Most scholars date John's work to the mid-90s under the emperor Domitian, though some think that all or part of it comes from the 60s and alludes to the emperor Nero.

CONCLUSION: UNITY IN DIVERSITY

Despite the diversity among the NT documents, six basic commonalities may be briefly mentioned in conclusion:

- *Centered on Jesus*—The NT writers, in all their diversity, are primarily focused on proclaiming Jesus (as Messiah/Christ, Lord, Son of God, etc.) and his significance for them and the world.

- *Eschatologically conscious*—Eschatology, as noted above, concerns itself with the "last things." The NT documents, however, do not describe a people waiting around for the end of the world. Rather, they are aware of living in a new age—the "last days," the age of the Spirit promised by the prophets and inaugurated by the life, death, and resurrection of Jesus.

- *Scripturally defined*—The NT writers universally quote and echo the Scriptures (the OT) as they understand both Jesus and themselves in light of those texts.

- *Focused on discipleship*—The purpose of the various NT writings is not merely to recount a story or to teach doctrine, but above all to encourage communities to follow Jesus faithfully.

- *Counter-imperial*—There is a growing consensus among scholars that most if not all of the NT documents are either implicitly or explicitly counter-imperial in the sense of proposing a different Lord, Savior, gospel, and polity (community lifestyle) than that offered by Rome in the cult of the emperor and other pagan cults.

- *Expectant of suffering*—Almost all of the NT writings give indication of a persecuted writer, or audience, or both. This phenomenon has prompted some to speak of the NT as the "martyrs' canon"—the collection of texts that were able to inspire and sustain those suffering for the faith.

These twenty-seven writings, in their diversity and unity, have shaped the Christian church and inspired believers and non-believers alike for two thousand years; they continue to do so.

FOR FURTHER READING AND STUDY

Achtemeier Paul J., Joel B. Green, and Marianne Meye Thompson. *Introducing the New Testament.* Grand Rapids: Eerdmans, 2001. A basic but solid introduction emphasizing the theological content of the NT texts, as well as literary and historical matters, with helpful maps and illustrations.

Brown, Raymond E. *An Introduction to the New Testament.* New York: Doubleday, 1998. A massive, semitechnical introduction summarizing the results of twentieth-century critical scholarship and respectful of faith-based perspectives.

Ehrman, Bart D. *The New Testament: A Historical Introduction to the Early Christian Writings.* 3d ed. New York: Oxford University Press, 2003. A popular and significant introduction written from a nontheological perspective.

Gorman, Michael J. *Apostle of the Crucified Lord: A Theological Introduction to Paul and His Letters.* Grand Rapids: Eerdmans, 2004. An introduction to and commentary on all thirteen of the Pauline letters in their original contexts that also raises questions about their contemporary relevance.

Johnson, Luke Timothy, and Todd Penner. *The Writings of the New Testament: An Interpretation.* Rev. ed. Minneapolis: Fortress, 1999. A brilliant engagement with the NT texts, emphasizing their literary and religious dimensions, now available with a CD.

Nickle, Keith F. *The Synoptic Gospels: An Introduction.* Rev. and exp. ed. Louisville: Westminster John Knox, 2001. A standard text now updated.

Patzia, Arthur D. *The Making of the New Testament: Origin, Collection, Text and Canon.* Downers Grove, Ill.: InterVarsity, 1995. A helpful guide to the process by which the NT books and canon came into being.

Powell, Mark Alan. *Fortress Introduction to the Gospels.* Minneapolis: Fortress, 1997. An insightful guide to the structure and contents of each of the gospels.

Chapter 5

Significant Noncanonical Books

EDWIN C. HOSTETTER

This chapter surveys Jewish and Christian writings that did not make it into Scripture. Most of these writings were authored during the period stretching from about two hundred years before the start of the Common Era until two hundred years after that era's beginning (200 B.C.E.–200 C.E.). These **non-canonical** (also called **"parabiblical"** or **"extracanonical"**) books are significant aids to our interpretation of Scripture because they help us to understand the rich diversity of perspectives that existed during biblical times. We will examine four categories of documents: the Old Testament Pseudepigrapha, the Dead Sea Scrolls, the New Testament Apocrypha, and the Apostolic Fathers. After describing each category, we will focus briefly on one of its representative writings.

THE OLD TESTAMENT PSEUDEPIGRAPHA

The set of documents known as the OT Pseudepigrapha (singular "pseudepigraphon") is a modern collection of ancient writings. The term **pseudepigrapha** means "false titles or superscriptions" or "falsely ascribed writings": that is, books attributed or ascribed to somebody other than the real author. Most of the OT pseudepigrapha come from a period between the third century B.C.E. and the second century C.E., although a number of the latest items may possibly date to sometime after the fourth or fifth century. These texts, resembling biblical writings yet not incorporated into the Bible, were composed originally in Hebrew, Aramaic, and Greek. Some are represented among the Dead Sea Scroll manuscripts.

Typically in the pseudepigrapha, prominent individuals allege to have received revelations. In other cases, biblical narratives furnish the basis for expanded stories, or the Psalter provides models for poems, or Jewish wisdom literature shapes new compositions. Broadly conceived genres of pseudepigrapha include apocalypses, testaments, histories, philosophies, and psalms.[1] Besides an array of additional specimens in every principal category, OT pseudepigrapha include:

- Apocalypses—*1 Enoch, Apocalypse of Elijah,* and *Syriac Apocalypse of Baruch* (*2 Baruch*);

- Testaments—*Testament of Job, Assumption of Moses,* and *Testaments of the Twelve Patriarchs;*

- Histories—*Jubilees* and *Ascension of Isaiah;*

- Philosophies—*4 Maccabees;* and

- Psalms—*Odes of Solomon.*[2]

These books are unified by their recurring themes, notably the origin of evil, the end of the world, the messiah, the transcendence of God, the resurrection of the dead, angels, and paradise as the reward for the righteous. Moreover, an interest in esoteric matters and figures—like the priest/king Melchizedek—pervades pseudepigraphous writing.

As these themes might suggest, the pseudepigrapha have been transmitted to us as an amalgam of Jewish and Christian elements. While Jews produced the majority of these documents, Christians later revised several of them (e.g., *Ascension of Isaiah*). A few pieces (e.g., *Odes of Solomon*) seem to have been compiled directly by Christians, who depended in varying degrees on written or oral Jewish tradition from before 70 C.E. They may have been influenced by Jewish legends they had come across or by Hebrew Scripture itself. Either would have been expanded through a liberal use of the Church's own imagination—in much the same way as the already existing Jewish pseudepigrapha had come into being.

Frequently, a pseudepigraphon would intentionally but incorrectly claim authorship by a famous predecessor, especially a great OT character. That is how the term "pseudepigrapha" became applied to the whole body of literature. Of course, scholars generally believe that pseudepigraphous works written under a fictitious name are also found among canonical scripture—for example, Daniel and Song of Solomon (or Canticles).

---

[1] There are additional genres. For example, *Letter of Aristeas,* mentioned in previous chapters because it contains the story of the translation of the Bible into Greek (the LXX), is in letter form, but it is actually an apology for Judaism.

[2] Actually, 1 Enoch and Jubilees are part of the canon of the Ethiopian Christian Church, and 4 Maccabees is part of some Orthodox canons.

The large quantity of pseudepigrapha attests to their wide use and great popularity. Some of them were nearly as influential as the writings of the canonized Bible in both Jewish and Christian circles (particularly before the Jewish Bar Kokhba revolt against Rome ended in 135 C.E., and the early church's Council of Nicea convened in 325, respectively). Countless members of early synagogues and churches considered these documents to be divinely inspired.

Important, but unknown by many casual readers, is the effect of this literature upon the NT writers. For instance, Jude 14–15 explicitly quotes *1 Enoch* 1:9. Similarly, the Gospels' "great commandment" (Luke 12:29–31 and parallels), in which Jesus combines love of God with love of neighbor, is already found in *Testament of Issachar* 5:2 and *Testament of Dan* 5:3 (part of *Testaments of the Twelve Patriarchs*).

Reading the pseudepigrapha enhances our comprehension of Christianity's origins, to be sure, but even more so our understanding of this period's Judaism. The texts that are Jewish constitute some of the main sources for reconstructing the lives of Jews in both the Promised Land and the diaspora—especially Alexandria—before the Jerusalem temple's demolishment by the Romans in 70 C.E. These writings introduce us to Jewish ideas, symbols, perceptions, fears, dreams, and problems prior to that destruction. The books show that the Judaism of the Second Temple period was open to a range of influences from the surrounding world, yet desirous of preserving its traditions in the face of perceived threats from the outside.

An Example from the Old Tesament Pseudepigrapha: *1 Enoch*

A prime example of the OT Pseudepigrapha is *1 Enoch*. Five main sections about the mysteries of the universe and the future of the world constitute the work: Book of Watchers (chapters 1–36), Parables of Enoch (37–71), Book of Astronomy (72–82), Book of Dreams (83–90), and Epistle of Enoch (91–107). Book of Watchers concerns fallen angels and their intercourse with women, as well as various visions of Enoch during a tour of heaven, earth, and hell. Parables of Enoch deals with the coming judgment of the righteous and wicked and provides an exposition of additional heavenly secrets. Book of Astronomy contains a calendar (attested also in the pseudepigraphal Jubilees) that was the same one the Qumran sect (the community that produced the Dead Sea Scrolls) used. Book of Dreams records biblical history from Adam to the outbreak of the Maccabean revolt. Epistle of Enoch represents an exhortation by Enoch to his sons and has something of the form of a testament. The background to the emergence of much of this material can be found in the circumstances of the third and second centuries B.C.E., when the Greeks increasingly affected Palestinian Jews in diverse ways. Following is a short excerpt from *1 Enoch:*

> And the vision appeared to me as follows: Behold clouds called me in the vision, and mist called me, and the path of the stars and flashes of lightning hastened me and drove me, and in the vision winds caused me to fly and hastened me and lifted me up into heaven. And I proceeded until I came near to a wall which was built of hail stones, and a tongue of fire surrounded it, and it began to make me afraid. (1 Enoch 14:8–9)

THE DEAD SEA SCROLLS

The Dead Sea Scrolls (often abbreviated DSS) are large deposits of manuscripts from different periods and of various types that were discovered, beginning in 1947, at ruins in the Judaean desert near the western shore of the Dead Sea. The discoveries yielded rules, poems, liturgies, apocalypses, and commentaries dating between the second century B.C.E. and the first century C.E. These ancient texts were written in Hebrew, Aramaic, or Greek—and occasionally in Latin or Arabic. The label "Dead Sea Scrolls" is normally restricted to papyri and parchments found in eleven caves in the vicinity of Khirbet Qumran. It is also sometimes broadened to include those texts from other nearby sites, such as the famous remains at Masada. Although the stashes of contracts and correspondence found there and elsewhere provide inestimable information for understanding things like the Second Jewish Revolt against Rome, the remainder of this section will concentrate only on materials from Qumran.

Certain Essenes (a Jewish group opposed to the temple officials in Jerusalem) presumably settled Qumran prior to 135 B.C.E. The Dead Sea Scrolls they left in the desert comprise only religious works, a sizable number of which can be classified as representing a sectarian (separatist) theology or custom: for example, they refer to the coming of a priestly messiah, and they promote a calendar different from the standard one. Even those texts that did not originate at Qumran but were merely copied there must have basically agreed with the sectarian group's ordinances or tenets, in order to have been included in the separatists' library.

The Qumran library of writings clearly displays a tightly structured community with a hierarchical organization, whose members isolated themselves from the rest of contemporary Judaism. Rule books such as *Messianic Rule* and *MMT* (or *Some Precepts of the Law*) were prepared for the sect, which believed itself to be living at the end of days. The literature (e.g., *Commentary on Habakkuk*) shows an awareness that the final age's emergence was delayed but insists that all of God's times will come in their fixed order, and it encourages the

Some of the caves near the Qumran community on the edge of the Dead Sea, where the community hid its scrolls from the world until their accidental discovery in 1947. (M. Gorman)

essential virtues of hope and perseverance meanwhile. Some documents (e.g., *War Scroll*) show a dualistic opposition between the spirit of light and the spirit of darkness, while others (e.g., *Damascus Document*) ascribe a role to Belial as a supernatural enemy against God. The scrolls reflect their adherents' sense of participating in angelic worlds, which is evident in hymnic compositions such as *Songs of the Sabbath Sacrifice* and *Thanksgiving Hymns.*

The primary importance of the Dead Sea Scrolls is that they greatly enrich our understanding of Judaism around the turn of the era and in some cases shed light on the pre-Maccabean period. The scrolls also show variety in text and canon at the turn of the era and help dispel the mirage of a monochromatic Judaism in this period. They attest another Jewish party similar to the Nazareans (earliest Christians) who struggled against principalities or powers and who reinterpreted the Scriptures in this context. That the Dead Sea Scrolls and the NT date to roughly the same era and derive from a comparable milieu accounts for linkages between them.

An Example from the Dead Sea Scrolls: *Thanksgiving Hymns*

Among the Dead Sea Scrolls are *Thanksgiving Hymns,* poems similar to biblical psalms. They are divided into two groups of hymns: one type uses the first-person singular ("I") and the other type the plural ("we"). The latter presumably expresses thoughts and sentiments common to all members of the sect. The former is characterized by biographical details taken from the life of the speaker. Recurring themes are his solitude, his exile and persecution by enemies, and God's grace in saving him plus electing him for special knowledge—which he transmits to a group of followers. The speaker feels himself unworthy of the divine favors he has been singled out to receive, alluding again and again to his frailty and total dependence on God. The hymns exhibit a full variety of spirituality and doctrine. They perceive God as having created everything according to a preordained plan, and they view human flesh as susceptible to sin but human spirit as capable of purification. Here is an excerpt from the hymns:

> But they are sowers of deceit
> and seers of fraud,
> they have plotted evil against me
> to alter your Law, which you engraved in my heart,
> by flattering teachings for your people;
> they have denied the drink of knowledge to the thirsty,
> in their thirst they have given them vinegar to drink
> to consider their mistake,
> so they may act like fools in their feasts
> so they will be caught in their nets. (*Thanksgiving Hymns* 4.9–12)

THE NEW TESTAMENT APOCRYPHA

The NT apocrypha comprise various ancient Christian writings that are excluded from the canonical NT. They do not, however, constitute an agreed or settled entity penned within a defined time scale. While certain books or the traditions on which they are based have been dated as far back as the first century C.E., the creation of apocryphal literature and the revision of prior texts did not cease with the formation and acceptance of the NT canon in the fourth century. Thus, although most of the NT apocrypha derive from about 100 to 400 C.E., some medieval texts known as NT apocrypha were produced perhaps as late as the ninth century.

The word "apocryphon" (Greek for "hidden"; plural *apocrypha*) strictly understood refers to an esoteric writing regarded as having been authored centuries earlier but supernaturally kept secret until the latter days. Despite the fact that a few documents now normally found under the label "apocrypha" may have been designed as secret writings for an inner circle, the majority were not really "hidden." On the contrary, the works seem intended by their character or titles to be counterparts to or rivals of the canonical books. Respecting apostolic derivation, this corpus of early Christian literature shares with the writings of the NT proper a self-consciousness in asserting the authority that derives from the age of Christianity's origins. Nonetheless, the apocrypha generally did not achieve the level of widespread ecclesiastical use that would have prompted their incorporation in most of the church's canonical lists. Even though these books were not accepted into the canon, several were accorded a limited recognition as suitable for private use.

Numerous apocrypha were inspired by primitive church events or personalities. The books exhibit motifs and concepts in common with the NT itself. From the point of view of genre, the apocrypha parallel the kinds of literature created and received in the NT. Indeed, the apocrypha are conventionally subdivided into gospels, acts, letters, and apocalypses.

Samples of the gospel genre are the infancy gospels like *Protevangelium of James,* sayings gospels like *Gospel of Thomas,* and passion gospels like *Questions of Bartholomew.* A sample of the acts class is *Acts of Paul (and Thecla).* A sample of the letter category is *Epistle of the Apostles,* but this sort of writing never flourished as lushly as did the other sorts. A sample of the apocalypse type is *Apocalypse of Peter;* it is actually included as a second (though disputed) canonical apocalypse in the important Muratorian canon (or fragment), which may date to ca. 200 C.E. (see further discussion in chapter six).

The apocrypha were written in order to instill true piety and convey true history. One purpose was to enforce what the particular writer esteemed to be sound Christian belief. These writings show what was acceptable to certain Christians of the first ages, what interested them, what they admired, what ideals of conduct they cherished for this life, what they thought they would find in the next. This at times took the shape of expanding upon some virtue such as fortitude, temperance, or love, or else of embroidering some doctrine such as the virgin birth, the physical resurrection, the second coming, or the future state—with special attention to the torments of the damned. Additionally, some of the apocrypha claim to present authentic memories of Jesus (not least his infancy and postresurrection activity) and of his followers (especially apostles). Scholars debate the value of apocryphal gospels for addressing the issue of the historical Jesus. At a minimum, the apocrypha record the imaginations, hopes, fears, affections, and aversions of those who wrote them. They surely throw light on the diverse lifestyles and outlooks of the first Christians.

An Example of the New Testament Apocrypha: *Gospel of Thomas*

Dating anywhere between 50 and 150 C.E., *Gospel of Thomas* is among the greatest of the apocrypha. From the Nag Hammadi library in Egypt, it is a collection of 114 concise sayings attributed to Jesus. They are listed *seriatim* in the form of direct statements made by him or responses to questions asked of him.

The sayings preserved are of several types: proverbs, parables, prophecies, and prescriptions. The kingdom is a central concept in Gospel of Thomas, but only its present and strongly spiritualized character seems to be important. In contrast to the canonical Gospels, sayings about the future coming of the Son of Man are completely missing. Jesus appears as a risen being who has laid aside all earthly form, and the elect alone can recognize his heavenly form. The world and human bodies are negatively assessed, and the text stresses finding the kingdom of the Father in the knowledge of oneself. Surprisingly, there are scarcely any signs of the formation of a community, and ecclesiological ideas are entirely lacking. Access to the kingdom is promised to individuals reached by a call from Jesus. *Gospel of Thomas* begins like this:

> These are the secret words which the living Jesus spoke and Didymus Judas Thomas wrote down.
>
> And he said, He who finds the interpretation of these sayings will not taste death.
>
> Jesus said, Let him who seeks not cease in his seeking until he finds and, when he finds, he will be troubled. When he is troubled he will marvel and he will reign over the All. (*Gospel of Thomas* 0–2)

THE APOSTOLIC FATHERS

The Apostolic Fathers is a group of writings traditionally thought to have been set down by people who were faithful to the teaching of the apostles, and who were directly or indirectly associated with them or their immediate disciples. Actually, no significant link between any of these writings and the apostles seems particularly likely—except perhaps in the cases of [the Letter of] *1 Clement,* the seven letters of Ignatius, and *Letter of Polycarp.* (Of course, the same lack of apostolic connection is probably true for more than one book in the NT itself.) The Apostolic Fathers were penned during the late first and the second centuries C.E.; some are therefore contemporary with the NT's later documents. Thus scholarship is moving consciously toward an integration of these two sets of materials, as portions of the broad anthology called "early Christian writings."

"Apostolic Fathers" is a late title because no such collection was ever made by the primitive church. Modern editions usually print at a minimum *Didache* (or *Teaching of the Twelve Apostles*), *Epistle of Barnabas, Martyrdom of Polycarp, Shepherd of Hermas,* and [Sermon of] *2 Clement,* plus the aforementioned *1 Clement,* the letters of Ignatius, and *Letter of Polycarp.* The purported authors whose names the last three works bear had some sort of official standing, like bishop, in their assemblies. We clearly do not know who wrote the pseudonymous *Barnabas* and *Didache* as well as *2 Clement,* whether the authors held responsible and honored positions of leadership or not.

Apart from the **apologies** defending early Christian beliefs and practices (*Epistle to Diognetus* and *Apology of Quadratus*) often inserted among the Apostolic Fathers, every one of these practical texts was aimed largely at a Christian audience. Several had a quasi-canonical authority in certain churches. The fourth-century C.E. biblical manuscript Sinaiticus incorporated *Barnabas* and *Shepherd of Hermas;* the fifth-century manuscript Alexandrinus contains *1 Clement* and *2 Clement;* and a catalog in the sixth-century manuscript Claromantanus lists among the NT books *Barnabas* and *Hermas* (though a dash sets off both items).

Regarding form, most of the Apostolic Fathers are ostensibly letters, but *Hermas* is a kind of apocalypse, and *Didache* is a manual. Through visions and parables, *Hermas* teaches the oneness of God who contains all but is himself contained by nothing. *Didache* combines ethics with church order and liturgical instruction. While *Letter of Polycarp* breathes the spirit of the NT Pastoral Epistles, *Fragments of Papias* is fond of **millennialism** (belief in a future one-thousand-year era of peace). Ignatius perceives a hidden entrance by Christ into the world and infuses his writing with qualities reminiscent of John and other mystical (perhaps even quasi-gnostic) strands of thought. Yet his emphasis on monepiscopacy—a single local bishop's having sole authority—sets the stage for the further development of a hierarchical conception of ministerial authority.

By virtue of their dating prior to the formation of the NT canon, the Apostolic Fathers are indispensable sources for the history, theology, and institutional development of the church in the postapostolic age. They are important, too, for studying the vocabulary of the NT and for tracing the process by which much of the NT came to take on canonical authority. The Apostolic Fathers display a rich and powerful articulation of Christian faith and devotion.

An Example from the Apostolic Fathers: *Epistle of Barnabas*

An important illustration of the Apostolic Fathers is *Epistle of Barnabas.* Its message is characterized by a zeal for true religion. The anonymous author seeks to show that Christians are the intended heirs of God's covenant. Although Barnabas displays the form of a letter, the epistolary framework (chapters 1 and 21) is largely a literary device. The longest part of the document (chapters 2–17) seems bent upon two objectives: opposition to Jewish legalism, and explanation of how the OT teaches about Christ. Selecting texts from both Law and Prophets, Barnabas rejects literal Jewish interpretations in order to build the case that Christ crucified for our sins is prefigured in the OT and that even the ceremonial law is disguised moral teaching. A second, shorter section (chapters 18–20) contrasts the Two Ways, the way of light and the way of darkness. The presentation of the former way comprises almost entirely do's and don'ts, while the latter describes evil actions and persons. Here is an excerpt from the epistle:

> The meaning of his allusion to swine is this: what he is really saying is, you are not to consort with the class of people who are like swine, inasmuch as they forget all about the Lord while they are living in affluence, but remember Him when they are in want—just as a swine, so long as it is eating, ignores its master, but starts to squeal the moment it feels hungry, and then falls silent again when it is given food. (*Epistle of Barnabas* 10:3)

CONCLUSION

The OT Pseudepigrapha, Dead Sea Scrolls, NT Apocrypha, and Apostolic Fathers dramatically augment motifs of the Jewish and Christian Bibles. In them we encounter creation myths, community laws, tribal prophecies, visionary journeys, gospel legends, apostolic adventures, and much more. Familiarity with these texts profoundly increases our modern understanding of both Judaism and Christianity in antiquity. Early Jews and Christians decided, however, not to include the parabiblical material in their Scriptures. Criteria such as authorship, consistency with other beliefs and practices, and extent of usage at synagogue or church all factored into the process of exclusion (see further on the canon in chapter six).

FOR FURTHER READING AND STUDY

Charlesworth, James H., ed. *The Old Testament Pseudepigrapha.* 2 vols. Garden City, N.Y: Doubleday, 1983–1985. The English text of Jewish and Christian extracanonical literature, plus an inclusive guide to their ideas, styles, and genres.

de Jonge, M[arinus], ed. *Outside the Old Testament.* Vol. 4 of Cambridge Commentaries on Writings of the Jewish and Christian World 200 BC to AD 200. Cambridge: Cambridge University Press, 1985. Excerpts from and introductions to twelve pseudepigraphic pieces that deal with prominent OT figures.

Ehrman, Bart D. *Lost Scriptures: Books That Did Not Make It into the New Testament.* New York: Oxford University Press, 2003. A translated selection of lengthy extracts or entire texts from among the Apocrypha and Apostolic Fathers.

Elliott, J. K. *The Apocryphal New Testament.* Oxford: Clarendon Press, 1993. A collection of Christian literature in English translation without excessive textual or critical notes.

Evans, Craig A. *Ancient Texts for New Testament Studies: A Guide to Background Literature.* Peabody, Mass.: Hendrickson, 2005. Previously *Noncanonical Writings and New Testament Interpretation.* A guide to the subjects of this chapter plus Philo, Josephus, the rabbinic literature, and other writings.

Holmes, Michael W., ed. *The Apostolic Fathers.* Updated ed. Grand Rapids: Baker Books, 1999. An annotated edition containing the Greek texts and their English translations plus introductions and bibliographies.

Schneemelcher, Wilhelm, ed. *New Testament Apocrypha.* Translated by R. McL. Wilson. Rev. ed. 2 vols. Louisville: Westminster John Knox, 1991–1992. A standard English tool (based on a German edition) with scholarly introductions, translations, and bibliographies.

Sparks, H. F. D., ed. *The Apocryphal Old Testament.* Oxford: Clarendon Press, 1984. Translations of Pseudepigrapha, introductions, and brief bibliographies designed by a team of scholars for general use.

Tugwell, Simon. *The Apostolic Fathers.* Harrisburg: Morehouse, 1990. An interpretation of these seminal Christian writings that takes cognizance of the relevant modern scholarship.

VanderKam, James C. *The Dead Sea Scrolls Today.* Grand Rapids: Eerdmans, 1994. An introductory account summarizing the background, discovery, nature, and controversies of the Qumran community's library.

Vermes, Geza. *The Complete Dead Sea Scrolls in English.* New York: Penguin Books, 1997. Translations of every nonbiblical text of the DSS that is sufficiently well preserved to be rendered into English.

Chapter 6

The Formation of the Biblical Canon(s)

SHIRA LANDER

The subject of the canonization of Jewish and Christian Scriptures is fraught with problems of definition. Scholars use the term "canon" to convey a variety of concepts. What unites this diversity of approaches is the notion that a canon refers to a definitive collection of literature. In the context of religion, a canon comprises texts regarded as authoritative for religious belief and practice, as well as for daily life. This chapter considers the formation of the Jewish and Christian canons. The following discussion is complex at points, corresponding to the complexity of the historical phenomena it analyzes.

CANONIZATION AS PROCESS

Canonization emerges in a social context, where groups of religious adherents gather for public readings (especially in liturgy, or worship) and/or communal study, thus providing interpretive frameworks through which both a group as a whole and individuals within it come to understand these texts. Canonization also occurs in the context of complex historical events. Events that catalyze collection activity range from conflict, both physical and ideological, to demographic and geographic population shifts. Additionally, the role of technology in this process cannot be underestimated: as scrolls were abandoned for the more economical and portable codex, or book (see chapter one), decisions had to be made about what literally belonged between the front and back covers.

This physical development created the visual impression of a singular "Bible," whereas the former concept of the Bible had been plural, as, for example, the Jewish writer Philo reveals with his term "sacred books" (Greek, *ta hiera biblia,* in his *Life of Moses* 2.6 [36] and elsewhere). Many scholars, therefore, distinguish the term "Scriptures," the group of texts considered canonical, from the term "Bible," their collection in codex form. With the adoption of this revolutionary technology, "the concept of 'canon' became concretized in a new way that shapes our thinking to the present day" (Kraft, "The Codex and Canon Consciousness," p. 233).

THE CANONIZATION OF THE JEWISH SCRIPTURES/ CHRISTIAN OLD TESTAMENT

Finding evidence for a Jewish Scriptures canon in the Second Temple period (ca. 536 B.C.E.–70 C.E.) is complicated. The group of writings considered to be authoritative for those living in Judea evolved over many centuries, changing to meet the needs of each generation. What may have been regarded as "canonical" in the Persian period may not be the same as the group of texts regarded as canonical in the Roman period. These writings, like other state's laws and archives, were likely to have been kept under safe guard in the temple's treasury. It is only with the experience of national disintegration (the destruction of the first temple and the Babylonian exile, the Maccabean revolt, and the Roman wars), the emergence of scribes not based in the temple, and the rise of controversies among various Jewish groups that the collection of writings in the temple archives would encounter competition to their claim of authority.

With exile and dispersion, descendents of Judean citizens came to distinguish between national and religious identity. Whether in Persia or in Egypt, they produced literature that portrayed Jews as living a covenantal life in obedience to "the Law" apart from the legal requirements of the Judean state (e.g., Esther, Tobit, 3 Maccabees). They also continued to rely on texts produced in Judah, if the *Letter of Aristeas* reflects historical circumstances. This view of Jewish life was not restricted to texts produced by Jews living outside the land of Israel (i.e., in the Greco-Roman Diaspora, or dispersion from Palestine), since Aramaic portions of Tobit were found at Qumran, near the Dead Sea. Alternative understandings of Jewish identity inspired various groups of Jews to regard different writings as authoritative for their own communities. For example, the residents of Qumran (or, more precisely, the authors of certain writings among the Dead Sea Scrolls), were Jews who found themselves at odds with the authority of the Jerusalem temple. As noted in the previous chapter, they produced alternative texts for understanding and living out a covenantal Judaism (e.g., 4QMMT [*Miqṣat Maʿaśê ha-Torah*], CD [Cairo Genizah copy of the *Damascus Document*]).

Two Holy Scriptures: Greek and Hebrew

Two primary versions of Holy Scriptures survive the Second Temple period.

The Old Greek/Septuagint

The Old Greek/Septuagint (LXX) consists of books categorized by the grandson of Ben Sira, in the prologue to his Greek translation of the *Letter of Aristeas,* as "the law, the prophets, and other books of our ancestors" (introduction to Sirach/Ecclesiasticus). Greek fragments corresponding to the Septuagint version of Exodus, Leviticus, Numbers, Deuteronomy, and the Letter of Jeremiah were discovered among the Dead Sea Scrolls at Qumran, suggesting that the use of Greek Scriptures may not have been limited to Jews who lived outside Palestine, in the Diaspora.

As preserved in fourth- and fifth-century Christian manuscripts of the Bible, and attested by early Christian writers, the Greek Scriptures included works not included in what later came to be the traditional canon of Hebrew Scriptures: the Wisdom of Solomon, Sirach (Ecclesiasticus), the Letter of Jeremiah, longer versions of Daniel and Esther, Tobit, Judith, 1–4 Maccabees, Psalm 151, and 1 Esdras. As noted in chapter one, these are called the deuterocanonical or apocryphal books.[1]

The Hebrew Scriptures

The Hebrew Scriptures are attested in early rabbinic literature (beginning after the destruction of the temple in 70 C.E.) and, according to some scholars, in the historian Josephus (d. ca. 100 C.E.). According to Josephus, there were twenty-two holy books, corresponding to the number of letters of the Hebrew alphabet (*Against Apion* 1.8 [38]).[2] However, the classification of certain books as holy is not the same as regarding them as a closed canon. Josephus writes that "no one has ventured either to add, or to remove, or to alter a syllable" of these holy books (*Against Apion* 1.8 [42]) in order to show that the record of Jewish history is more reliable than that of the Greeks.[3]

Because Josephus does not include a list of *which* books this selection contained, we cannot know whether his list was identical to the twenty-four-book

---

[1] Current scholarship has also explored the possibility of Jewish Latin versions of Scripture. The Christian writer Tertullian, in late-second-century North Africa, cites an already existing Latin translation of Jewish Scriptures.

[2] The Pentateuchal scrolls of Qumran offer significant evidence for the existence of a consistent (if not standard) version of the "five books of Moses" by the first century B.C.E.

[3] I am grateful to Robert A. Kraft for reminding me of this distinction in the course of previewing this article.

The first page of Genesis from the Leningrad Codex, the earliest complete copy of the Hebrew Bible (1009 C.E.), known as the Masoretic Text, showing both the text and critical notes in the margins. (Photograph by Bruce and Kenneth Zuckerman, West Semitic Research with the collaboration of the Ancient Biblical Manuscript Center. Courtesy Russian National Museum [Saltykov-Shchedrin])

canon later adopted in rabbinic circles and by the Masoretic scholars of Tiberius in Galilee in the Middle Ages (referred to as the **Masoretic Text**).[4] Based on accounts of the discussions held by a group of rabbis in Yavneh (also known as Jamnia, near the Mediterranean coast) in about 90 C.E., as well as other rabbinic accounts, some scholars argue that this collection did not include Ecclesiastes, Song of Songs, or Esther, and that these books were added to the rabbinic canonical collection at the end of the second or beginning of the third century. Against this argument, Josephus already alludes to material contained in Ecclesiastes; he attributes 1,005 "odes and songs" as well as 3,000 "parables and similitudes" to Solomon; and includes the Esther story in his historical summary.[5] Thus, even

---

[4] The discrepancy in the number of books (22 versus 24) could be due simply to different ways of combining or grouping (and therefore counting) the same writings.

[5] *Antiquities* 11.6.1[184]–11.6.13 [296].

though Palestinian rabbis might have debated the status of these three books, Josephus, reflecting the temple archival collection, probably included them and more of the Solomonic material than was included later in his list. He also mentions histories of the Maccabees, although he states that since these were composed after the Persian period, they are not to be considered of equal authority with the twenty-two (*Against Apion* 1.8 [42]).

Scholarly Theories and Challenges

There have been two predominant theories about the dating and formation of the Jewish scriptural canon. The earliest theory, prevailing among nineteenth- and early-twentieth-century scholars, advocated a tripartite canon that developed in three stages, corresponding to the categorization found in current Jewish Bibles (Tanakh). The first section, the Pentateuch, referred to by ancient Jewish authorities as "the Law" (*Torah*) or "the five books [of Moses]," was thought to have been canonized around 400 B.C.E., with the eclipse of prophecy in the Persian period. The second section, "the Prophets" (*Nevi'im*), was believed to have been recognized around 200 B.C.E. The third section is referred to by ancient Jewish authorities as "the other books of our ancestors," "psalms [of David]," and "psalms and precepts," and by the Talmud as "Writings" (*Kethuvim*). According to the tripartite-canon theory, this final collection was accepted no later than the rabbinical gathering held in Yavneh (Jamnia) around 90 C.E.

Variations on the tripartite theory assign an earlier date to the closure of the canon: in the Persian period (according to Freedman) or the Maccabean period (Leiman, Beckwith). To explain how Christians would eventually include the apocrypha in their First (or Old) Testament, despite the fact that these books were excluded from the tripartite canon of Jewish Scriptures, scholars argued that this narrower canon was Palestinian, while a distinct, broader canon had developed in Alexandria. The Alexandrian canon, they argued, is attested by the Christian Septuagint codices, which do not group books according to these three divisions. The Alexandrian-canon theory has been discredited by the fact that many groupings in early Christian canon lists diverge from that of the Septuagint codices (see Sundberg). This diversity demonstrates that Christians had not inherited a particular canon or ordering, let alone a tripartite one, from Second Temple-period Judaism.

Other observations challenge the tripartite theory. Most salient is the reexamination of the type of meeting the Yavneh rabbinical gathering was. Since later rabbinic texts attest the ongoing debate over which books were regarded as canonical, the "decision" of the rabbis who met in Yavneh could not have been either binding or universal (Lewis). In addition, the assumption that the third collection of "Writings" was created to include texts composed during the second century B.C.E. has been abandoned, since, with the exception of parts or all of Daniel, these texts are firmly dated prior to the Maccabean period (see Schechter and Taylor, p. 35).

In response to these critiques, scholars have revised their views of the triple-canon theory. Some scholars have suggested that the third section (the Writings) was not decided at Yavneh, but that it reflects what had been collected in the temple archives by the year 70 C.E., when the temple was destroyed. Others claim that the third group developed later in the second or third century C.E. and that earlier Jewish authorities only considered the two categories of Pentateuch and Prophets to be canonical. One scholar has argued that the triple canon only developed among one specific Jewish sect, namely Pharisees (Collins). A definitive resolution, however, has not yet been achieved.

Codices, Canon, and Early Christians

The Hebrew Scriptures and the first copies were written on scrolls. The earliest codex version of Hebrew Scriptures dates to the Middle Ages. (Jews today still use hand-printed scrolls for liturgical readings of the Pentateuch and Esther.) Fourth-century Christian Greek manuscripts provide the earliest attestation of the Bible in codex form. Thus it is difficult to assess when the concept of a single, authoritative canon became part of Jewish consciousness. Evidence suggests that various collections—"the Law," "the Prophets," "the Psalms," "the Twelve" (in one scroll), "the Writings"—emerged over the course of six or so centuries. Yet it is difficult to determine not only the exact content of these categories before the evidence in the rabbinical teachings in the **Talmud** (*Babba Bathra* 14b), but also when, or whether, they came to be regarded as a whole. Such determinations must be deduced from fragmentary papyri and literary citations, since no canon list created by a Second Temple-period author currently exists.

Such lists emerge, however, in the context of Christian debates over the content of the First/Old Testament collection. Christian consensus on the OT canon proved elusive, as it is even to this day. There are a number of reasons for this. First, early Christians began using Jewish Scriptures at a time when there were regional and sectarian variations about the content of the last part of that canon. While "the Law and the Prophets" were universally accepted, what constituted the "other books of our ancestors" (in the words of Ben Sira's grandson) seems to have varied.

Furthermore, Aramaic translations of Scriptures, or **Targumim** (singular **Targum**), developed during this period and were probably extemporaneously devised during synagogue worship. Thus, no preferred Aramaic versions existed.

Jesus and the first Christians used some form of these Scriptures, most likely in Aramaic, that have not been preserved. Soon thereafter, however, as Paul conveyed the gospel to Gentiles outside Palestine, the Greek Scriptures became prevalent among Christians.

Scholars disagree over whether the use by NT authors of Greek scriptural material not found in the later Hebrew canon constitutes the existence of a broader canon or simply the use of materials considered to be *instructional* but *noncanonical.* Alternatively, this usage may simply reflect an early stage in the development of canon consciousness in which such categories are anachronistic. By the fourth century, Christian authorities, except the church fathers Jerome (d. 420) and his contemporary Rufinus, considered the books that were collected in the earliest Septuagint codices to be authoritative. These earliest biblical manuscripts, produced by Christians, include 1–2 Esdras, Wisdom, Sirach, Judith, Tobit, Baruch, and the Letter of Jeremiah.[6] Christian use of other writings outside these collections or lists, sometimes referred to as "pseudepigrapha" (writings "falsely attributed"; see chapter five), suggests that while such books as *Enoch, Jannes and Jambres, Apocalypse of Elijah,* and *Jubilees* were not considered canonical Scriptures, they were regarded by Christians as "useful for teaching" as well as helpful for understanding NT references (Tertullian, *On the Apparel of Women* 3, who himself accepted Enoch, despite the opinions of other Christians; see Adler, pp. 218–28).

THE CANONIZATION OF THE NEW TESTAMENT

The development of a NT canon was quite different from that of the First or Old Testament. Composing, editing, reproducing, and canonizing were intertwined to a greater degree; canonical consciousness developed alongside, or even within, the production process.

Beginnings and the Gospels

Within about a century of Jesus' ministry, there was a self-conscious effort to create a definitive, authoritative collection. Christian writers produced lists of the writings they considered authoritative, and evidence for their lists exists in scriptural papyri as old as the second century and in nearly complete codices dating to the fourth century. However, while the process of collecting

---

[6] The manuscripts Vaticanus (B) and Alexandrinus (A) also include Ps 151; the manuscript Sinaiticus ℵ is missing leaves, making definitive determination impossible. It is worth noting that few codices containing an entire collection of OT and NT books have survived.

authoritative writings in categories such as "Gospel" and "Acts of Apostles" began already in the second century, there was diversity among canon lists and among the contents of various codices of the Bible. This suggests that even though Bishop Athanasius of Alexandria produced a list in the mid-fourth century (367) corresponding to the current twenty-seven-book NT (Athanasius, *Epistle* 39.5), his view was not universally accepted, particularly by communities in the East.[7]

Due to the lack of a centralized political authority and of an official temple archive in earliest Christianity, diversity was inherent and unavoidable in the initial spread of the gospel message. Orally transmitted to different communities around the Roman Mediterranean, different versions of the life and teachings of Jesus of Nazareth were considered authoritative for various groups of early followers of Jesus. In the mid-second century, the apologist Justin Martyr attests that these accounts were read aloud in Christian assemblies, although Justin's pupil, Tatian, is the first Christian writer to quote a Gospel text as Scripture (Justin, *First Apology* 67.3–4; Tatian, *Oration to the Greeks* 13.1).

Already by the time of Justin and Tatian, only four of these accounts were widely considered sufficiently authoritative to elicit the approval of various authors over and against other attempts to privilege a single gospel. While the collection of a fourfold gospel created other problems for Christians (most notably the apparent contradictions among the different accounts), a multiform collection was considered an important corrective against the heretical purposes more easily served by a single gospel (Tertullian, *Prescription Against Heretics* 38). Clement of Alexandria used the (ultimately noncanonical) *Gospel of the Egyptians,* the *Gospel of the Hebrews,* the *Protevangelium of James,* and perhaps a *Secret Gospel of Mark* in addition to the "four gospels that have been handed down to us" (*Miscellanies* 3.13.93; see Gamble, p. 281).

The Letters

The letters of Paul may have been collected and circulated under Paul's own tutelage. They continued to undergo further editing and publishing by Paul's scribes and their students after his death. Although Paul and his communities may have held only one collection of Scriptures as authoritative, namely the Jewish Greek Scriptures, Christians began to rely on Paul's interpretations of those Scriptures and of the gospel, as recorded in his letters, for guiding their daily life and practice. While the writings of other teachers (e.g., Peter, James, Apollos, Barnabas) may have been held in equal regard by non-Pauline communities, the

---

[7] Cf. *Apostolic Canon* 85 from Syria; Gregory of Nazianzus, *Poems* 12.31 in Asia Minor; Syrian Catalogue of St. Catherine's monastery; Laodicea Synod, canon 60 in Asia Minor, as listed in McDonald, *et al, Canon Debate,* Tables D-2, D-3.

Pauline corpus gained preeminence by the second century. Although the earliest full extant papyrus collection of Paul's letters probably did not include the Pastoral Letters or Philemon (an argument based on the theoretical reconstruction of what the incomplete manuscript actually contained), by the fourth century most lists and collections of Paul's letters consisted of thirteen or fourteen letters, depending on whether Hebrews was included.[8]

The fourth-century Alexandrian bishop Athanasius advocated the inclusion of Hebrews, which he attributed to Paul, in the canonical list of his festal letter of 367 noted above. The anti-Arian bishop wrote this letter largely to condemn the "fabrication" of books by those whom he considered to be heretics. The letter also articulated his notion of canonicity: "In these alone the teaching of godliness is proclaimed. Let no one add to these; let nothing be taken away from them" (*Epistle* 39.6, trans. Metzger, pp. 211–12). The canon of Athanasius delineates the same twenty-seven books accepted a few years later in Rome (see discussion below) and then throughout the Christian church.

The Catholic Epistles—James, 1–2 Peter, 1–3 John, and Jude—were sometimes included in second- and third-century lists and collections, but it was not until the fourth century that they were widely accepted as authoritative. Until the fifth century, the book of Revelation was regarded as problematic by eminent Eastern authorities, but was more widely accepted by the Latin church. Other writings (some of which are often called "the Apostolic Fathers") were cited as authoritative and were included in many canon lists and scriptural manuscripts: *Shepherd of Hermas, Letter of Barnabas, Apocalypse of Peter,* and *Didache* (see chapter five for brief descriptions of these writings).

Canon and Orthodoxy

As noted at the beginning of this chapter, canonization is a process that can only be understood in historical context. Debates over which books were to be considered authoritative centered on which writings expressed the essential Christian message. How a particular individual or community understood the essence of the gospel depended upon which texts were studied and read in worship. Thus, recent scholars refer to a "functional canon" to describe how texts influenced the life and practice of Christian communities rather than a fixed, theoretical canon.

The notion of a **Rule of Faith** (Latin, ***regula fidei***), *or* standard of orthodoxy, became the essential criterion by which texts were accorded authority (McDonald, "Identifying Scripture and Canon in the Early Church," p. 428).

---

[8] In contrast to most modern scholarship (see chapter four), the fourth-century leaders assumed that Paul was in fact the author of all thirteen letters ascribed to him. The only debate was about Hebrews, which does not name its author.

Their apostolic character, or "apostolicity"—often thought to be one of the primary criteria for canonicity—was determined not merely by attribution to Jesus' apostles but also by their adherence to the correct interpretation of the gospel, or "orthodoxy." Doctrinal debates had canonical consequences. In the early centuries of Christianity, various canons reveal controversy over the core of Christian teaching.

The second-century case of Marcion is the most well-known example of this. Marcion, based in Rome, proposed a canon that excluded the OT and consisted of only one gospel, namely Luke (in a shorter, nonorthodox version), and 10 letters of Paul (Galatians, 1–2 Corinthians, Romans, 1–2 Thessalonians, Colossians, Philippians, Philemon, and one called "Laodiceans," which scholars identify with the letter usually called Ephesians). Marcion premised his selection on the dualistic belief that the love of Jesus Christ released human souls from the legalistic, bodily imprisonment that the nefarious demiurge (creator god) of the OT had maliciously and capriciously imposed on the human race (as recorded in the first chapter of Genesis; cf. Tertullian, *Against Marcion* 1.2, 24). Marcion justifies this dichotomous antipathy between Gospel and Law with an idiosyncratic reading of Paul's letters. Scholars are divided as to whether subsequent insistence on the plurality of the gospels was a reaction to Marcion's canon or simply the vociferous articulation of a norm that his canon challenged. In either case, definitions of heresy and orthodoxy directly shaped canon development.

Canon and Civil Authority

When the Emperor Constantine convened bishops to determine a consensus about the fundamentals of Christian faith in the face of the Arian controversy[9] (the Council of Nicea, 325), the possibility of the state's enforcing a particular type of Christianity, along with the collection of writings it considered to be authoritative, was created. Although an orthodox consensus would not be legally enforceable until the Theodosian Codes of the last quarter of the fourth century, the need for generating such texts had already been created by Constantine's request from the bishop and scholar Eusebius of Caesarea for Scriptures for his churches in Constantinople (modern Istanbul).

This need had been created both by the construction of new basilicas and by the destruction of scriptural manuscripts in the persecutions of Christians under the emperor Diocletian at the beginning of the fourth century. According to Eusebius, these copies of the NT Scriptures did not include James, 2 Peter, 2–3 John, or Jude, coinciding with the canon of the early third-century biblical

---

[9] Arius (d. 336) and his followers believed that the Son of God was not eternal or fully divine but was created by God the Father.

scholar Origen, whose scholarly work was probably available to Eusebius in the library of Caesarea.

The first attempt to produce a universally accepted standardized text for the wider church emerges out of the historical context of the changing role of bishops in civil affairs over the course of the fourth century. In 380, Emperors Gratianus, Valentinianus, and Theodosius acknowledged the apostolic authority of Damasus, the bishop of Rome (*Theodosian Code* 16.1.2). He asked Jerome, the great biblical scholar who settled in Palestine, to produce a standard Latin text of the Scriptures (later known as the Vulgate). Jerome's subsequent promulgation of a twenty-seven-book NT canon at the Council of Rome (ca. 382) carried more authority than previous decrees by church councils.

A statement following a similar list adopted by the Synod of Carthage in 419 reflects this authority: "Let this be sent to our brother and fellow priest, holy Boniface, bishop of the city of Rome, and to the other bishops of those parts, so they may confirm this canon, since this is what we have received from the fathers for reading in church" (Canons on account of Apiarus 24/29, in *Corpus Christianorum: Series Latina* 149: 108, 126, author's translation). The list contained Revelation, probably under the influence of Augustine, who had written earlier that he considered it canonical (*On Christian Doctrine* 2.8–9, 12–14). An important list and brief discussion of canonical books, the Muratorian Fragment, also lists Revelation, but it includes the *Apocalypse of Peter* as well, even though it says that "some of us do not want it [*Apocalypse of Peter*] to be read in church."[10] Meager attestation for Revelation in actual NT manuscripts, however, suggests that its canonical status was in question throughout the Middle Ages (Epp, "Issues," p. 505). It was never included in the **lectionary** of the Greek church (and still is not, though it remains in the Orthodox canon). It was included in the official canon accepted by the Roman Catholic Church at its Council of Trent in 1546, and it is considered canonical by Protestants.

CANON AND COMMUNITY

When we consider the Bibles used by Christians and Jews today, we notice that the texts used for public readings are often different from those used in the context of Bible study. Some scholars would observe that this demonstrates that faith communities have a **canon within the canon.** Texts read aloud in a

---

[10] The Muratorian Fragment is from an eighth-century Latin manuscript. Its original date and provenance are debated: scholars who date it to the late second century claim it reflects a Western, perhaps Roman, canon (Bruce, Ferguson, Metzger), while those who assign a mid-fourth century date tend to locate its origins in the East, perhaps Syria (von Campenhausen, Sundberg, McDonald).

liturgical (worship) context might be said to carry a higher authority than those used in Bible study. Jews read the entire Pentateuch in the course of their synagogue lectionary in a one- or three-year period, yet only selections of the prophets are read, and the selections exclude Nahum, Zephaniah, and Haggai. The books of Proverbs, Job, Daniel, Ezra-Nehemiah, and Chronicles also have no place in the Jewish liturgical calendar. Likewise, the Revised Common Lectionary, used by many Christian churches, does not include any readings from Chronicles, Ezra-Nehemiah, Obadiah, Nahum, Habakkuk, 2–3 John, and Jude. These discrepancies may illustrate that a community's functional canon does not necessarily correspond to its theoretical canon.

Scholars have also pointed out that the commentaries through which the text is understood, whether oral (e.g., sermons), written (e.g., annotations in study Bibles), or even visual (e.g., plays and movies), are sometimes also treated as authoritative by those who use them. Thus for some Christians, the gospel proclamation is the sole lens through which OT texts are understood, and the centuries of biblical commentaries that have been transmitted help to frame texts in this manner. There are other Christians who engage in modern, scholarly (e.g., **historical-critical**) study of the Bible, without regard to the accumulated interpretation, in an attempt to recover the original contexts of the biblical texts themselves. This impulse lay at the heart of Luther's appeal to *sola Scriptura,* which prompted the Council of Trent to reject his relegation of the apocrypha to the status of "books which are not held to be equal to holy scripture but are useful and good to read." Instead, the Roman Catholic canon now includes the apocrypha as it is today (Harrington, "The Old Testament Apocrypha," pp. 204–5). Many Christians explore both traditional commentaries and historical-critical studies to discern how the Bible can inform their belief and practice.

A similar situation is found in Judaism. One scholar has argued that Jews who view the Bible through the lens of the Oral Torah, or Talmud, privilege the classical rabbinic interpretation to such an extent that the interpretation overtakes the Bible itself as canonical (Halbertal, *People of the Book*, p. 125). Others engage in modern academic text criticism, without regard to Talmudic interpretation. Many Jews regard the tradition, along with modern insights, as informative, but rely on contemporary authorities to determine which aspects of Torah are authoritative for their belief and practice.

CONCLUSION

In conclusion, the history of the development of the biblical canons is complex and, at times, uncertain. On the one hand, there is much evidence to take into account. On the other hand, there are questions for which no evidence currently exists. The First Testament/Old Testament canon eventually developed into at least two primary forms: the Hebrew Scriptures, or Tanakh, and the Greek Scriptures, or Septuagint. Jesus and the first Christians used some form of these Scriptures, most likely in Aramaic, no longer extant. Soon thereafter, however, as Paul and others conveyed the gospel to Gentiles outside Palestine, the Greek Scriptures became prevalent among Christians.

This preference for the Greek Bible (LXX) persisted up to the emergence of a canonical consensus in the fourth century and beyond, and it remains the case in Greek-speaking churches. The Vulgate became the accepted Latin version of Scriptures for Western churches. The canonization of the Second Testament/New Testament occurred alongside the Christian canonization of the Septuagint, although there is more agreement among early authorities about the contents of the NT. After a series of critical controversies, most notably that of Marcion, a consensus emerged, as reflected in fourth-century lists, prepared both by individual authorities and by councils of bishops, about the core books of the NT canon.

Historical events shaped the early and later development of these canons, sometimes producing new canons or recovering old ones that had been lost. The central idea of a canon, however, binds these varieties together; religious communities continue to seek direction in their lives from the texts "received by their ancestors" that they hold to be authoritative and sacred. The canon remains the principal collection of texts through which to apprehend the Divine W/word.

FOR FURTHER READING AND STUDY

Adler, William. "The Pseudepigrapha in the Early Church." Pages 211–28 in *The Canon Debate*. Edited by Lee Martin McDonald and James A. Sanders. Peabody, Mass.: Hendrickson, 2002. An account of how early Christian writers used the categories "pseudepigrapha" and "apocrypha" and used pseudepigraphic works themselves.

Beckwith, R. *The Old Testament Canon of the New Testament Church*. Grand Rapids: Eerdmans, 1986. An analysis of the Christian canon of the OT, concluding that Tanakh was canonized in the Maccabean period, around 160 B.C.E.

Bruce, F. F. *The Canon of Scripture*. Downers Grove, Ill.: InterVarsity, 1988. An argument for the existence and authority of Tanakh by the first century C.E. and for the existence of the core of the NT canon by the second century.

Collins, J. "Before the Canon: Scriptures in Second Temple Judaism." Pages 225–41 in *Old Testament Interpretation: Past, Present, and Future. Essays in*

Honor of Gene H. Tucker. Edited by J. L. Mays, D. Petersen, and K. Richards. Nashville: Abingdon, 1995. An argument for the acceptance by Jews of a tripartite canon in the first century, originating with the Pharisees.

Epp, Eldon Jay. "Issues in the Interrelation of New Testament Textual Criticism and Canon." Pages 485–515 in *The Canon Debate.* Edited by Lee Martin McDonald and James A. Sanders. Peabody, Mass.: Hendrickson, 2002. An analysis of manuscript evidence suggesting both the fluidity of canon formation and the influence of doctrinal commitments in producing standardized texts.

Freedman, D. N. *The Unity of the Hebrew Bible.* Distinguished Senior Faculty Lecture Series. Ann Arbor: University of Michigan, 1991. An argument for the canonization of Tanakh in the Persian period, following the Babylonian exile (587/6 B.C.E.) and driven by the experience of exile.

Gamble, Harry Y. "The New Testament Canon: Recent Research and the *Status Quaestionis.*" Pages 267–94 in *The Canon Debate.* Edited by Lee Martin McDonald and James A. Sanders. Peabody, Mass.: Hendrickson, 2002. A concise introduction to the history of NT canon research.

Grant, Robert M. *The Formation of the New Testament.* New York: Harper & Row, 1965. An overview highlighting the role of early Christian communities, rather than councils, as well as the contribution of nonorthodox Christian movements.

Halbertal, Moshe. *People of the Book: Canon, Meaning, and Authority.* Cambridge, Mass.: Harvard University Press, 1997. An examination of the concept of canon in Judaism.

Harrington, Daniel J. "The Old Testament Apocrypha in the Early Church and Today." Pages 196–210 in *The Canon Debate.* Edited by Lee Martin McDonald and James A. Sanders. Peabody, Mass.: Hendrickson, 2002. An examination of the history of Jewish and Christian usage of the so-called OT Apocrypha from Qumran to the modern period.

Kraft, Robert A. "The Codex and Canon Consciousness." Pages 229–33 in *The Canon Debate.* Edited by Lee Martin McDonald and James A. Sanders. Peabody, Mass.: Hendrickson, 2002. An exploration of the impact of the technological change from scroll to codex on canon consciousness, particularly the idea of a closed canon.

Leiman, S. *The Canonization of Hebrew Scripture: The Talmudic and Midrashic Evidence.* Transactions of the Connecticut Academy of Arts and Sciences 47. 2d ed. New Haven: Connecticut Academy of Arts and Sciences, 1991. A highly technical study of the rabbinic sources relevant to the development of a Hebrew Bible canon.

Lewis, J. "What Do We Mean by Jabneh?" *Journal of Bible and Religion* 32 (1964): 125–32. A groundbreaking article that challenged the theory that the Hebrew Bible was canonized at the "council of Jamnia."

McDonald, Lee Martin. *The Formation of the Christian Biblical Canon.* 3d ed. Peabody, Mass.: Hendrickson, forthcoming. A comprehensive but accessible introduction to the formation of the OT and NT canons.

———. "Identifying Scripture and Canon in the Early Church: The Criteria Question." Pages 416–39 in *The Canon Debate.* Edited by Lee Martin McDonald and James A. Sanders. Peabody, Mass.: Hendrickson, 2002. An examination of the criteria used by early Christian communities for ascribing authority to certain writings.

Metzger, Bruce M. *The Canon of the New Testament: Its Origin, Development, and Significance.* New York: Oxford University Press, 1987. A comprehensive treatment considered by many to be the quintessential work on the subject.

Schechter, S., and C. Taylor. *The Wisdom of Ben Sira: Portions of the Book of Ecclesiasticus from Hebrew Manuscripts in the Cairo Genizah Collection Presented to the University of Cambridge by the Editors.* Cambridge, England: Cambridge University Press, 1899. A critical study of the book and its relevance for canonical studies.

Sundberg, Albert C. *The Old Testament of the Early Church.* Harvard Theological Studies 20. Cambridge, Mass.: Harvard University Press, 1964. An argument for the openness of the canon of Tanakh when early Christians began to interpret it within the context of the early Jesus movement.

Ulrich, E. "The Notion and Definition of Canon." Pages 21–35 in *The Canon Debate.* Edited by Lee Martin McDonald and James A. Sanders. Peabody, Mass.: Hendrickson, 2002. A concise introduction to the definition and idea of "canon."

Chapter 7

The Transmission and Translation of the Bible

MICHAEL L. BARRÉ

Most modern readers of the Bible recognize that they are not reading the exact words of Jeremiah or Jesus, of Isaiah or Paul, for none of them spoke or wrote in English, French, Swahili, or even modern Hebrew and Greek. Rather, there was a long process of transmitting the texts of the Bible and of translating them into foreign languages—a process that continues to this day. How did (and does) this process take place? That is the subject of this chapter.

THE BIBLE: ORIGINS IN SPEECH AND WRITING

The Oral Character of Biblical Traditions

When we think of "the Bible," we naturally picture a book. In fact, as noted in chapter one, the word "Bible" comes from the ancient Greek word for "books." It is a collection of historical and religious traditions that has come down to us in written form. It is important to remember, however, that a good percentage of these traditions were originally handed down by word of mouth. Only later were they written down, eventually assuming the form of a book.

In the nineteenth century there was a great deal of interest in the oral origins of the Bible. Biblical researchers began to notice and then to investigate the similarity between the shape of many biblical passages and folklore traditions in modern societies. This led to the realization that many of the biblical stories once existed in oral form. Of course, not all biblical books had an oral background—for example, the letters of Paul in the NT. But investigations resulted in the conclusion that the Bible was not—at least not entirely—the product of writers who sat down and penned the texts that we now call the Bible.

In many instances, even after oral traditions came to be written down, they continued to be recited (for example, in rituals or storytelling). Because it was not fixed like the written version, the oral version continued to develop. Over time various additions or changes would occur in the oral form of the tradition. Eventually this process could affect the written word.

Two brief examples may be given to exemplify the oral background of the OT:

- Many of the stories about the patriarchs (or ancestors) were classified as "sagas." A saga was a short, easily memorized, simple folk story that had little in the way of plot or character development and was handed down from generation to generation by word of mouth. This category includes the various stories about Abraham, Isaac, and Jacob in Genesis.

- The oral aspect of biblical traditions can also be seen in the Psalter. The psalms were originally sung prayers in poetic form that were later written down. They continued to be sung—from memory—in temple services. Psalm 18 and 2 Sam 22 are two versions of the same psalm, though there are many divergences in the wording of these two versions. Many experts in the Psalms today believe that the divergences stem partly from the fact that this prayer continued to have an oral existence even after being cast in written form.

As for an example from the NT, most critical scholars of the Bible today agree that Matthew's version of the Lord's Prayer originally did not contain the words "For thine is the kingdom, and the power, and the glory, for ever. Amen" (Matt 6:13, King James Version). But at least by the early second century C.E. this brief "doxology" had come to be added to the original prayer as it was prayed privately and publicly by Christians (as can be seen in the *Didache,* one of the writings from the Apostolic Fathers discussed in chapter five). As a result, some scribes added it to the written biblical text—probably in the margin at first. Later copyists took this marginal addition to be part of the biblical tradition, and so added it to the text. This is why it appears in older, traditional Bible translations such as the King James. But since it is no longer believed to be part of the original tradition, this doxology does not appear in most modern translations of the Bible except in a footnote.

The oral background of the gospels is also evident from the way in which the traditions about Jesus (or "Jesus traditions") were handed down by the early church. Before the age of critical study of the Bible, it was assumed that the gospels were essentially biographies of Jesus with eyewitnesses as their sources. In the last century, this view was thoroughly discredited. The position of the majority of critical scholars today is that while the gospels give us certain reliable traditions about the words and deeds of Jesus, there is not enough from which to construct his biography (at least in the modern sense of that word). This realization marked the end of the "Lives of Jesus" movement in the nineteenth century, which attempted to reconstruct the life of Jesus from NT sources. The predominant view among NT scholars today is that our four gospels are the final product in a chain of tradition, as described in chapter four:

- the first disciples and apostles recalled the words and actions of Jesus in their preaching;

- these traditions were kept alive in the early Christian churches by being recounted and meditated on; and

- the evangelists selected from these traditions and used them in putting together their gospels.

The first two of these stages involved oral tradition only.

The Work of Biblical Scribes

Once biblical traditions began to be written down, there arose the need for scribes to make copies of these written texts for future generations. In general these transmitters of the tradition did a commendable job of accurately passing down the Scriptures. However, error-free copies of long texts were virtually impossible in ancient times. In the OT and NT, therefore, it was inevitable that over the centuries errors would find their way into the text. These errors are apparent from occasionally unintelligible passages, which have suffered some kind of corruption in the transmission process, and also (in the case of the OT) from a comparison of the standard Hebrew text with the ancient **versions** (translations).

Not all scribal changes to the text were the result of accidental error. Some were deliberate, with the purpose of updating the text (e.g., by replacing an obsolete word or grammatical form with a current one), expanding the text in some cases (as in the Lord's Prayer), and generally making it relevant to those who would read what the scribe was writing. Thus as regards the transmission of the biblical text, scribes were not human copying machines but to some extent interpreters and shapers of the tradition. In a real sense they were part of the canonical process.

On rare occasions, scribes would change the text in order to avoid something that sounded blasphemous to them. For example, in Job 2:9, after a host of tragedies befalls Job, his wife says to him, "Curse God, and die!" (NRSV). But the Hebrew text that has come down to us actually says, "Bless God, and die!" (see NRSV note). The textual evidence (including that of the LXX) for this and similar OT texts suggests that some pious, pre-Masoretic scribe found the original wording in Job too blasphemous to be included in the sacred text and so replaced

"Curse" with "Bless." The NRSV, recognizing this scribal change, rightly trans-lates the intention of Job's wife according to the biblical writer.

The Textual Traditions of the Bible

Earlier generations viewed the text of the Hebrew OT and the Greek NT quite simplistically. They naively tended to assume that any copy of the Hebrew Scrip-tures was virtually the original Hebrew text as written by the biblical authors and editors, and that a copy of the Greek NT was identical to what the NT authors had written.

Later generations assumed that the Masoretic Text (MT), the standard edi-tion of the Hebrew Scriptures since the end of the first millennium C.E., was identical with the original biblical text. At least early Jewish and Christian tradi-tion believed it was dictated directly by God to the inspired biblical authors, let-ter by letter. Today only the most conservative believers hold such a view. The evidence of the Dead Sea Scrolls has demonstrated that the matter is not so simple. Parts of all the books of the OT except Esther have been found among the scrolls. Study of these scrolls has shown that between the years 300 and 100 B.C.E. there grew up a variety of Hebrew texts of the OT. Scholars divide them into three "families": the Palestinian, the Egyptian, and the Babylonian. While all of these contained *basically* the same text, they differ in many details. Some con-tained a shortened text of a particular book or passage, while others expanded the text by adding material. This discovery makes it difficult to maintain, as many scholars had in the past, that the MT is a text superior to all others. Increas-ingly, translators of the OT today are making more use of the ancient Hebrew and Greek versions, together with the MT, in their work.

Eventually there came a time when many Jews were no longer able to read or understand the Hebrew text. Already in the time of Nehemiah (fifth century B.C.E.), when the Hebrew Scriptures were read publicly, it was necessary to pro-vide a running translation so that the people could understand what was being read (Neh 8:7–8). This situation eventually led to the first translation of the He-brew Scriptures into another language. As earlier chapters have already dis-cussed, in the third century B.C.E. the Pentateuch was translated into the universal language of the day, Greek. This probably took place in Alexandria, Egypt, a major Jewish intellectual center outside of Palestine at the end of the OT period. Later the Prophets (i.e., the Former Prophets and Latter Prophets) were also translated. This Greek translation, as we have also noted in earlier chapters, came to be known as the Septuagint (LXX), Latin for "seventy," since in popular legend it was allegedly translated by seventy (or seventy-two) Jewish elders. The LXX is thus the oldest and most important of the biblical versions.

As time went on, translations were made into other languages. Aside from the Septuagint the most important version was St. Jerome's translation into Latin in the late fourth to early fifth centuries C.E. Earlier Latin translations already existed, but many of these were judged to be of poor quality. In 382 Pope Damasus commissioned Jerome to prepare a new translation. The result was the Vulgate, from the Latin meaning "vernacular, popular," as we have also seen in earlier chapters. The translation of the OT was made partly from the Hebrew text and partly from the Septuagint. The translation of the NT, of course, was made from the Greek. This came to be the official Bible of the Roman Catholic Church and was officially recognized as such at the Council of Trent in 1546. Until 1943 Catholics were not permitted to translate the Bible from the original languages but only from the Vulgate.

In the history of the NT textual tradition there was no single form of the text that commanded the same esteem as the MT did for Jews. The earliest manuscripts were written on papyrus or parchment. Fragments of the NT on papyri as early as the second century C.E. are known. At first these were written as scrolls. But scrolls that held more than one average-size biblical book were cumbersome to use. In the second century C.E. the codex appeared, in which individual pages were bound together similarly to modern books. With the codex, one could find a particular passage rather quickly, without unrolling a large scroll. Two of the major codices containing all or part of the NT were Codex Sinaiticus (abbreviated ℵ [aleph, the first letter of the Hebrew alphabet]) and Codex Vaticanus (abbreviated B). The former is a fourth-century codex containing most of the OT and the entire NT. It was discovered between 1844 and 1859 by Konstantin von Tischendorf, Professor of New Testament at Leipzig, at the Monastery of St. Catherine on Mount Sinai. Codex Vaticanus is a mid-fourth-century codex that has been housed in the Vatican Library since the fifteenth century. Today over five thousand manuscripts containing all or part of the NT text are known.

Ancient Biblical Texts and Textual Criticism

Since we do not possess the original texts written by the biblical authors, virtually all translators of the Bible today use the science of **textual criticism** to try to get back to the earliest form of the text, a text that is as free of scribal additions and errors as possible. The result is known as a **critical text** of the Hebrew OT and the Greek NT.

Since the MT is still the official Bible of Judaism and continues to be the standard edition of the biblical Hebrew text, the text printed in critical editions of the OT is still that of the Leningrad Codex, dated 1009 C.E., the earliest dated complete copy of the Hebrew Bible. This edition of the MT can be called a critical text, however, insofar as beneath the Hebrew text on each page appears a **critical apparatus,** containing evidence of other ancient versions (DSS, LXX, Vulgate, etc.), citations from ancient authorities, and suggestions for alternative readings of words or passages in the MT. The standard critical text of the OT is the second edition of *Biblia Hebraica Stuttgartensia,* edited by K. Elliger and W. Rudolph.

The critical edition of the Greek NT is a scholarly reconstruction of the text based on textual-critical evidence; it does not match any one manuscript. Newer editions continue to improve the text to arrive at what experts in NT textual criticism regard as the most accurate reading of a word or passage. The two main editions of the critical text of the NT, the fourth edition of the American Bible Society's *Greek New Testament* (known as UBS[4]) and the twenty-seventh of the Nestle-Aland *Novum Testamentum* (known as NA[27]) now agree to the point that their texts are identical.

One striking achievement of this modern textual-critical approach to the Bible is found in the *New Revised Standard Version* (NRSV): the unprecedented addition of a paragraph to the biblical text that has never appeared in any translation of the Bible for over 2000 years. At the end of 1 Sam 10:27 is a brief narrative about Nahash king of the Ammonites found (though fragmentary in character) in one of the DSS manuscripts of 1 Sam. It is supported also by the writings of Josephus, the great Jewish historian (first century C.E.).

TRANSLATING THE BIBLE IN MODERN TIMES

Significant Translations in the Middle Ages and Early Renaissance

The Middle Ages saw sporadic translations of parts of the Bible into vernacular languages. St. Bede the Venerable (ca. 673–735) is said to have translated the Gospel of John into Anglo-Saxon shortly before his death, though nothing of this translation has come down to us. His translation was made from the Vulgate and was not disseminated.

None of the laity but the most highly educated read Latin in the Middle Ages. Since the only Bible permitted by the Church was the Vulgate, the Bible was unavailable for reading by the great majority of people. In fourteenth-century England, John Wycliffe (ca. 1330–1384) was part of a movement (the Lollards) that believed the Scriptures should be accessible to the general public in their own language. Wycliffe and his Lollard colleagues produced the first complete translation of the Bible into English (1380–1392). It was translated from the Vulgate. (At this time in Europe the biblical languages [Hebrew, Aramaic, and ancient Greek] were virtually unknown to European Christians.)

Because the Church did not permit any translation of the Scriptures except the Vulgate, Wycliffe's Bible was later condemned and copies of it were burned.

The Renaissance and Its Effects: Erasmus

The Renaissance (French for "rebirth") began immediately after the Middle Ages and marked a period of intense intellectual renewal and activity throughout Europe. To a large extent it was a revival of interest in the Latin and Greek classics as well as the beginning of humanism. Up to this point the intellectual life of Europe had been largely dominated by clerics. The Renaissance ushered in the intellectual rise of the laity, as evidenced in such early Renaissance figures as Dante (1265–1321) and Petrarch (1304–1374). Certain contemporary events outside of Europe also contributed to this movement, notably the fall of Constantinople to the Turks in 1453. After this event, many Christian scholars from the East sought refuge in Italy and brought with them the tradition of Greek scholarship, not to mention numerous important manuscripts from that tradition. The Renaissance, in about 1450, saw the invention of the printing press by Johann Gutenberg, which made possible the wide dissemination of Bible translations, at first only the Vulgate but later—after the Reformation—translations into various languages.

The effects of the Renaissance on intellectual Europe, and on Bible research, may be seen in the work of Desiderius Erasmus (1469–1536), which marked a turning point in NT studies in Europe. A philosopher and humanist, Erasmus learned Greek and studied the Greek classics. The influence of Renaissance humanism on him was evident first of all in his insistence on turning to early sources. Erasmus was one of the first practitioners of textual criticism, insisting that any translation of the Scriptures had to be preceded by establishing the most accurate text of the book(s) in question. In this task he employed the techniques of Italian humanists of the fifteenth century in his linguistic research on the Bible and the church fathers. In 1516, Erasmus prepared the first critical text of the Greek NT, which served as the basis for later critical editions.

English Translations after the Renaissance

The first translation of the Bible into English made from the original languages was that of William Tyndale (1494?–1536). Since translations of the Bible were still not permitted by the Catholic Church during his lifetime, the local bishop refused to support his translation project, which forced Tyndale to do his work in Germany and the Netherlands rather than in England. The project took

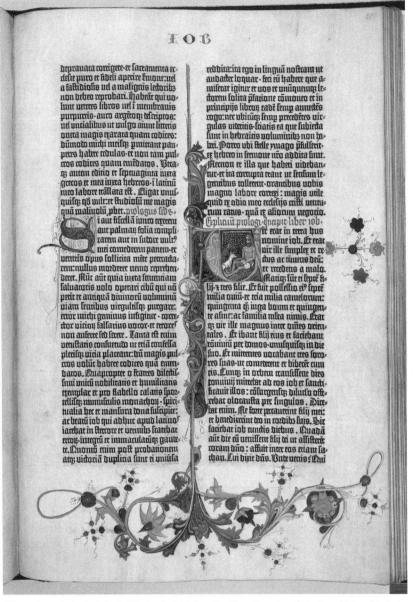

The prologue to the Latin text of the book of Job from the fifteenth-century Gutenberg Bible, printed ca. 1455–56 with moveable letters and adorned with hand painted initials, a small depiction of Job, and marginalia. (Bildarchiv Preussischer Kulturbesitz / Art Resource, NY)

him ten years—from 1525 to 1535. Copies of his translation were smuggled into England, where Church authorities confiscated and destroyed them whenever possible. A year later Tyndale was declared a heretic and killed near Brussels. His translation survived, however, and had a great influence on the **Authorized** (or "King James") **Version** (AV) almost a century later.

Slightly later than Tyndale's Bible was the Roman Catholic *Douay-Rheims* translation into English, which began to be printed in 1582. Given the polemical atmosphere of the time, its notes were apologetic (defensive) in nature, but this was partly a response to the anti-Catholic tone of those in the earlier English language *Geneva Bible* (1557–1560), published by Protestant refugees from England in Geneva. The non-Catholic translators of the AV at times followed the Catholic Douay-Rheims Bible.

At the Hampton Court conference in 1604, the president of Corpus Christi College at Oxford proposed a new translation of the Scriptures. The project was begun in 1607 and published in 1611 during the reign of James I. The result was the Authorized Version, commonly known in America as the King James Version (KJV) or King James Bible. The work was done by over fifty of the best scholars in England, including professors of Hebrew and Greek at Oxford and Cambridge. It was based on the translation of the *Bishops' Bible* (1568), and in style it was much indebted to Tyndale's translation. It is even today one of the best-selling Bible translations in English, despite its archaic language and its reliance on manuscripts that are not the most ancient or accurate.

The translation of the Bible into German by Martin Luther (1483–1546) is ranked as a monumental achievement of German literature. He began translating the NT in 1521 and published it the following year. He was aided by Philipp Melanchthon (1497–1560), who was more proficient in the biblical languages than Luther. After the completion of the NT, Luther began translating the OT, and the entire project was completed in 1534. For the next decade he kept revising his translation, the last edition appearing in 1545, a year before he died.

TWENTIETH-CENTURY TRANSLATIONS OF THE BIBLE INTO ENGLISH

Modern Bible translations are often classified as "formal-equivalence" or "dynamic-equivalence" translations. (The latter type is also referred to as "functional-equivalence" translations.) In ancient times, translations basically attempted to translate the biblical text word-for-word, or "literally," although some paraphrasing could occur. The reasoning was that only such a translation was regarded as "accurate" in antiquity. In many cases the result was hardly idiomatic in the target language, and it was sometimes incomprehensible to anyone who was not familiar with the underlying language. Modern formal-equivalence translations of the Scriptures (such as the *Revised Standard Version* or the *New Revised Standard Version*) do not go this far, though they emphasize close agreement with the exact form and wording of the original text.

In contrast, the primary aim of a dynamic-equivalence translation (such as the *Good News Bible* or the *Contemporary English Version*) is to reproduce as accurately as possible the sense (or function, hence "functional-equivalence") of the biblical passage. The result is a translation that makes liberal use of paraphrasing.

The following are brief descriptions of some of the better-known recent translations of the Bible into English:

The *Revised Standard Version* (RSV) was a revision of the *American Standard Version* (1901), itself a revision of the AV, and was intended for use in private and public worship. The NT was published in 1945, followed by the OT in 1952. In 1977 an edition appeared with the Apocrypha. This translation intended to preserve as much as possible the elevated style of the AV, while eliminating archaic English. Nevertheless, the RSV was based on the latest text-critical research of its time. It is basically a formal-equivalence translation and is still highly regarded by biblical scholars even today.

The *New International Version* (NIV) was sponsored by a consortium of conservative evangelical bodies in the United States. The NT appeared in 1973 and the OT in 1978; it has gone through two further revisions. While it gives precedence to accuracy of translation, it strives to be more than a word-for-word translation, contemporary but not dated, in clear and natural English. The project was sparked by the negative reaction of many conservative Protestants to the RSV. It often translates OT passages so that their fulfillment in the NT is more readily apparent (e.g., "virgin" in Isa 7:14 [cf. Matt 1:23], although strictly speaking, the Hebrew word does not mean this). The NIV has recently (NT, 2002; OT, 2005) been revised with a more gender-neutral approach and other changes, as Today's New International Version (TNIV).

A revision of the RSV, the *New Revised Standard Version* (NRSV), was published in 1989. It was in some respects an ecumenical and even interfaith translation, as its translation committee included men and women of Protestant, Roman Catholic, Greek Orthodox, and Jewish faith traditions. The translators tried to retain the style of the RSV while updating it and taking advantage of recent scholarship. One new feature was the use of moderately conservative gender-inclusive language.

The *New American Bible* (NAB), by members of the Catholic Biblical Association of America, was the first Roman Catholic translation of the Bible into English from the original languages, inspired by Pius XII's encyclical *Divino Afflante Spiritu* (1943; see discussion in chapter twelve). It was begun in 1944 and completed in 1970. A revised edition of the NT appeared in 1986 and of the Psalms in 1991, both of which featured the use of inclusive language. A revision of the rest of the OT, begun in the 1980s, is nearing completion.

A significant Jewish translation is the one published as *Tanakh: The Holy Scriptures: The New JPS Translation according to the Traditional Hebrew Text* (NJPS). The project was done in three stages, representing the three parts of the Hebrew Bible: the Torah (Pentateuch) in 1962, the Prophets in 1978, and the Writings in 1982. As the MT is the Bible of Judaism, the translation was made from this authoritative text. The aim was to make the best possible sense of the MT. In places where the meaning of the text was difficult, footnotes—which are kept to a minimum—indicate readings of the versions and conjectural solutions. A revised edition appeared in 1999.

In 1966 the American Bible Society published *Good News for Modern Man,* also known as *The New Testament in Today's English Version* (TEV). This was followed in 1976 by a translation of the OT, and then by an edition containing the Apocrypha in 1979. Known as the *Good News Bible* (GNB), it is perhaps the most popular example of a dynamic-equivalence translation today. This translation puts great emphasis on clarity and simplicity of language, and English that is comprehensible to all speakers of the language. To achieve this, it frequently makes use of paraphrasing. The TEV has been criticized for its use of paraphrasing in poetic texts (Psalms, the Prophets, Song of Songs, etc.). Paraphrasing often destroys any trace of the form of the poetic lines, which runs against the very nature of poetry. In 1995, the American Bible Society issued a new translation, the Contemporary English Version (CEV). It reflects translation principles similar to those of the TEV/GNB and attempts to be more sensitive to certain aspects of the biblical text, especially NT references to Jews.

CONCLUSION

In this chapter we have briefly explored the process by which the words uttered and recorded were transmitted by the biblical writers and their predecessors so that people of later generations (including our own) and other languages could hear and read them. The average reader of Scripture may not fully appreciate the complexity of this process, even though he or she benefits from it on a regular basis. Perhaps the best way to begin to learn firsthand the task that transmitters and translators face is to study Hebrew and Greek and then to read the Bible in its original languages. Those who do so gain not only a greater appreciation of the transmission of the Bible but also of its meaning.

For Further Reading and Study

McCarter, Kyle P., Jr. *Textual Criticism: Recovering the Text of the Hebrew Bible.* Guides to Biblical Scholarship, Old Testament Series. Philadelphia: Fortress, 1986. Rather technical, but one of the best guides to OT textual criticism available.

Metzger, Bruce M. *The Bible in Translation: Ancient and English Versions.* Grand Rapids: Baker, 2001. A valuable study of ancient and modern (English) Bible translations by a world-renowned expert in NT manuscripts and in translation.

————. *The Making of the New Revised Standard Version of the Bible.* Grand Rapids: Eerdmans, 1991. An overview by the chair of the translation committee.

Nicolson, Adam. *God's Secretaries: The Making of the King James Bible.* New York: HarperCollins, 2003. An interesting account of the story behind the King James Bible as a landmark of biblical scholarship and a masterpiece of English literature.

Rogerson, John, ed. *The Oxford Illustrated History of the Bible.* Oxford: Oxford University Press, 2001. An easy-to-read but informative history of the Bible, abundantly illustrated and with suggestions for further reading.

Soulen, Richard N., and R. Kendall Soulen. *Handbook of Biblical Criticism.* 3d ed. Lousiville: Westminster John Knox, 2001. Easily the best companion book for anyone studying the Bible, especially beginners, containing short articles (with bibliographies) on hundreds of topics and terms relating to biblical studies.

Ulrich, Eugene. *The Dead Sea Scrolls and the Origins of the Bible.* Studies in the Dead Sea Scrolls and Related Literature. Grand Rapids: Eerdmans, 1999. An excellent collection of essays (some very technical in nature) on the subject of the Scrolls' impact on the history of the OT text.

Part Two

The Interpretation of the Bible

Chapter 8

The Interpretation of the Bible before the Modern Period

CAROLE C. BURNETT

Jewish and Christian approaches to biblical **exegesis**—the careful analysis and interpretation of texts—share a common ancestry: the self-interpretation evident within the Hebrew Bible/Old Testament itself. Exegesis is performed there when psalmists and prophets ruminate on Israel's oral traditions and recorded experiences. Among many possible examples, Ps 78 can be cited as an interpretation of previously written Scripture, in that it is a retelling of the exodus story from the perspective of David's kingship. The postexilic books of Ezra and Nehemiah reflect a focused effort to interpret preexilic writings as moral specifications for the reconstructed nation of Israel. It is from such OT roots that the impulse for subsequent exegesis sprang.

In this chapter we survey many of the issues and approaches that have marked the development of the ongoing relationship between the Bible and faith communities of diverse times and places, ranging from the beginning of the Common Era to the sixteenth century. Some of these issues still stimulate discussion among people of faith today.

JEWISH EXEGESIS AROUND THE BEGINNING OF THE COMMON ERA

In ancient Israel, as in any **theocracy** (religiously based government), political and social leaders interpreted and applied sacred Scripture in their daily decisions. In the centuries immediately preceding the Common Era, however, formal biblical exegesis emanated from two sources, the synagogue and teams of scholars who collaborated on resolving exegetical questions. Line-by-line exposition of Scripture, a method known as **pesher,** was practiced very early, especially at Qumran. The Hebrew term **midrash** (from the Hebrew verb "search") refers to the interpretation of texts, which can be divided into two primary areas. One is **halakah,** the derivation from Scripture of concrete regulations governing individual behavior and social practices. The other is **haggadah,** the detailed interpretation of biblical narratives, employing historical, philosophical, and philological approaches, as well as humor, and usually drawing a moral from the story. Passages from one portion of Scripture were elucidated by references to other portions of Scripture.

The rabbinical scholars active before about 200 C.E., called **Tanna'im,** transmitted and contributed to both oral and written exegetical traditions. Many of these materials provided specific rules and wise sayings to assist Jewish communities in regulating their everyday transactions and maintaining their Jewish identity. Near the end of the Tannaitic era (ca. 200 C.E.) the halakhic teachings, with haggadic traditions, were compiled in written form to produce the **Mishna.** Subsequently there developed commentaries on the Mishna known as the **Gemara.** The Mishna and the Gemara together are called the Talmud, of which there are two editions, or recensions: the Palestinian (ca. 450 C.E.) and the Babylonian (ca. 550 C.E.). The painstaking scholarship they represent took place in Tiberias (of Galilee) and in Babylon, respectively; Jerusalem could no longer serve as a locus of scholarship after its destruction by the Romans in 70 C.E. Yet another exegetical tradition resides in the Targums, Aramaic translations of Scripture dating from ca. 250 B.C.E. to ca. 300 C.E. These qualify as exegesis because, in addition to the intrinsically interpretive nature of any translation, the Targums also contain explicitly interpretive material.

It is within the realm of haggadah that two first-century Jewish writers widely known today, Josephus and Philo, flourished. Josephus's *Antiquities of the Jews* and *Against Apion* render patriotic accounts of Israel's history aimed at Greco-Roman sensibilities. Philo, a luminary of the Hellenistic Jewish academy of Alexandria, Egypt, was heir to the tradition of synthesizing Scriptural revelation with Greek philosophy, which is conspicuous in the apocryphal/deuterocanonical books of Sirach (Ecclesiasticus) and 4 Maccabees. Greek philosophers had long been utilizing **allegory** to interpret Greek myths and legends. In the **allegorical** method of **interpretation,** characters and events are assigned a symbolic significance as representing spiritual realities; for example, an enemy army may symbolize moral vices attacking the human spirit. Whatever Philo's goal may have been, the allegorical approach appears in his Scriptural commentaries and essays, most strikingly in his *Life of Moses,* where he identified the two cherubim on the mercy seat of the ark as symbols of the creative and the kingly powers of God, and the uplifted arms of Moses at the battle against the Amalekites as a symbol of the celestial realm.

ANCIENT CHRISTIAN EXEGESIS

Early Apologetic and Polemical Uses of Scripture

Just as Philo and Josephus used exegetical approaches intelligible to educated Gentiles, second-century Christian writers likewise strove to offer an account or defense (Greek *apologia,* as in 1 Pet 3:15; hence the English word
"apology") of their faith that would make sense to Jews. In dialogues with the
Jewish community, these writers agreed with the rabbinical view of canonical
Scripture as a single, undivided divine revelation, but included Christian literature as expressing the culmination of that revelation. (The formation of the Jewish and Christian canons is described in chapter six.) The task of defending the
Christian proclamation and explaining its relationship to Israel's salvation history lent itself to the **typological** method of exegesis, which was adopted by,
among others, Justin Martyr and the anonymous author of the *Epistle of Barnabas.* These authors interpreted OT narratives as types, or symbolic precursors,
of NT events. They depicted as precursors of Christ's crucifixion both (a) the
scapegoat of Lev 16, who bore the sins of Israel; and (b) Moses supervising with
outstretched arms the battle against the Amalekites in Exod 17 (a different symbolism from that of Philo; see above).[1]

Another occasion for invoking symbolism was the conflict between orthodox Christian authorities and the world-denying gnostics, who, in taking Plato's
dualistic philosophy to extremes, rejected the physical creation and its Creator,
along with the OT that described them. In order to refute the gnostics and their
kin (including the infamous presbyter Marcion), ecclesiastical writers were
compelled to defend the canonical status of the OT. One response, formulated by
the second-century bishop Irenaeus, stressed the original goodness of the creation prior to Adam and Eve's sin and promised a future restoration of this
fallen world to its former blessedness. Another approach, emanating from the
third-century Christian catechetical school of Alexandria, was the use of allegorical interpretation, borrowed from the Jew Philo (a native of the same city).
When the OT was viewed as allegory, the apparently vengeful acts of its God could
be explained as allegorical rather than as evidence of moral inferiority, of which
the gnostics accused Israel's God. Clement of Alexandria, the director of the
catechetical school, postulated that the highest level of spiritual development
was to become a "Christian gnostic" attuned to the allegorical sense of Scripture.

---

[1] This approach does not differ substantially from that of the NT itself. Recall the
portrayal of Jesus as successor to Moses in the Gospel of Matthew, Paul's linkage of Israel's rock in the desert to Christ (1 Cor 10:4), and the metaphor of Christ as the ultimate
high priest in Heb 9.

Origen's Allegorical Exegesis

Allegorical exegesis was more systematically expounded, and its parameters defined, by Clement's successor, the brilliant Origen (d. 254). Influenced by Platonism, Origen found it eminently reasonable to regard the physical, earthly phenomena described by Scripture as signposts pointing to intangible, spiritual realities. Nevertheless, Origen cautioned that all such theological speculations must be kept within the boundaries of the church's traditions—boundaries often referred to in early Christian literature as "the Rule of Faith" (Latin *regula fidei*). Thus Origen precluded individualistic departures from the orthodoxy of his day. Moreover, he supported his allegorical approach on the basis of Scripture itself, citing Paul's interpretation in Gal 4 of Sarah and Hagar as an "allegory" (Paul's word: *allēgoroumena*) of the two covenants.

The burning issue for Origen's exegesis was how to handle Scriptural statements that simply do not make sense or that attribute to God qualities uncharacteristic of divinity. Because he regarded it as axiomatic that the same Holy Spirit was responsible for the entirety of sacred Scripture, and because he stipulated that the majority of scriptural passages could be taken literally, he utilized easily understood passages in interpreting more challenging ones. Some intractable exegetical problems, however, were not conducive to this intrabiblical approach; these, Origen thought, had been intentionally designed by the Holy Spirit as incentives to push the reader into a quest for a nonliteral meaning.

According to Origen, then, there are three possible meanings in Scripture: the **literal,** the **moral,** and the **spiritual** senses. A passage may possess all three, because a historical event, reliably recounted by the biblical author, may itself symbolize moral and spiritual truths. No literal meaning, however, can reside in passages that are patently illogical, such as the account in Gen 1 of three evenings and mornings having occurred before the creation of the sun and moon. And Paul's declaration of his own unworthiness in 1 Cor 15:9 is not to be taken at face value, but is to be regarded as a moral lesson, namely, that all souls are capable of both good and evil; here, the second, or moral, sense of Scripture is operative.

The concept of extracting multiple meanings, including allegorical ones, from biblical texts would survive in Christian theology for centuries to come. Originating from the Alexandrian Jew Philo, then adapted by Clement and Origen, this approach would be disseminated first in the Mediterranean world and then in medieval Europe, as we will see below.

Scriptural and Theological Controversy in Late Antiquity

Allegorical exegesis provoked fierce controversy in the fourth and fifth centuries, rending the theological world of the eastern Mediterranean area into two camps, sometimes labeled the **Alexandrian** and the **Antiochene** schools of thought, after their cities of origin (Alexandria in Egypt and Antioch in Syria, respectively). Diodore of Tarsus and his disciple Theodore of Mopsuestia, both leaders of the Antiochene school, rejected allegory as too subjective and individualistic, preferring to approach scriptural texts as literal accounts of human experiences to be examined within their respective historical contexts. Utterly rejecting Origen's view of the Song of Songs as an allegorical metaphor for the intimate union between God and the soul, or between God and the church, Diodore regarded the book merely as erotic poetry. Likewise, Theodore understood royal language in the Psalms not to allude typologically to Christ, but rather to refer to its contemporary setting in King David's court. Yet another Antiochene exegete and pupil of Diodore, John Chrysostom, who was acclaimed more for his powerful preaching than for theological speculation, drew homiletical exhortations from the literal interpretation of Scripture, taking care, for example, to interpret the Pauline Epistles in light of the pastoral problems that Paul encountered. John (later to be dubbed "Chrysostom," or "Golden Mouth") began his ecclesiastical career in his native Antioch and subsequently became Bishop of Constantinople. He disliked allegorical exegesis, but, in an ironic turn of events, met his downfall by providing safe haven to four controversial Egyptian monks loyal to Origenism with its use of allegory.

The disagreements on the value of allegory were paralleled by the christological controversies (arguments about the doctrine of Christ's humanity and/or divinity) spanning the fourth and fifth centuries. Diodore and Theodore both believed that Scripture passages describing Jesus as suffering could be applied only to Jesus' humanity, not to the divine Word, or Logos, for the reason that God Almighty cannot change or suffer. A younger contemporary of Theodore, Nestorius, who became Bishop of Constantinople in 428, took this "two-natures" Christology further by insisting that Jesus as an infant had not yet received his divine nature, and that therefore scriptural passages referring to Jesus' growth and development (Luke 2:40, 52) must be applied only to his human nature. According to Nestorius, NT texts must be categorized according to which of Christ's two natures, divine or human, is being described.

This division of scriptural texts was abhorrent to the passionate Cyril of Alexandria (d. 444), the archadversary of Nestorius. Trumpeting his view of Christ as a single entity resulting from a true union—a **hypostatic union**—of God with humanity, Cyril condemned Nestorius's exegetical approach on the grounds that texts describing Jesus as changing or suffering pertain to the self-limitation imposed by God upon himself in making himself incarnate. Cyril's views eventually gained only a partial victory: an ecumenical council at Chalcedon in 451 repudiated Nestorius's perspective on the infant Jesus, but affirmed the two natures of Christ and the validity of categorizing scriptural texts as Nestorius had done.

Augustine as Exegete

Meanwhile, in the western, Latin-speaking area of the Roman Empire, Augustine (d. 430), Bishop of Hippo in North Africa, was composing a prodigious number of theological works, including his *On Christian Doctrine*. In this work he set forth exegetical guidelines that included, as Origen had done, the concept of multiple meanings in Scripture, the authority of the church's "Rule of Faith," and the use of lucid scriptural passages in wresting the meaning from obscure ones. Like Origen, Augustine believed that God had intentionally sprinkled difficult passages here and there in the Bible; his explanation was that these strenuous exegetical challenges are meant to spur the reader to overcome pride and to cherish the interpretations that were obtained by such effort. In addition to these observations, Augustine explained the *Rules* for exegesis written by Tyconius, a fellow North African who belonged to a schismatic sect. Tyconius's rules dealt with figures of speech and literary devices found in Scripture. Above all, said Augustine, the ultimate criterion for accepting an interpretation must be whether it promotes the growth of charity: "Whoever, then, thinks that he understands the Holy Scriptures, or any part of them, but puts such an interpretation upon them as does not tend to build up this twofold love of God and our neighbor, does not yet understand them" (*On Christian Doctrine* 1.36.40).

MEDIEVAL EXEGESIS

In the fifth century the Roman Empire crumbled in the west, while eastern imperial power remained intact, to thrive as the Byzantine Empire. There ensued the era called by Westerners "the Middle Ages," which hummed with exegetical activity in three arenas: Latin-speaking Christendom in the West, the Greek-speaking Byzantine Empire, and Jewish academic circles, especially in Spain.

The Christian West

In Western Europe the Latin biblical translation made by Jerome (d. 420), called the Vulgate, gained authoritative status, and with it a new genre of biblical commentary became widespread. Previous exegetical formats had been those of the homily, the line-by-line commentary, the essay (or tractate), the epistle, and the dialogue. Now that monastic scribes were producing copies of the Bible itself, interpretive comments crept into the copies, written between the lines or in the margins of the biblical text. These comments, which sometimes consisted merely of a single word, were called **glosses;** in the early medieval period they were extracted and compiled into books.

During this period the content of Western scriptural commentary and other theological thought was dominated by Augustine's weighty legacy. His influence is embedded in the works of Caesarius of Arles, a sixth-century bishop in France, and of Bede, the erudite and prolific eighth-century English monk who nourished the growth of scholarship in a time when continental Europe was teeming with tribal warfare. Bede embraced the exegetical guidelines provided by Augustine in *On Christian Doctrine,* including the rules of Tyconius reproduced there. He advocated an expansion of the threefold exegetical methodology expounded by Origen and approved by Augustine; this expansion added a fourth possible meaning to be found in Scripture: the **anagogical** sense, which describes the afterlife. This **fourfold exegesis,** which seeks to uncover (1) the historical (or literal), (2) the **tropological** (or moral), (3) the allegorical, and (4) the anagogical meanings in Scripture, had originated in late antiquity with the fifth-century monk John Cassian. Thanks to its dissemination by Bede and others, it persisted throughout the Middle Ages as the standard methodology.

In the so-called High Middle Ages (roughly 1000–1300), the mode of theological instruction was transformed as the centers of scholarship moved from the monasteries to urban cathedral schools, which spawned the medieval universities. In its early stages, classroom teaching consisted of the *lectio* (similar to a lecture), in which the professor read and commented upon each individual line of Scripture or other ancient writing—a classroom procedure that today's students would refuse to tolerate. In preparing his *lectio,* the professor found compilations of glosses extremely useful. Pedagogical methodology shifted, however, as the *disputatio* gained popularity. In the *disputatio* theological questions were identified, to which opposing responses were proposed, supported by evidence gleaned from the Bible, from ancient Christian scholarship, and from classical philosophy. A concluding resolution was offered for each question, and a professor's conclusions were expected to be comprehensive and logically consistent with one another.

Into this movement, called "Scholasticism," a milieu of lively debate and meticulous logic, the theological giant Thomas Aquinas stepped. Not since Augustine had such deep footprints been imprinted in Christian academia. Aquinas (d. 1274) and his colleagues at the University of Paris eagerly pored over the newly discovered writings of the pre-Christian philosopher Aristotle that, though long lost in the Christian world, had been carefully preserved by Muslim scholars. This introduction of Aristotle's logic and science injected an urgency into the issue of the authority of faith versus that of reason—an issue with regard to which Aquinas is celebrated as having discovered a satisfying synthesis.

A page from a fourteenth-century illuminated manuscript of a missal, preserved in the Abbey at Altenburg, Austria, showing two monks reading the Bible. (Erich Lessing/Art Resource, NY)

Combining the new focus on Aristotle, whom Aquinas referred to respect-fully as "the Philosopher," with the format of the academic *disputatio*, Aquinas articulated his formidably comprehensive theological system in his tome titled *Summa Theologica* (or *Theologiae*). Although he wrote commentaries on some NT books, the starting point of his theology was not Scripture. Rather, he set out to demonstrate by the methodology of the *disputatio* how human beings can come to know and to participate in God's holiness; in so doing, he presented in-sights from Scripture as one source among many. Like other medieval theologians, he upheld the fourfold interpretation of Scripture presented earlier by Cassian and Bede; however, in doctrinal formulations Aquinas admitted only the literal sense, which for him consisted of the meaning intended by the biblical author within his own particular historical context. The other three senses of Scripture could serve as edification and inspiration, but no doctrine could be based upon them. In this way Aquinas tried to attain objectivity, or at least to steer clear of individualistic interpretations not demonstrable by academic reasoning.

In the twilight of the Middle Ages, Nicholas of Lyra (d. 1340), utilizing the insights of the Jewish scholar Rashi (see below), expanded on the theories of Aquinas. Nicholas posited the existence of two literal senses, both implanted by God: one was the meaning of a text within its original historical context, and the other was the message intended for subsequent generations. Like Aquinas, Nicholas was not appreciated in his own lifetime.

The Christian East

In the Byzantine Empire the theological work of monastic scholars continued in a smooth progression from the days of the ancient Christian writers. There is no real distinction between "ancient" and "medieval" theology in the Byzantine church. Controversies and councils continued to arise. One of these upheavals, the Iconoclastic Controversy, elicited the support of John of Damascus (d. 749) for the veneration of icons, which are distinctive painted images of Christ and of saints. In response to the critics of icons (iconoclasts) who argued on the basis of the divine prohibition of images in Exod 20 and Deut 5, John highlighted the historical context of this commandment, which had been issued to the Israelites in the wilderness at the time when the golden-calf episode had clearly exhibited their inclination to worship statuary. Distinguishing between "worship" and "veneration" of images, he pointed out that God had commanded that figures of cherubim be carved on the mercy seat, and that Solomon's temple, approved by God, had contained many images of animals. God had not forbidden the use of images, concluded John; rather, for a particular people in a particular situation (Israelites in the wilderness) God had prescribed a particular remedy. Thus John pursued verbal and historical analysis to determine whether a given scriptural passage was applicable in his own day. Besides John, a host of Byzantine scholars produced a wealth of theological insights. Two of these, Photios (d. 891) and Symeon the New Theologian (d. 1022), were noted exegetes—Photios in addressing a variety of issues, including the procession of the Holy Spirit from the Father only; and Symeon in his advocacy of immediate spiritual experience and of the unbroken continuity of his own day with the NT age of miracles and charisms.

Medieval Jewish Exegesis

During the same era, Jewish scholarship was thriving in a golden age of biblical and philosophical study in both East and West. By the time of the completion of the two Talmuds at the end of the fifth century or so, Hebrew was no longer a spoken language, having been replaced by Aramaic. This shift endangered the accessibility of the sacred text to laymen, who might be stymied by the uncertainty surrounding its pronunciation. Between the sixth and the ninth centuries C.E., therefore, the Masoretes, rabbinical scholars of massive erudition headquartered in Tiberias and in Babylon, inserted vowels, punctuation marks, and section divisions into the biblical text, in addition to identifying the authoritative textual version. The resulting text, still in use today, is known as the Masoretic Text.

In the tenth, eleventh, and twelfth centuries, Jewish learning flowered in France and especially in Moorish (Muslim) Spain. Two major fields of investigation for the Spanish Jewish scholars were biblical philology (the exploration of the exact meanings of words in Hebrew Scripture) and the relationship between philosophy and biblical faith. The most illustrious representatives of this school were the rabbis Abraham Ibn Ezra (d. 1167) and Moses Maimonides (d. 1204). The latter's famous philosophical and exegetical work, *Guide of the Perplexed*, allows the use of Aristotelianism for interpreting some texts, and allegory for others, but carefully limits both. Meanwhile, the French Jewish exegete Rashi (d. 1105) and his grandson, Samuel ben Meïr, emphasized the indispensability of literal interpretation and philological analysis.

In summary, while Byzantine Christian scholars were exploring a broad array of theological questions, both Jewish and Christian scholars in the medieval West focused on Aristotelian philosophy with its concomitant problem of the relationship between faith and reason, and adopted a multifaceted exegetical approach that permitted allegory. Soon the European Renaissance would bring new factors into play.

RENAISSANCE AND REFORMATION

The Renaissance, which began in fourteenth-century Italy and spread to northwestern Europe in the next century, was driven by a humanistic revival of interest in classical (ancient Greek and Roman) art and literature. A consequence of this *ad fontes* ("to the sources") movement for Christian biblical studies was an increased focus on the primary source of faith, that is, the Bible in its original languages. Among other scholars, the fifteenth-century philologist Lorenzo Valla examined the NT books of the Vulgate, the official Latin biblical text, in light of the original Greek text, and the sixteenth-century German Johannes Reuchlin studied both the Hebrew and the Greek Scriptures, publishing a Hebrew grammar textbook and dictionary.

During Reuchlin's lifetime, the Lutheran Reformation—with its slogan *sola Scriptura* ("Scripture alone")—ushered in a widespread rejection of Aristotelian philosophy, of fanciful allegory, and of church tradition as a criterion for biblical exegesis. Biblical passages were to be understood through the application of other biblical passages, not of any external standard such as ancient or medieval theological statements; thus the Bible was to be regarded as self-interpreting. As we have seen, the exegesis of Scripture by means of Scripture had been done throughout the centuries, though not to the exclusion of other methods. In particular, Martin Luther's interest in the self-evident meaning of Scripture can be partially attributed to the influence of Nicholas of Lyra, and through Nicholas to Rashi. Luther's doctrine of "the priesthood of all believers" placed scriptural interpretation in the hands of the individual, and justification by faith alone (*sola fide*) became a guiding principle.[2] Moreover, Luther identified a canon within the canon, meaning that biblical books that preach Christ and support the concept of *sola fide,* such as Romans and Galatians, were to be esteemed more than those that do not; in fact, Luther all but relegated the Epistle of James, with its exhortation to good works, to the junkpile, calling it an "epistle of straw." For Luther the OT was a prefiguration of and preparation for the advent of Christ, who is the reason for the Bible's very existence, although he also stressed the difference between the (OT) Law and the (NT) Gospel.

John Calvin endorsed the *sola fide* and *sola Scriptura* theology of Luther, but added an emphasis on the revelatory role of Scripture and on the ongoing usefulness of the Law for Christians (the so-called "third use of the Law"). Because the human eye is obscured by sin, said this second-generation Reformer, God has graciously provided scriptural revelation to function as a pair of eyeglasses in enabling nearly blind humanity to perceive him. Not everyone, however, will accept Scripture as authoritative or understand it accurately; therefore, God bestows the internal guidance of the Holy Spirit to enable believers to interpret the Scriptures correctly. To the Christian exegete is imparted a sense of assurance that the gift of the Spirit has been given. Calvin

---

[2] Interestingly, although Luther preached the doctrines of *sola fide* and *sola Scriptura,* his theology consistently supported the ancient creeds and councils.

remarked that "the testimony of the Spirit is superior to reason" (*The Institutes of the Christian Religion* 1.7.4) and that

> the Lord has so knit together the certainty of his word and his Spirit, that our minds are duly imbued with reverence for the word when the Spirit shining upon it enables us there to behold the face of God; and, on the other hand, we embrace the Spirit with no danger of delusion when we recognize him in his image, that is, in his word. (*The Institutes of the Christian Religion* 1.9.3)

Naturally the individualistic approach to scriptural interpretation represented a radical departure from medieval Catholic exegesis. The widening chasm between Catholics and Protestants and the resulting decades of bloody warfare exhausted Europeans and produced receptivity to seventeenth- and eighteenth-century Enlightenment perspectives, which laid the groundwork for the modern era.

FOR FURTHER READING AND STUDY

Grant, Robert, and David Tracy. *A Short History of the Interpretation of the Bible.* 2d ed. Philadelphia: Fortress, 1984; chapters 1–10. A highly readable account of the development of exegetical methodologies in the ancient, medieval, and Reformation eras, including the approaches to the OT adopted by NT authors.

Hall, Christopher A. *Reading Scripture with the Church Fathers.* Downers Grove, Ill.: InterVarsity, 1998. A lively introduction to the ancient schools of biblical interpretation and a persuasive argument for the relevance of the Church Fathers to contemporary Christian thought.

Kugel, James L., and Rowan A. Greer. *Early Biblical Interpretation.* Vol. 3 of the Library of Early Christianity. Philadelphia: Westminster, 1986. An exploration of biblical interpretation in ancient Judaism around the beginning of the Common Era and in early Christianity as it germinated from its Jewish roots.

Montague, George T. *Understanding the Bible: A Basic Introduction to Biblical Interpretation.* New York and Mahwah, N.J.: Paulist, 1997; chapters 1–4. A survey of the questions posed to the biblical text, and of the answers perceived in it, by the most renowned scholars of early and medieval Christianity, as well as by the ancient biblical authors themselves.

Simonetti, Manlio. *Biblical Interpretation in the Early Church: An Historical Introduction to Patristic Exegesis.* Edited by Anders Bergquist and Markus Bockmuehl. Translated by John A. Hughes. London: T&T Clark, 1994; paperback reprint, 2001. A thorough but succinct exposition of the varieties of patristic exegetical thought and the influences that forged each.

Smalley, Beryl. *The Study of the Bible in the Middle Ages.* Oxford: Clarendon Press, 1941. Repr., Notre Dame, Ind.: University of Notre Dame Press, 1964. A chronological description of the interaction among movements and personalities in the development of biblical interpretation in the Middle Ages, including a thoughtful discussion of the influences of medieval Jewish scholars on their Western Christian counterparts.

Steinmetz, David C. "The Superiority of Pre-Critical Exegesis." *Theology Today* 37 (1980): 27–38. A vindication of the ancient and medieval belief that biblical texts can offer more meanings than the one that the biblical author consciously intended.

Young, Frances. *Biblical Exegesis and the Formation of Christian Culture.* Cambridge: Cambridge University Press, 1997. Repr., Peabody, Mass.: Hendrickson, 2002. Bold research into the interplay between ancient biblical interpretation and the literary, religious, and philosophical milieu that shaped it and in turn was shaped by it.

Chapter 9

Modern and Postmodern Critical Methods of Biblical Study

JOHN R. DONAHUE

Modern "critical" study of the Bible, sometimes called **biblical criticism** for short, is a child of the eighteenth-century **Enlightenment,** or the Age of Reason, when human reason was assiduously cultivated and applied to traditional teachings including religious claims, texts, and authoritative teaching. "Criticism" is itself a neutral term coming from the Greek word *krisis,* meaning "judgment." When joined with "historical," it simply designates the application to biblical texts of the same methods of investigation and the same norms for truth that are used with other documents from a past and different culture. This chapter surveys the origin and development of modern and postmodern biblical criticism, as well as some of its various expressions.

THE ENLIGHTENMENT AND THE LAST TWO CENTURIES OF BIBLICAL STUDY

During the Enlightenment a threefold approach to a faith-based interpretation of the Bible developed. This approach still influences contemporary biblical studies:

- For some, the Enlightenment leads to *rejection of faith-based claims about texts* (e.g., the existence of miracles, the reality of resurrection);

- For others, it leads to *dialogue between religion and reason,* what German theologian Friedrich Schleiermacher (1768–1834) called "the eternal covenant" between faith and modern thought; and

- For still others it leads to *rejection of modernity* in favor of a faith-based literalism or fundamentalism.

Most biblical scholarship today falls into the second category. As a child of the Enlightenment, it was born and raised in the nineteenth and twentieth centuries.

The major legacy of the nineteenth century was the evolution of what falls under the general heading of **historical criticism,** that is, judgments about texts based on their historical setting and the meanings possible in a culture very different from subsequent ages. The nineteenth century was immensely productive as various disciplines took shape.

For example, faced with thousands of biblical manuscripts, none of which date to the age of the attributed author, the field of "textual criticism" (see chapter seven) sought to discover the earliest form of a text and to trace its subsequent evolution. This was aided by the discovery of significant manuscripts, such as Codex Sinaiticus, a beautiful fourth-century-C.E. manuscript discovered in the middle of the nineteenth century by Konstantin von Tischendorf at St. Catherine's monastery in the Sinai. Important for the NT was the discovery and publication of fragmentary sections of the Scriptures, such as two very early manuscripts of the Gospel of John, the John Rylands Papyrus and Papyrus Bodmer II.[1] Textual criticism (like other aspects of biblical study) was immensely furthered in the twentieth century through developments in methodology and by the unearthing of a great number of biblical and early Christian texts at Nag Hammadi in Egypt in 1945, as well as by the more famous discovery of the Dead Sea Scrolls from 1947 to about 1956.

Along with textual studies, a host of allied disciplines emerged during the last two centuries. Intensive archaeological expeditions unfolded in the lands of the Bible that spawned a subdiscipline called "biblical archaeology." Ancient texts that contained material similar to biblical material were also published and studied, most dramatically the Babylonian creation stories such as *Enuma Elish* and *The Gilgamesh Epic,* dubbed "The Babylonian Genesis," and a large collection of wisdom texts from Egypt such as *The Book of the Dead* and *The Instruction of Amenemope,* a collection of maxims strikingly similar to Proverbs 1–9.

Though a discussion of all the forms of biblical criticism that emerged in the last two centuries is beyond the scope of this chapter, attention must be focused on those of major importance: **source criticism, form criticism, redaction criticism,** and **tradition criticism** (all part of what is often called the "historical-critical method"), as well as the more recent approaches known as **social-scientific criticism, literary criticism, rhetorical criticism,** and **reader-response criticism,** plus **liberationist** approaches.

---

[1] The very fragmentary John Rylands Papyrus, or $\mathfrak{P}^{52}$, is the earliest surviving NT manuscript, dating from the early second century. It includes only verses 31–33 and 37–38 of John 18. Papyrus Bodmer II, or $\mathfrak{P}^{66}$, dating from about 200, is much larger, including most of the first fourteen chapters of the Gospel of John.

SOURCE CRITICISM

Culturally, the nineteenth century was characterized by a fascination with "sources," manifest in Darwin's explorations of human evolution and in wide-ranging discoveries of manuscripts and archeological artifacts, which were used to map the histories of whole civilizations. The emerging disciplines of "depth psychology" showed that the source of many personal human problems lay hidden in a person's consiousness or experience. Concern for sources of existing texts gave rise to the subdiscipline of source criticism.

Old Testament Source Criticism

As noted in chapter three, the presumption of Mosaic authorship of the Pentateuch was replaced by stress on different sources, the most prevalent theory being that proposed by Julius Wellhausen (1844–1918). He maintained that the Pentateuch was comprised of four primary sources (discerned on the basis of linguistic usage and theological content), and his theory was ultimately called the "Documentary Hypothesis" (see further discussion in chapter three). The oldest source is "J" ("Yahwist," after the German transliteration, "Jahve," and the related word "Jahwist"). The creation account in Gen 2:4b–25, for example, uses YHWH ("Yahweh") for the divine name, contains vivid narration, and gives an anthropomorphic (humanlike) view of God. This J source, which runs through the whole Pentateuch, was thought to originate in Judah, most likely Jerusalem, perhaps under Solomon in the ninth century B.C.E.

The "P" (for "priestly") source unfolds in rhythmic solemnity and embraces the origin of the whole universe (not simply humanity) in the creative word of God. P dates after the exile (ca. 586–546 B.C.E.), and the priestly writers were responsible for the final edition of the Pentateuch. The "E" source, so called for its use of the Hebrew word "Elohim" for God, and often dated to the northern kingdom (Israel) after the death of Solomon, is so interlaced with J and P that its exact content is often debated. A collection of sources and traditions prior to P is often attributed to the "D" source, the work of the Deuteronomist, composed in the eighth and seventh centuries B.C.E. This work extends also through the books of Kings and stresses the need for fidelity to the Mosaic covenant as well as the central place of Jerusalem in the worship of the people.

After the emergence of Wellhausen's Documentary Hypothesis, virtually every book of the OT was subjected to various forms of source criticism, based often on indications in the texts themselves that sources were used. Correlative with the discovery of sources, judgments were then made about the evolution of Israel's history, religion, and culture.

New Testament Source Criticism

During this period, NT source criticism focused mainly on the development of the gospel traditions. When Matthew, Mark, and Luke are viewed "synoptically," that is, side by side, there are clear indications of massive overlap as well as significant differences. These "synoptic facts" gave rise to a discussion of "the synoptic problem": the question of which gospel was written first, and how the gospels are interrelated. This was no new problem but actually goes back at least to St. Augustine (354–430), who argued that Matthew was the earliest and that Mark was a digest of Matthew. This theory was revived by Johann Jakob Griesbach (1745–1812), who argued that Matthew was written first, that Luke used Matthew, and that Mark was a digest of both Matthew and Luke.

A counterposition emerged in the early nineteenth century that affirmed Markan priority and ultimately became known as the "Two-Source Theory." As noted in chapter four, this theory holds that Matthew and Luke composed their gospels by independently drawing on (1) the Gospel of Mark and (2) a collection of sayings (discerned from roughly 235 present in both Matthew and Luke but absent from Mark), which was later called "Q," from the German word *Quelle* ("source"). Material found only in Matthew (e.g., Matthean infancy and resurrection narratives) is dubbed "M," while "L" is used for special Lukan material (likewise primarily in the infancy and resurrection narratives but also comprising major Lukan parables). The recognition of these two groups of special material in Matthew and Luke leads some to call the Two-Source Theory the "Four-Source" Theory, though it is not at all certain that M and L represent coherent source documents (see illustration in chapter four).

Some version of the Two-Source (or Four-Source) Theory represents the majority view today, though significant counterpositions have emerged. Also, studies of Q have dramatically grown as scholars now talk about the "the theology of Q" and "the Q community." These studies have greatly influenced the quest for the historical Jesus since Q has no Passion and Resurrection Narrative and since so many of the sayings are similar to the second-century extra-canonical *Gospel of Thomas* (discussed in chapter five), which is thought by some to provide an independent entrée to the teaching of Jesus.

Source studies of other NT material proceeded as the relation of the Gospel of John to synoptic material became a burning question. Despite the great amount of gospel material found only in John, there are also significant overlaps with the Synoptics (e.g., the ministry of John the Baptist, the cleansing of the temple, the feeding of the five thousand, and much of the Passion Narrative). Interpreters argue whether John knew all the Synoptic Gospels or a particular synoptic gospel, or whether he simply had access to similar traditions that he integrated into his work. Equally, studies abound on the sources of John's distinctive material, with leading proposals about a "signs source" behind John 1–11, and a collection of "revelation discourses" for John 13–17. Though no consensus exists on what sources or extended traditions the Fourth Evangelist used, the quest continues to issue in new insights about the growth of that gospel.

FORM CRITICISM

All human communication involves different forms, such as letters of introduction, congratulatory notices, biography, historical fiction, and even jokes, all of which are used in different settings. One finds the way to a state park not by reciting a poem on the beauty of nature but by obtaining precise directions. One of the major disciplines of biblical criticism has been *form criticism,* the study of different forms of communication, their setting or living context and function (often called the *Sitz im Leben* [German for "setting in life"]), and the stages of their evolution and transmission.

The terminology in this subdiscipline of biblical studies is often a bit confusing since there is a strong overlap between "form criticism," which concentrates on relatively small, oral forms of communication, and "genre criticism," which focuses on larger categories of literature (e.g., poetry vs. prose; historical report vs. legend) as well as divisions within these categories (e.g., lyric vs. epic poetry). In biblical literature, psalms and wisdom literature would constitute a genre, each of which contains specific forms. In general, form criticism is concerned about the preliterary stage of material, while genre criticism pertains to literary collections. Proper understanding of both form and genre is essential for valid interpretation. Neglect of these is one of the cardinal errors of those interpreters who read the Gospels, for example, as if they were literal history.

Old Testament Form Criticism

Form criticism has been a vital but often controversial aspect of OT studies, as forms such as "legend" and "myth" were applied to the major parts of Genesis. Though the formal category of legend or myth itself does not preclude historical value (e.g., an epic portrayal of a battle or war can be based on hard historical facts), the manner in which the narratives unfold and their similarity with other ancient literature (see above) show that their major function is to communicate religious truth rather than historical data. Form criticism has flourished especially in studies of the Psalms and the Prophets.

As noted in chapter three, the Psalms are divided into categories or forms, including first of all *hymns,* which are songs of praise of God (e.g., Pss 8–9;

103–105), and which exhibit a similar structure of a call to praise, an account of God's glorious works, and (often) another, concluding call for praise and gratitude. Another distinctive group within the psalms is the *royal psalms* (e.g., Pss 47; 93; 96–99), which some scholars have called "enthronement psalms," thought to be sung at an annual festival celebrating the enthronement of God (though no concrete festival has been found among Israel's feasts). Other royal psalms read like a job description for a just king (e.g., Pss 2; 72; 110).

The largest category of psalms is that of *laments,* which consist of introductory statements on the sad plight of the psalmists with prayers that God, though seemingly absent, hear them in their distress. Most then end with a prayer of confidence even amid suffering. Some laments are communal (e.g., Pss 12; 14; 44; 53; 58; 106; 127) and may have been prayed during liturgies of communal repentance accompanied by fasting and other prayers. Individual psalms of lament (e.g., Pss 3–7; 22; 25–28; 42–43; 69; 88; 140–43), which have major influence on the Passion Narratives of the Gospels, articulate prayerful responses to personal suffering and misfortune.

Other forms, such as the *psalm of thanksgiving* (e.g., Pss 30; 107; 116), contain a more nuanced notion of thanksgiving than that which appears in both the hymns of praise and laments, namely thanksgiving to God in response to a particular situation of distress. Yet another form is the *wisdom psalm,* which repeats themes from the wisdom literature. Wisdom psalms are often constructed in poetic acrostics (where each verse begins with a letter of the Hebrew alphabet (e.g., Pss 37; 112; 119), which fostered their use in moral instruction.

Though the categories of psalms are not rigid, attention to the forms provides a privileged window into the liturgical life and personal piety of ancient Israelites.

The wisdom literature generally consists of *short sayings* that crystallize human experience in vivid images and appear in collections on a particular theme (see Prov 5; Sir 31). Many of the sayings of Jesus can be categorized as teachings of wisdom (e.g., Mark 2:21–22).

Different literary forms also permeate the Prophets. One is the *prophetic call* (e.g., Isa 6), where a prophet receives, often through words in a dramatic vision, a call from God to speak in God's name. This is followed first by reluctance and then by a commission from God, often with some sign or confirmation by God.

The *prophetic oracle* is another standard form. In proclaiming God's word, the prophet most often begins with a phrase such as "thus says the Lord," and then uses various specific forms. One of these is the *rib,* or lawsuit, in which the prophet, like a prosecuting attorney, calls Israel to account for its sins (e.g., Mic 6:1–7). Oracles against the people for their infidelity (e.g., Isa 5:8–23) and against the nations (e.g., Isa 10:5–11) constitute additional major forms of prophetic speech.

New Testament Form Criticism

In the early part of the twentieth century, NT form criticism developed under the leadership of two German scholars, Martin Dibelius and Rudolf Bultmann. Of the two, Bultmann's analysis determined the shape of the discipline. He divided the narrative material of the Gospels into two major forms: *miracle stories* (including healings, exorcisms, and nature miracles like the calming of the sea) and *legends* (including stories of Jesus' infancy, life [baptism, temptation, etc.], passion, and resurrection). The miracle stories themselves follow a familiar pattern of:

1. Meeting or contact between the miracle worker and the sick person;

2. Some description of the illness or the problem;

3. A request for healing (implicit or explicit);

4. A saving action either by gesture or word;

5. The actual healing; and

6. Acclamation by the crowd or demonstration of the healing.

This pattern is found in narratives as brief as the healing of Peter's mother-in-law (Mark 1:29–31) or as long as the Gerasene demoniac (Mark 5:1–20).

Legends are described by Bultmann as "those parts of the tradition that are not miracle stories in the proper sense, but instead of being historical in character are religious and edifying" (*History of the Synoptic Tradition*, p. 244). Major parts of the Passion Narratives were considered legendary by Bultmann, and still are by those who follow his lead.

Bultmann also had two major divisions of discourse (sayings) material in the Gospels: *dominical sayings* ("sayings of the Lord," such as Mark 8:35 about losing and saving one's life) and *apophthegms* (sometimes spelled simply apothegms), from the Greek term for "speaking out plainly." The latter term refers to a terse, pointed saying and/or an anecdote. In Bultmann's analysis, these are often in narrative form, but they refer to a narrative that culminates in, and is subservient to, a specific saying. Bultmann distinguished the following types of apophthegms:

- Controversy dialogues (e.g., Mark 3:1–6, with the Pharisees about the Sabbath);

- Scholastic dialogues (e.g., Mark 10:17–22, with the rich man about selling all); and

- Biographical apophthegms (e.g., Mark 2:1–12, about the paralytic lowered through the roof).

Bultmann argued that in the formation of the gospel tradition many narratives that are often thought to be historical were created mainly as a framework for, or illustration of, a saying. For example, he argued, the story of the paralytic in Mark 2:1–12 and parallels is an example of a biographical apophthegm that serves to illustrate the claim that Jesus had the power to forgive sin.

The setting for these sayings was thought by Bultmann to be, not the life of the historical Jesus, but the apologetic and doctrinal needs of the emerging Christian community. Form criticism inaugurated a revolution in exegesis and theology, and also influenced immensely the understanding of the development of early Christianity. Yet it met with strong rejection by many mainline and most conservative traditions because of its undermining of the historicity of gospel accounts.

When applied to other parts of the NT, form criticism was less controversial. Paul's letters contain clear examples of early Christian hymns (Phil 2:5b–11; Col 1:15–20); pre-Pauline tradition (Greek *paradosis*), or fragments of early Christian teaching (e.g., 1 Cor 11:23–26; 15:1–7); traditional lists of vices and virtues (Gal 5:19–26; Rom 1:29–31); and conventional advice on familial relations (Col 3:18–25; Eph 5:22–6:9). Study of such forms helps to locate Christian teaching in the mainstream of Greco-Roman culture.

REDACTION CRITICISM AND TRADITION CRITICISM

Out of form criticism developed a new method of analysis known as redaction criticism. The term "redaction" is from the German word for "editor," *Redaktor.* As a literary and historical method associated mainly with Gospels research, redaction criticism is

> concerned with the theological motivation of an author as this is revealed in the collection, arrangement, editing and modification of traditional material, and in the composition of new material or the creation of new forms within the traditions of early Christianity. (Perrin, *What is Redaction Criticism?* p. 1)

Redaction criticism has evolved to comprise distinct operations:

- Collection and analysis of the editorial alterations of an oral or written tradition;

- Attention to the literary context of every **pericope** (story/passage)—its immediate context as well as its location in the structure of a given gospel;

- Comparison of this context to that in other gospels; attempts to define verses or whole pericopes that are "composed" (i.e., written by the final author/redactor); and

- Synthesis of these results with suggestions about the theological purpose of a given pericope or of the gospel as a whole.

Redaction criticism also stresses the "setting in life" (sometimes also called the *Sitz im Leben*), not of individual sections of a gospel (as in form criticism) but of the gospel as a whole. This has led to important discussions about the nature and social location of the respective communities that received and handed on each of the gospels.

Though primarily associated with the Synoptic Gospels, redaction criticism has also been applied to the Gospel of John and even to OT studies, where it more often goes under the name "tradition criticism." An example would be the comparison of differing accounts of Israel's history in the Books of Kings and Chronicles. The same events are described, and similar sources are used, by the respective authors, yet each block of literature has distinctive theological perspectives.

From its origin redaction criticism was a counter to the fragmentation of a text into small, traditional units (the net effect of form criticism), to the detriment of a holistic look at the individual gospels. It provided a way for both specialists and lay readers to engage the text at hand. While still an important method in NT study, other methods have developed from redaction criticism and taken on lives of their own.

MORE RECENT (POSTMODERN) APPROACHES TO STUDYING THE BIBLE

Principal among the newer methods are (1) social-scientific criticism, (2) literary criticism, and (3) rhetorical criticism and reader-response criticism, which can be grouped together. The first of these, closely related to historical criticism, looks at the social world and community to which the text bears witness (as a kind of window), or in other words, the world behind the text. The second considers the world within the text itself. And the third is concerned with the world in front of the text, the persuasive purposes of the text, and its effect on readers. Recent decades have also brought the development of approaches to biblical interpretation that are sensitive to the concerns of the oppressed and marginalized. Many of these newer methods and approaches are the result of the new cultural situation of **postmodernism** (defined below).

Social-Scientific Criticism

Since redaction criticism was interested in the *Sitz im Leben* ("life setting") of the final edition or composition of a biblical work, new methods of social analysis developed in the latter half of the twentieth century came to be applied to the quest for the communities addressed by the biblical texts. "Social-scientific criticism" is an umbrella phrase for a host of emergent subdisciplines. As described by Jonathan Z. Smith ("The Social Description of Early Christianity," p. 19), these are:

- The study of social facts in early Christian texts;

- Social history involving "political history and theology within an informed theoretical framework";

- Study of social organization, forces and institutions; and

- Probing of the social world—"what it felt like to live in a world described by the symbols, rituals, and language of early Christianity."

In recent years the methods have been broadened and enriched to include considerations from cultural anthropology.

The Effects of Postmodernism

While historical criticism in all its forms (including its close cousin, social-scientific criticism) remains a vital part of biblical interpretation, its adequacy has been challenged by a number of new sub-disciplines that have emerged over the last quarter-century or so, reflecting a "postmodern" consciousness, itself a protean term (see also chapter ten on **ideological** strategies of **interpretation**). Postmodernism emerged in the twentieth century in reaction to a modernism that "put critical thinking on the throne of human consciousness," as someone has said. In place of a split between the object and subject of knowledge, postmodernism questions pure objectivity in both science and literature. It stresses participatory knowledge, with emphasis on the reader and reading process rather than on the author or the referent of the text. Postmodernism resists the authority of tradition and is suspicious of "master narratives" or universal principles of interpretation.

These emergent movements cannot really be called "methods," since they do not offer clear directives for interpretation. Though "postmodern," they also recall an earlier wedding of philosophy to exegesis. Just as the patristic interpreters adopted Plato, biblical exegetes engage a wide and diverse spectrum of thinkers, such as the philosophers Heidegger, Derrida, Gadamer, and Ricoeur, to mention only a few. Many of these approaches are more interested in the world within in the text, or the world the text can create ("the world in front of the text"), than in the world "behind" the text. These approaches are often, though not always, literary in character. (We discuss a few of them in the following subsections.)

Thus in postmodern study of the Bible the situation of readers becomes crucial for interpretation, which raises questions of the *validity* of interpretation. While scholars recognize multiple interpretations of a given text, not *every* interpretation is a valid one. There are criteria in the texts that historical and literary criticism will always provide. NT scholar Sandra Schneiders (*The Revelatory Text*, pp. 165–66) offers helpful guidelines for what an interpretation should do:

- Respect the text as it stands;

- Be consistent with itself and elucidate the whole text;

- Explain anomalies in the text;

- Be compatible with what is known from other sources (e.g., the expulsion of Christians from the synagogue [John 9:22], which occurred after 85 or 90 C.E.); and

- Use appropriate methods.

Three other factors influence judgments about validity. The first is the realization that biblical criticism itself is part of a larger process of interpretation involving human experience, traditions of believing communities, and theological reflection. The time when Scripture alone was adequate for believers has passed, as even many Protestant theologians and biblical scholars have said. Second, interpretation is less private and now occurs dialogically in and within wider "communities of interpretation," ranging from the work of highly specialized scholars to readings by particular groups in and outside of church contexts. Finally, the notion of "validity" is concerned with the *effect* of a particular interpretation—whether it leads readers to the divine-human encounter and engenders respect for the image of God present in every human. Some aspects of these factors will be explored in subsequent chapters.

Literary Criticism

Here terminology is a problem. The term "literary criticism" was initially used in biblical studies for things such as the detection of sources and judgments on the authenticity of a document (e.g., Did Paul write the Pastoral Epistles?). Recently, however, it has taken on the sense used in general literary studies in the humanities.

One variation of literary criticism is "narrative criticism." In narrative criticism concern for what the text meant (e.g., in the first century) shifts to questions of how meaning occurs. It assumes that Mark, for example, is not a pastiche of undigested traditions (as form criticism alone might suggest), but a crafted dramatic composition. With the advent of narrative approaches, biblical specialists began reading texts with an eye to character, plot, setting, and point of view. Interest in the *actual* author yielded to a concern for the "implied author," understood as the sum of values and perspectives that emerge from the text itself, along with the "implied reader," the picture of the reader that is constructed from the text independent of specific external (historical) data. While theoretical aspects of this approach continue to be debated, it provides a way of introducing the average interested reader to the fabric of a text whereby new meanings can emerge from a text rather than be imposed on it.

Rhetorical Criticism and Reader-Response Criticism

In the ancient world, "rhetoric" was the art of persuasion—of organizing material in a speech to form a certain disposition in the audience or to win them over to a point of view. In effect, the audience determined the inner shape of a speech or text. Rhetorical criticism seeks to uncover the "rhetorical strategy" and "rhetorical situation" of a given text. The method proceeds from the world behind the text (the situation out of which it arose) through the world of the text (its internal literary structure and argument) to the world in front of the text (the audience originally addressed by the text). It thereby seeks to uncover the power of the text to persuade, convince, or move its original readers, also attempting, through this analysis, to paint a tableaux of these readers.

While literary criticism discloses the narrative structure and symbolic world of the text, and social analysis uncovers the world out of which the text emerges and for which it is produced, rhetorical criticism is interested in how a text guides the reaction of the readers or hearers toward a certain response. Elizabeth

Schüssler Fiorenza (in "Rhetorical Situation and Historical Reconstruction in 1 Corinthians") presents a concise and systematic exposition of the task and method of rhetorical criticism, which involves four operations that interpreters employ as they attempt to assess the rhetorical situation and strategy of a given document:

- Identification of the rhetorical interests and models of contemporary interpretation;

- Delineation of the rhetorical arrangement, interests, and modifications introduced by the author;

- Elucidation and establishment of the rhetorical situation of the document; and

- Reconstruction of the common historical situation and symbolic universe of the writer/speaker and the recipient/audience.

While study of ancient rhetoric and its impact on biblical texts (rhetorical criticism) remains vital, its modern variation is "reader-response criticism," which directs its attention to those devices in the text that shape the anticipated involvement and response of original and subsequent readers, including contemporary interpreters. The "reader-involving" devices to be studied would include: unresolved omissions in the text, such as the unfulfilled promise that Jesus will baptize in the Spirit (Mark 1:8); the creation of impressions for readers that are ultimately challenged or shattered, such as the enthusiastic initial response of a disciple like Peter in Mark, whose last words are apostasy (Mark 14:71); or the ending of the Gospel of Mark (according to the best manuscripts) with the women saying nothing because of their fear or awe (16:1–8). This kind of approach challenges contemporary readers to plot their own responses to the biblical text as they move through it.

Reading for Liberation

The past century has witnessed a dramatic drive toward the ideals of the Enlightenment, crystallized in the cries of the French Revolution for liberty, community ("fraternité"), and equality—which unfortunately have remained largely unrealized for most of the human family. The spectrum of liberation concerns range from protest against massive social inequality, to consciousness of the independence, rights, and dignity of women, to rejection of colonialism in all its forms. Liberationist approaches also stress the importance of readings from different social locations, such as African-American, Asian-American, and Native American. Common to all of these movements of liberation is the dilemma proposed by biblical injunctions so opposed to these ideals (e.g., "slaves, obey your masters"; "women, be submissive to your husbands").

The Bible has played a twofold role in liberation. Liberationist (including **feminist**) interpreters draw on themes such as the exodus, leading people from slavery to freedom; the prophetic critique of oppressive wealth; and traditions that run counter to a dominant cultural ethos, such as the important leadership roles of women in the Pauline communities. They also insist that all interpreters recognize how their own social and economic situation influences their reading of the Bible.

CONCLUSIONS

The term "method" can be easily misinterpreted when applied to biblical texts, since it suggests a set procedure or approach that leads to objective results, as in the phrase "the scientific method." A better term would be "approaches," or "ways of reading." From their origin until the present, biblical traditions and texts have been read in different ways. As *historical* texts in languages different from those of most interpreters and from an age and culture distant from readers, the biblical texts will always summon interpreters to use all available resources to assess what the text could have meant in its original context. As *literary documents* that have lasted for centuries, they are subjects of methods of interpretation current in every age (e.g., Augustine was versed in classical rhetoric and used its techniques when interpreting the Bible). As *religious* texts they engender structures of faith and commitment that in turn influence their interpretation.

No one method is adequate for the interpretation of the Bible, nor can any interpreter be adept in the full spectrum of methods. The historical and literary methods that emerged after the Enlightenment are necessary, but not sufficient, for our task. Contemporary communities of interpretation and dialogue that bridge social and religious differences are essential for enduring and fruitful reading of the Bible.

FOR FURTHER READING AND STUDY

Ackroyd, Peter, G. W. H. Lampe, and S. L. Greenslade, eds. *Cambridge History of the Bible*. 3 vols. Cambridge: Cambridge University Press, 1963–1970. A standard history of biblical study from early centuries to the present.

Aichle, G. et al., eds. *The Postmodern Bible.* New Haven: Yale University Press, 1995. A collection of excellent essays on many important aspects of contemporary critical methods applied to the Bible.

Anderson, Janice Capel, and S. D. Moore. *Mark and Method: New Approaches in Biblical Studies.* Minneapolis: Fortress, 1992. Readable introductory essays to approaches such as narrative criticism, feminist exegesis, and social-scientific study.

Baird, William. *History of New Testament Research. Volume One: From Deism to Tübingen; Volume Two: From Jonathan Edwards to Rudolf Bultmann.* Minneapolis: Fortress, 1992, 2003. Magisterial and eminently readable histories of all aspects of NT research, with a third volume projected.

Barton, John. *Reading the Old Testament: Method in Biblical Study.* Rev. ed. Louisville: Westminster John Knox, 1997. A treatment of standard methods as well as more recent literary and postmodern approaches.

Epp, Eldon J., and George W. MacRae, eds. *The New Testament and Its Modern Interpreters.* Atlanta: Scholars Press, 1989. Excellent scholarly essays on research, methods and practitioners.

Exum, J. Cheryl, and D. J. A. Clines, eds. *The New Literary Criticism and the Hebrew Bible.* Sheffield: JSOT Press, 1993. Studies in more recent methods.

Gorman, Michael J. *Elements of Biblical Exegesis: A Basic Guide for Students and Ministers.* Peabody, Mass.: Hendrickson, 2001. A reader-friendly guide to an eclectic model of exegesis, with brief overviews of various approaches and criticisms.

Green, Joel B., ed. *Hearing the New Testament: Strategies for Interpretation.* Grand Rapids: Eerdmans, 1995. An excellent collection of essays on traditional and contemporary methods of interpretation.

Hayes, John H., ed. *Dictionary of Biblical Interpretation.* 2 vols. Nashville: Abingdon, 1999. Excellent studies of issues, methods, and interpreters.

Knight, Douglas A., and E. M. Tucker, eds. *The Hebrew Bible and Its Modern Interpreters.* Philadelphia: Fortress, 1985. Companion volume to Epp, above.

Kümmel, Werner G. *The New Testament: A History of the Investigation of Its Problems.* Translated by S. M. Gilmour and H. C. Kee. Nashville: Abingdon, 1972. A classic study of movements in NT study, especially strong on the nineteenth century.

McKenzie, Steven L., and Stephen R. Haynes, eds. *To Each Its Own Meaning: An Introduction to Biblical Criticisms and Their Application.* Rev. ed. Louisville: Westminster John Knox, 1999. A collection of readable essays on traditional and newer methods.

McKnight, Edgar V., and E. S. Malbon, eds. *The New Literary Criticism and the New Testament.* Sheffield: Sheffield Academic Press, 1994; Valley Forge, Pa.:

Trinity Press International, 1994. A volume similar in scope and method to Exum and Clines, above.

Morgan, Robert, with John Barton. *Biblical Interpretation*. Oxford Bible Series. Oxford/New York: Oxford University Press, 1988. An excellent history of biblical interpretation since the Enlightenment.

Perrin, Norman. *What Is Redaction Criticism?* Guides to Biblical Scholarship. Philadelphia: Fortress, 1969. The best short introduction to the method; see also other volumes in the same series.

Powell, Mark Alan, with Cecile Gray. *The Bible and Modern Literary Criticism: A Critical Assessment and Annotated Bibliography*. Westport, Conn.: Greenwood, 1992. An indispensable resource for the study of contemporary methods.

Schneiders, Sandra. *The Revelatory Text: Interpreting the New Testament as Sacred Scripture*. 2d ed. Collegeville, Minn.: Liturgical, 1999. A very helpful book for combining historical-critical and literary methods with religious appropriation.

Schüssler Fiorenza, Elisabeth. "Rhetorical Situation and Historical Reconstruction in 1 Corinthians." *New Testament Studies* 33 (1987): 386–403. An example of the application of rhetorical criticism to a specific biblical writing.

————. *Wisdom Ways: Introducing Feminist Biblical Interpretation*. Maryknoll, N.Y.: Orbis, 2001. An introduction from a major scholar who has written significant works on feminist interpretation.

Smith, Jonathan Z. "The Social Description of Early Christianity." *Religious Studies Review* 1 (1975): 19–25. A brief, early description of the application of social-scientific methods to the NT.

Soulen, Richard N., and R. Kendall Soulen. *Handbook of Biblical Criticism*. 3d ed. Louisville: Westminster John Knox, 2001. Superb coverage of methods, technical terms, movements, and scholars in biblical studies.

Chapter 10

Theological and Ideological Strategies of Biblical Interpretation

STEPHEN FOWL

The present chapter follows chapters on premodern, modern, and post-modern biblical interpretation. It also precedes discrete chapters on the interpretation of the Bible within specific Christian churches. It seems appropriate to take advantage of this placement in order to consider **theological interpretation.** In the light of the chapters that precede this one, this chapter will lay out several issues concerning the importance of premodern strategies for reading Scripture and the relationship between theological interpretation of Scripture and historical-critical study of the Bible. In the light of the chapters that follow, this chapter will address theological concerns and strategies related to interpreting Scripture in the context of church division.

THEOLOGICAL INTERPRETATION, PREMODERN INTERPRETATION, AND THE RISE OF HISTORICAL CRITICISM

Premodern interpretation of Scripture was theological from beginning to end. That is, the various interpretive practices common in the premodern period arose from and were governed by Christian theological convictions. Reading the Bible was a religious activity. Scripture was seen as God's gift to the church. Scripture was the central, but not the only, vehicle by which Christians were able to live and worship faithfully before the Triune God. Moreover, faithful living, thinking, and worshipping shaped the ways in which Christians interpreted Scripture. This was because, ultimately, scriptural interpretation, worship, and Christian faith and life were all ordered and directed toward helping Christians achieve their proper end (or goal; Greek *telos*) in God.

Nevertheless, it is also clear that premodern interpretation was very different from the types of interpretation one encounters in a modern biblical commentary or article. For many students, their encounter with premodern interpretation can strike them as alien. It may be tempting to think that the difference between premodern interpreters and us is that they had a naïvely literalistic understanding of the Scripture and that they neglected or glossed over textual puzzles. Although there may be some examples of these interpretive flaws, they are not characteristic of premodern interpretation at its best. Premodern interpreters understood that Scripture was extraordinarily diverse and that it contained various textual puzzles and obscurities.

The chief difference between premodern interpreters and the historical critics who came to dominate academic study of the Bible from the late eighteenth century down to the present is that premodern interpreters granted theological concerns, interests, and strategies priority when it comes to interpreting Scripture. They did so because they understood that Scripture could only fulfill its role in bringing Christians to their proper end in God if scriptural interpretation shaped and was shaped by theological concerns. Modern biblical study is most clearly distinguished from premodern interpretation because of the priority granted to *historical* concerns over *theological* ones.

The Seismic Shift in Biblical Interpretation

The first step in interpreting Scripture theologically is to grant priority to theological concerns. As a way of leading to that point, it will be useful to explore, at least briefly, why textual puzzles, ruptures, and obscurities that were relatively well-known began—sometime in the mid- to late eighteenth century—to generate concerns that led to the rise of historical-critical methods of interpretation. During this period there was a fundamental shift in the practices of biblical interpretation. Prior to this shift, in the premodern era, Scripture was believed to be the most important of God's providential gifts for ordering, understanding, and making the world accessible to humans. Scripture (interpreted theologically) presented a unified narrative through which people could develop coherent views of the world. The evident diversity and rich detail of Scripture called forth a variety of reading practices, both literal and nonliteral (**figural**), that nonetheless presented a common narrative. The rich variety of reading strategies characteristic of premodern biblical interpretation was essential if the Bible was to provide Christians with a way of rightly understanding and living within their past, present, and future.

> [S]ince the world truly rendered by combining biblical narratives into one was indeed the one and only real world, it must in principle embrace the experience of any pres-

ent age and reader. Not only was it possible for him, it was also his duty to fit himself into that world in which he was in any case a member, and he too did so in part by figural interpretation and in part of course by his mode of life. He was to see his disposition, his actions and passions, the shape of his own life as well as that of his era's events, as figures of that storied world. (Frei, *The Eclipse of Biblical Narrative*, p. 3)

To perhaps oversimplify the matter, this sort of interpretation moves from *text* to *world*. The presumption was that it is often difficult to figure out how to live and move in the world in ways that will enhance one's prospects of living and worshipping faithfully before God. Scripture, despite its evident obscurities, was believed to provide a relatively clear and God-given set of lenses for viewing the world and faithfully negotiating one's path through it.

But a seismic shift in interpretation occurred when the relationship between text and world was reversed in the eighteenth century with the rise of the historical-critical methods of interpretation. At that time, scientific, social, and philosophical changes made it seem that the world was, more or less, immediately (directly) intelligible to all rational people, apart from both faith and Scripture. The "real" world became detached from its biblical rendering. In the light of this transformation, interpreters of the Bible began to believe that

[t]he real events of history constitute an autonomous temporal framework of their own under God's providential design. Instead of rendering them accessible, the narratives, heretofore indispensable as means of access to the events, now simply verify them, thus affirming their autonomy and the fact that they are in principle accessible through any kind of description that can manage to be accurate either predictively or after the event. It simply happens that, again under God's providence, it is the Bible that contains the accurate descriptions. (Frei, *The Eclipse of Biblical Narrative*, pp. 4–5)

The causes of this transformation are numerous and complex. They are related to the scientific, political, economic, and philosophical upheavals that accompanied the rise of what we have come to call modernity. For the purposes of this chapter it is less important to explain how this transformation took place than to explain some of its consequences for the study of the Bible. For example, as we have just noted, "the real" or "the historical" became its own realm, accessible to all, if not immediately evident to all. Thus, scriptural, theological, and ecclesial concerns were not only separated from concerns of historical investigation, they became actively *excluded* from such investigation. As a result, scholars began to devote a great deal of intellectual effort to such projects as inquiring into the historical accuracy of the Bible. Further, if "the real" or "the historical" was now its own autonomous (independent, self-sufficient) realm, then a great deal of effort would also be devoted to developing procedures and methods for supposedly understanding and interpreting reality as such, rather than viewing reality through the lenses of scriptural interpretation.

Once the shift was made from reading Scripture in order to more faithfully understand and live before God within the world, to reading Scripture in order to see if it matched up with an already known and understood reality, a gap opened up between the alleged "real" world and its past, on the one hand, and the world depicted in Scripture, on the other hand. It was within this historical context, and within this set of concerns, that "historical criticism" developed. Theological concerns were no longer given priority in biblical interpretation.

THE ASCENDANCY OF HISTORICAL CRITICISM

Although people often speak of historical criticism as if it were a single organized whole, it really reflects three recurring and interrelated issues.

The first issue concerns the policing of the scholar's confessional stance (worldview and beliefs). Once "the historical" is presumed to be an autonomous realm, it is a small step from presuming that that realm is providentially ordered (whether by the Christian God or the impersonal god of **Deism**) to presuming that history itself must provide its own standards of meaning and intelligibility independent of one's confessional stance. Once this step is taken, historical critics must seek to root out any seepage from their own or another scholar's confessional commitments into their historical work. This has forced the vast majority of biblical scholars to learn how to separate their public historical research from their private beliefs.

The second issue concerns questions about the historical reliability of the biblical texts. Initially, this issue was concerned with the nature and scope of evidence about Jesus. Scholars focused on the character of the evangelists and their honesty. Very soon, however, the focus of this question shifted to the gospel texts themselves as scholars tried to develop a variety of methods for getting behind the final form of the gospel texts to find data about what really happened in the life of Jesus and/or the early church. Further, as more extrabiblical sources became available, they, too, became part of the mix of possible pieces of evidence. Rather than being a set of lenses for interpreting the world theologically, the biblical texts became relatively discrete pieces of evidence for a variety of historical questions ranging from concerns with the authors of these texts and the sources they used to the insight these texts might provide into particular periods in the early church or, in the case of OT texts, the history of Israel.

The third issue concerns the interpretive framework used to organize the evidence. Once history is thought to be an autonomous realm with its own set of methods for establishing intelligibility or meaning, then scholars must not only figure out which pieces of information will count as evidence, but they must also develop ways of ordering and interpreting the evidence.

As long as biblical scholars treated the world, past and present, as more or less immediately (directly) accessible to them, then the practices, methods, and results of historical criticism confidently dominated academic biblical study. Theological concerns were largely pushed to the margins. To the extent that theological concerns received a hearing among biblical scholars, it was only as those concerns arose from the assumptions common to historical critics.

CHALLENGES TO THE DOMINANCE OF HISTORICAL CRITICISM

Scientific, cultural, political, and philosophical movements created conditions for the rise of historical criticism. It is not surprising, then, as noted at the end of the previous chapter, that changes in these areas would make an impact on historical criticism. The past century has witnessed great changes in the intellectual, social, and political climate. These changes worked both to undermine the dominance of historical criticism and to open possibilities for theological and ideological (or political) strategies of interpretation.

Recall that historical concerns took precedence over theological concerns only when people assumed they could comprehend the world and its past in more or less immediate, or direct, ways, apart from the lenses provided by Scripture read theologically. Numerous genocidal conflicts, the rise of quantum physics, the ideological critiques of Marx, the psychoanalytical explorations of Freud, and many other factors now make it clear that we never perceive or comprehend the world and its past without our own set of lenses. That is one of the chief claims of "postmodernism" (discussed briefly in the previous chapter).

However, the recognition that all view the world and its past through a set of lenses, and not immediately, does not mean that all lenses result in 20/20 vision, or that all lenses are equal. For the purposes of this chapter, it is sufficient to note that if the dominance of historical criticism depended on the assumption that the world and its past were immediately available to us, then the recognition that the world is not immediately available must affect the claims of historical criticism.

New Developments: Feminist and Marxist/Liberationist Interpretation

Since the late 1960s, therefore, professional biblical scholarship has seen an explosion of interpretive strategies driven by scholars with particular sets of interests and commitments that go beyond presenting the past as it (supposedly) "actually was." These strategies do *not* grant historical concerns priority over all others. The most prominent are feminist and **Marxist**/liberationist strategies for interpreting the Bible.

The field of biblical studies as it exists today, therefore, appears much different, and more fragmented, than it did even fifty years ago. The concerns and practices characteristic of historical criticism are still around, but they exist in a chastened form. Historical critics can no longer claim to offer an immediate view into the past. Rather, they pursue their specific historical investigations as one among many sets of scholarly interpretive interests.

It is as problematic to speak of "feminist biblical interpretation," as a single enterprise, as it is to speak of historical criticism as a single enterprise. Nevertheless, beginning students can expect to find at least two strategies that are commonly labeled "feminist." The first strategy seeks, through rigorous historical investigations, to uncover and document the lives of women in the biblical period. In this respect the Bible is simply one piece of evidence among many. The second strategy brings various contemporary feminist concerns to bear on the practice of biblical interpretation. Thus, this strategy can focus on structures within the academy or the churches that work to silence or marginalize women scholars or women in general. Alternatively, it can address and develop ways of reading the Bible that might advance a feminist agenda.

In the same manner, Marxist strategies of interpretation engage in historical work from a Marxist perspective, examining social structures and means of production in the Ancient Near East or the Mediterranean world. Again, the Bible is simply one piece of evidence for a scholar inclined in this way. Alternatively, contemporary Marxist interpretive strategies and agendas can be brought to bear on the biblical texts with an eye toward the contemporary world.

The demise of the conceptual apparatus that allowed for the dominance of historical-critical interpretation of the Bible has not led to the elimination of historical criticism, nor should it. It has, however, opened the door to critical approaches to the Bible that do not grant historical concerns priority over all others. This means in theory that there is now room for theological concerns to reenter the scholarly realm. However, this has been slow to happen, and it is still a work in process.

REINVIGORATING THEOLOGICAL INTERPRETATION

The first thing that must be said is that theological interpretation of Scripture never really stopped. Although it was largely exiled from academic biblical studies, Christians have been consistently interpreting Scripture theologically because their identity as Christians compels them to do so. Reading Scripture theologically does not depend on the support of academics for its survival. Nevertheless, disciplined, scholarly attention to interpreting Scripture theologically can only benefit the practice within the church.

Second, numerous generations of scholars came of age when historical criticism, which is not particularly concerned with theology, was the dominant form of academic biblical studies. Thus, the interpretive practices and strategies that arise when theological concerns and aims are given priority in scriptural interpretation fell into disuse.

Moreover, the academic practice of theology was separated from the practice of academic biblical studies. These two disciplines came to jealously guard their autonomy, making it difficult for scholars to try to work in both fields. It has only been since about the mid-1980s that the scholars have started to bridge the gap between theology and biblical studies with the aim of reinvigorating the practice of theological interpretation.

Here is the heart of the matter: *if there is to be a revival of theological interpretation of Scripture among scholars and students, theological concerns must be given priority over other concerns.* At the same time, it will not always be clear how and in what ways the priority of theological concerns will need to take shape in specific times and places. Theological interpretation will always to some degree be constituted by ongoing arguments and debates about how to bring theological concerns to bear on scriptural interpretation, and vice versa. At the very least, however, granting theological concerns priority will involve a return to the practice of using Scripture as a way of ordering and comprehending the world, rather than using the world as a way of comprehending Scripture.

Although, as we have seen, this was the standard practice prior to the eighteenth century, we today will have to relearn this habit for our own time. Exactly how it can be done remains to be seen. Nevertheless, at least two common theological interpretive strategies will need to be reinvigorated.

The Rule of Faith

First, Christians will need to read Scripture, as the early church did, in accord with the church's Rule of Faith (the church's basic teachings and traditions, formally represented in creeds and functioning as a standard of orthodoxy; see chapters six and eight for discussion). Reading according to the Rule of Faith is not like following an instruction manual, simply following a set of instructions in order to construct a product. Rather, the Rule of Faith works more like a moderately flexible framework within which one can order the pieces of a puzzle in order to render an image. While one could argue that the Rule of Faith operates from the very beginning of Christian scriptural interpretation, it receives an early formulation in St. Irenaeus's dispute with the gnostic Valentinus (late second century).

Both Irenaeus and Valentinus recognized that Scripture is an extraordinarily diverse set of writings, and they both tried to order that diversity. Their dispute concerned how to order the diversity. Valentinus and his followers devised a philosophical cosmology (belief system about the universe) that provided a sort of order to Scripture. Irenaeus's objection to this strategy was that the cosmology did not originate in the Scriptures themselves, and therefore it was imposing an external order.

Although Valentinus's type of interpretive strategy provides a sort of order to Scripture, it does so at some cost. Above all, it commits one to adopting a set of views that requires so much revision of essential Christian claims about God and the world that the result is not recognizably Christian. Irenaeus argued that such an account is "scriptural" only to the extent that it is stocked with biblical verses. Ordering these verses within a framework provided by a Valentinian cosmology results in a twisted version of the biblical story. Irenaeus likened this procedure to someone who constructs a story from Homeric verse. It is possible to take some texts from the Odyssey—in no particular order—and intersperse them with texts from the Iliad—again, in no particular order—and thus create a story. This story would contain only Homeric language; it would contain only Homeric characters. Moreover, it could easily convince the uneducated that it was a true Homeric story. Nevertheless, its connections to Homer would be only superfluous, and its assertions and narrative would not be Homeric at all (Irenaeus, *Against Heresies* 1.9.4.).

Irenaeus's brilliant alternative is to make use of the so-called Rule of Faith. He develops an account of God's economy (plan) of salvation that has its definitive and climactic moment in the incarnation, death, and resurrection of the Word. By clarifying the economy of salvation in the light of the crucified and risen Lord, Irenaeus can give a coherent account of the various movements of God's economy. This summary account of the whole of God's economy is what he calls the apostolic faith, a faith that is formally represented in the creed. This then provides the framework within which the diversity of Scripture can be rightly ordered so that it can be directed toward advancing the apostolic faith in the life, teaching, and worship of the church, a life, teaching, and worship that is acknowledged throughout the world (*Against Heresies* 1.10.1–3). Of course, what is so striking about Irenaeus's account of the divine economy and the Rule of Faith is that it is derived from Scripture.

Clearly there is a circular movement here. The diversity of the NT poses a problem that is solved by ordering that diversity in the light of the apostolic faith. Only in the light of the NT, however, does that apostolic faith receive its definitive formulations. As Rowan Greer puts it:

> We could say that the quest which Irenaeus accomplishes is basically the discovery of a principle of interpretation in the apostolic Rule of faith. At the same time . . . it is in another sense Scripture itself that supplies the categories in which the principle

is expressed. Text and interpretation are like twin brothers; one can scarcely tell the one from the other. (Kugel and Greer, *Early Biblical Interpretation*, p. 157)

This circularity is not vicious as long as one recognizes that theological considerations and church tradition are intimately and complexly connected to Christian interpretation of Scripture. At the same time, the rich and varied history of biblical interpretation following in the wake of Irenaeus indicates that interpreting within the Rule of Faith does not demand an erasure of Scripture's diversity.

Figural Interpretation

The second consideration that will be important if theological concerns are to regain and retain their priority in the theological interpretation of Scripture has to do with the importance of figural reading. Figural reading is a practice that is integral to Jewish and Christian reading of their respective Scriptures. It is common to contrast figural interpretations with the "literal sense" of Scripture. In the Christian theological tradition, however, the "literal sense" does not precisely correspond to our modern notions of "literal." For now, let me propose the following working notion of the "literal sense" of Scripture: the meanings that Christians conventionally ascribe to a passage in their ongoing struggles to live and worship faithfully before the Triune God.[1]

This means that the literal sense of Scripture will be primary; that is, it will be the basis and norm for all subsequent ways of interpreting the text. At the same time, and because God is the ultimate author of Scripture, a passage may have several meanings within its literal sense (as defined above). Think of this famous example from Isa 7:14, "Behold, a maiden [LXX, "virgin"] is with child and will bear a son and will name him Immanuel" (author's translation). Read in the context of Isa 7–8, the text seems pretty clearly to indicate that the child in question here is the son born to Isaiah of Jerusalem in 8:1–4. Some would argue, especially from a "modern" perspective, that this is the only "literal" meaning of the verse. It is equally clear, however, that Matthew's gospel and the Christian tradition generally take this verse to be a prophetic announcement of the coming birth of Jesus almost 750 years later. Christians, therefore, can grant that *both* of these are the literal sense of Isa 7:14, because God is capable of intending both of these meanings.

---

[1] Although in contemporary usage we often understand the word "literal" as referring to the meaning of a text strictly in its original context, my proposal is intended to reflect a broader understanding of "literal" that is characteristic of Christian biblical interpretation through the centuries. Even a dictionary definition of "literal" can allow for this: "taking words in their usual or primary sense and employing the ordinary rules of grammar" (*Concise Oxford Dictionary*).

If we use this working definition of the literal sense, then figural interpretations will rely on a variety of interpretive techniques to extend the literal sense of Scripture in ways that enhance Christians' abilities to live and worship faithfully in the contexts in which they find themselves. The primary importance of figural reading comes from the fact that there will be times when the literal sense of Scripture may not offer us a sufficiently sharp vision to account for the world in which we live.

A FIGURAL ACCOUNT OF CHRISTIAN DIVISION

Let me offer an example of figural interpretation. The chapters that follow this one will explore the interpretation of Scripture in Protestant, Roman Catholic, Orthodox, and African-American Christian traditions. The fact that these different chapters need to be written at all is tacit recognition that the church of Christ is divided. I do not have the space to explore all of the "hows" and "whys" of church division. Instead, as a way of illustrating the nature and importance of figural reading, I want to look at some scriptural passages that might provide Christians with ways of thinking theologically and faithfully about divisions within Christ's one body.

First, we need to note that the problems of a divided church are not really the same problems as those faced by Catholics and the various Reformers of the sixteenth century. Rather, the problems of a divided church as we know it today are really the result of ecumenism. The more that Catholics and non-Catholics, for example, recognize each other as true Christians (rather than heretics or members of different religions), the greater the problem of their division, the sharper the pain of this fracture.

If Christians today are to think about this division theologically and scripturally, we need to begin by recognizing that the NT will be of very limited use here. The NT has, for example, some things to say about divisions within the Corinthian church, but those are not at all of the same nature and scope as the divisions we face today. Indeed, if we are to find scriptural lenses for viewing contemporary church divisions, I suggest that we begin by turning to the OT. Interpreted figurally, biblical Israel and her divisions may provide us with ways of thinking and living in our own divided churches.

Passages such as Ps 103 and Jer 3 lead us to view Israel's division into northern and southern kingdoms as one of the results of Israel's persistent resistance to the Spirit of God. Division is simply one manifestation of this resistance, along with such things as grumbling against God and Moses in the wilderness, lapses into idolatry when Israel occupies the land, and the request for a human king. Interestingly, each of these manifestations of resistance becomes a form of God's judgment on Israel.

Take the example of Israel's request for a human king in 1 Sam 8. Although Samuel takes this as a personal affront, God makes it clear that it is simply part of a pattern of Israel's rejection of God's dominion that has carried on from the moment God led the Israelites out of Egypt. This rejection of God results in the granting of a king. The granting of this request becomes the form of God's judgment on Israel as kings become both oppressively acquisitive and idolatrous (cf. 1 Sam 8:10–18; 12:16–25).

We see here that one of the forms of God's judgment is giving us what we want. If we treat division in this light, it becomes clear that division is both a sign that we are willing to live, and even *desire* to live, separate from our brothers and sisters in Christ. And it is also God's judgment upon that desire. Our failure to love, especially to love our brothers and sisters with whom we are at odds, lies at the root of our willingness and desire for separation. This separation—in the form of church division—is God's judgment on our failure to love as Christ commands.

One of the by-products of Israel's resistance to God's Spirit is that the people's senses become dulled so that they are increasingly unable to perceive the workings of God's Spirit. The prophet Isaiah makes this particularly clear in Isa 6:10, 28:9, and 29:9–13. Readers who know the prophets well will recognize that this sort of stupefaction and blindness is a precursor to judgment. At those times when Israel is most in need of hearing God's word and repenting, the people's sin has rendered them least able to hear that word. Because God's covenant is everlasting, however, the judgment that follows leads to restoration. Importantly, it is restoration of a *unified* Israel, as noted in passages such as Jer 3 and Ezek 39. Such a vision of restoration may be both a sign of coming judgment on the churches and the basis for hope in a future restoration.

If we look at the divided church in the light of a figural reading of biblical Israel and her division, then we face several conclusions. First, division is one particularly dramatic way of resisting the Spirit of God. Such resistance further dulls our senses so that we are less able to discern the movements and promptings of God's Spirit. Thus we become further crippled in reading God's word. The response called for throughout the prophets to this phenomenon is repentance. Whether our senses are so dulled that we cannot discern the proper form of repentance, whether God's judgment is so close at hand that we cannot avoid it, we cannot say. Instead, we are called to repent and to hope in God's unfailing plan of restoration and redemption in Christ.

CONCLUSION

There is much more to say here if one were to develop this account further. I have merely tried to indicate how figural reading might look today as it extends the literal sense of passages about divided Israel in order to help Christians today view their own divided state.

As a way of concluding, let me note that reading according to the Rule of Faith, developing habits of figural reading, and more generally maintaining the priority of theological convictions in scriptural interpretation are central practices of theological interpretation. It is also important to recognize, however, that historical-critical, feminist, Marxist, or other strategies of interpreting the Bible may well yield insights that will be important for theological interpretation. There is little point in advocating the elimination of these other strategies. Rather, Christians can appropriately make use of their results as long as they are keeping their own ends and purposes for interpreting Scripture primary. This calls for wisdom as Christians move in and among the various strategies for interpreting Scripture with an aim toward ever deepening their love of God, and of their neighbors (and enemies).

FOR FURTHER READING AND STUDY

Blowers, Paul. "The *Regula Fidei* and the Narrative Character of Early Christian Faith." *Pro Ecclesia* 6 (1996): 199–228. A useful article relating the importance and function of the Rule of Faith.

Fowl, Stephen. *Engaging Scripture.* Oxford: Blackwells, 1998. More scholarly than *Reading in Communion* (see below), this book offers a more detailed account of the importance of theological interpretation and outlines some of the central practices and assumptions of such interpretation.

————, ed. *The Theological Interpretation of Scripture.* Oxford: Blackwells, 1997. A collection of essays about theological interpretation as well as examples of theological interpretations of Exod 3, Isa 53, Matt 5–7, and Rom 9–11 from patristic, medieval, Reformation, and modern interpreters.

Fowl, Stephen, and L. Gregory Jones. *Reading in Communion.* Grand Rapids: Eerdmans, 1991. An accessible volume on the importance of reading Scripture in the context of Christian communities.

Frei, Hans. *The Eclipse of Biblical Narrative.* New Haven: Yale University Press, 1974. A difficult but groundbreaking work that lays out some of the most crucial interpretive shifts that occurred in modernity, why they happened, and what was lost as a result.

Gottwald, Norman. *The Tribes of Yahweh.* New York: Orbis, 1979. One of the first Marxist materialist interpretations of Israel's history.

————. *The Hebrew Bible: A Socio-Literary Introduction.* Philadelphia: Fortress, 1985. A continuation and development of the work started in *The Tribes of Yahweh.*

Johnson, Luke. "Imagining The World Scripture Imagines." *Modern Theology* 14 (1998): 165–80. Part of an entire issue of *Modern Theology* devoted to theological interpretation of Scripture, Johnson's work is among the most thoughtful from those who interpret Scripture theologically and can provide a Catholic perspective to balance Watson (below).

Kugel, James L., and Rowan A. Greer. *Early Biblical Interpretation.* Vol. 3. Library of Early Christianity. Philadelphia: Westminster, 1986. A clear and incisive introduction to the history of biblical interpretation in early Judaism and Christianity.

Schüssler Fiorenza, Elisabeth. *In Memory of Her.* New York: Crossroad, 1983. A feminist reconstruction of Christian origins that was very important in articulating issues in feminist interpretation of Scripture.

———, ed. *Searching the Scriptures.* 2 vols. New York: Crossroad, 1994. A feminist introduction to Scripture and a one-volume commentary on the Bible written by a wide variety of feminist scholars, constituting a good place to begin a study of feminist interpretation.

Seitz, Christopher, and Kathryn Greene-McCreight. *Theological Exegesis.* Grand Rapids: Eerdmans, 1999. A collection of essays celebrating the work of Brevard S. Childs, whose scholarly treatment of the OT as canon has been very influential in opening up questions about how to interpret Scripture theologically.

Watson, Francis. *Text, Church and World.* Edinburgh: T&T Clark, 1994. A vigorous, detailed argument for the importance of the theological interpretation of Scripture, heavily influenced by Karl Barth, that repays careful study.

Chapter 11

The Interpretation of the Bible in Protestant Churches

MICHAEL J. GORMAN

Protestant Christians—those whose churches have their roots in the protests and reformations of the sixteenth century—have often thought of themselves as "people of the book," as Christians who derive their beliefs and practices from the Bible. This is entirely natural and appropriate for people whose churches were born with the words *"sola Scriptura"*—"Scripture alone"—on their lips. Under the influence of Martin Luther, Protestants also stressed the "priesthood of all believers." The corollary of that principle for biblical interpretation was the right, even the duty, of all Christians to read and interpret the Bible themselves.

Although it is true that the Bible has always been the foundation of Protestant beliefs and practices, it is self-evident from the large variety of Protestant churches, doctrines, and moralities—all claiming to be "biblical"— that this commitment to the centrality of Scripture has not yielded uniformity in its interpretation. Furthermore, despite the great heritage of Protestant commitment to Scripture, there is increasing concern among many Protestants that the people (and even the pastors) in their churches have become biblically illiterate and/or disrespectful of the authority of the Bible.

In this chapter we briefly examine some of the persistent issues and current trends in the interpretation of Scripture among Protestants. Our focus will be on American Protestantism, though largely exclusive of the distinctive aspects of African-American churches (which are treated in chapter thirteen), but with reference both to so-called **mainline** churches and traditions and to so-called **evangelical** and **fundamentalist** churches and traditions.[1]

---

[1] Brief working definitions of these terms will be helpful, though it is important to recognize that Protestant Christianity constitutes a broad theological spectrum that is

PROTESTANTS AS PEOPLE OF THE BOOK

Despite their wide diversity, Protestants have historically been unified in naming the Scriptures as their primary authority for faith and life. Protestants, one could say, seek to be a "Scripture-shaped community" (so Richard Hays of Duke in his article by that name). The centrality of Scripture manifests itself in several ways.

First, Protestant worship is biblically shaped and centered. The sermon is frequently the central and longest element of the worship service, averaging fifteen to twenty minutes in many mainline churches and thirty to forty-five minutes in many evangelical and fundamentalist churches. For most Protestant churches, communion is only a monthly or quarterly event, and the sermon is the primary aspect of worship by which members are spiritually nourished. Protestant ministers are generally expected to be informed, well-prepared, relevant, and inspiring preachers.

---

difficult to characterize fairly into three categories. Furthermore, there is significant overlap among these branches of Protestantism.

> By mainline Protestantism, I mean those churches and traditions characterized over the last century by (1) general acceptance of biblical criticism; (2) moderate to liberal theological, social, and political agendas; and (3) ecumenical dialogue and cooperation with ideologically similar Protestant churches and traditions, as well as with mainstream Roman Catholicism and Orthodoxy. Mainline Protestantism has been represented by denominations like the Presbyterian Church (USA) and the United Church of Christ; by publications like *The Christian Century;* by institutions like Princeton Theological Seminary (more moderate) and The University of Chicago Divinity School (more liberal); and by organizations like the National Council of Churches.

> By evangelical Protestantism, I mean those churches and traditions characterized over the last century by (1) gradual and cautious acceptance of biblical criticism; (2) moderate to conservative theological, social, and political agendas; and (3) interdenominational cooperation primarily with ideologically similar Protestant churches and traditions, but also recently with more traditionalist Roman Catholic and Orthodox Christians. Evangelical Protestantism has been represented by denominations like the Southern Baptist Convention and the Presbyterian Church in America and more recently by nondenominational megachurches; by publications like *Christianity Today;* by institutions like Fuller Theological Seminary (more moderate) and Gordon-Conwell Theological Seminary (more conservative); and by organizations like the National Association of Evangelicals and the Billy Graham Evangelistic Association.

> By fundamentalist Protestantism, I mean those churches and traditions characterized over the last century by (1) general rejection of biblical criticism and adherence to a theory of the Bible's **verbal inerrancy;** (2) adherence to very conservative theological, social, and political agendas in reaction to modernity and to perceived liberalism in other churches (often effectively deemed .nonchurches); and (3) a separatist approach to intrachurch cooperation that requires agreement on certain theological convictions (derived from five "fundamentals" enunciated in the early twentieth century). Fundamentalist Protestantism has been represented by independent Baptist, Pentecostal, and nondenominational churches; by institutions like Bob Jones and Liberty Universities, as

Protestants have a long tradition of reading Scripture at worship and of using biblical language in their corporate prayer (whether spontaneous or prepared) and song. Many Protestant churches have regularly read or sung a psalm at every service, and some have regularly recited the Ten Commandments. In recent decades, some churches have instituted the use of a lectionary, or compilation of Scripture readings for each Sunday, which in some denominations is obligatory while in others optional. Some churches, however, read only a single biblical passage that is the text for the sermon. Protestant hymnody is generally rich in biblical language and imagery, from the great traditional hymns of Martin Luther, Charles Wesley, and Isaac Watts to the "praise songs" of contemporary worship.

Second, the Bible is central to Protestant Christian education and "fellowship." Protestant churches have historically stressed learning Bible stories and memorizing key Bible verses to children. For youth and adults, the focus is often on understanding biblical "principles" and applying them to daily life. Protestant publishers, representing the entire theological spectrum, have issued books claiming to expound the biblical principles for living—everything from raising children to making love to accumulating wealth (or giving it away).

Protestant publishers have also produced untold numbers of Bible study guides for personal or group use inside or outside the church. These tend to be based on what is often called the "inductive" method of Bible study, a kind of commonsense approach in which participants ask questions of the text, frequently with little or no reference to its historical context. A relatively recent trend, however, has been the production of more serious adult education materials on the Bible prepared by (or with the help of) biblical scholars, but geared to lay people (e.g. "Kerygma" from the Presbyterian Church [USA] and "Disciple" from The United Methodist Church). Moreover, Bible study leaders are generally encouraged to consult commentaries, of which there are many (of varying quality) accessible to lay people.

Third, the Bible is at the heart of Protestant personal spirituality and, when it is present in a church, social action. One of the norms of Protestant piety is a daily time of "devotions," sometimes called a "quiet time," in which believers read Scripture and/or a scripturally based meditation, and engage in (primarily intercessory) prayer. This time can vary from a few minutes to an hour, but it is entered into with the presupposition that God speaks to individuals through Scripture (and perhaps an inspirational writer or "devotional booklet").

From their commitment to the authority of Scripture, Protestant Christians also often find their mandates for social and political action in addition to

---

well as Grace Theological Seminary; and by organizations like the Moral Majority and the (creationist) Institute for Creation Research.

personal conduct. While they may agree on certain basics (e.g., the importance of feeding the hungry and clothing the naked), Protestants are less likely to agree about matters that the Bible does not explicitly address (e.g., abortion), only cursorily addresses (e.g., homosexual relations), or addresses ambiguously (e.g., male-female relations). Nevertheless, statements from Protestant churches on social, political, and ethical matters are always filled with biblical references and biblical interpretation; a proposed statement will not be passed, or an existing statement long endure, unless it is thought by the decision makers in the church or denomination to address and rightly interpret Scripture. This is the stuff of which church wars are made, and it suggests that biblical interpretation is as much a *problem* as it is a distinguishing trait for the Protestant churches.

THE PROBLEM OF AMERICAN PROTESTANT BIBLICAL INTERPRETATION

It has often been said that common sense is not so common. So too, perhaps, with Scripture: the plain sense may not always be so plain, so clear.

An Example

An example will illustrate the problem: it was self-evident to many white, Protestant slaveowners that the plain sense of the Bible was that whites were superior to blacks (believed to be the descendants of Ham, cursed by Noah in Gen 9:25) and entitled to own them. Similar arguments for apartheid were mustered by Dutch Protestants in South Africa until late in the twentieth century. The clear "biblical principles" to which whites zealously clung were not so clear to the blacks they oppressed; nor are they clear to us today. What has changed? Our understanding of the biblical text?

Yes and no. To be sure, we have a more informed and sophisticated understanding of texts about Ham and Shem, about ancient and more recent forms of slavery, about oppression and justice. More importantly, however, we have a better comprehension of the process of reading and interpreting texts. We have learned, for example, that our perception of the "plain sense" of Scripture is greatly affected by the traditions and communities, small and large, within which we read the biblical texts. Exegesis without presuppositions is impossible, as the Protestant biblical theologian Rudolf Bultmann proclaimed early in the last century. That is to say, we are shaped by the ideologies or "-isms," together with the practices those "-isms" entail, that surround us. (Later in the chapter we will return to the importance of practices for interpretation.)

The Context(s) of (Mis-)Interpretation

For several decades now, Christians have been becoming increasingly aware of the effects of racism and sexism on their biblical interpretation. More recently, the theologian Stanley Hauerwas has convinced many American Protestants, especially in the mainline churches, that we are also inappropriately formed by modern liberalism and democratic pluralism. And biblical theologian Walter Brueggemann has argued convincingly that much of our biblical interpretation is distorted by what he calls "military consumerism" or "commodity militarism." (See his *Theology of the Old Testament,* pp. 486, 718–20, and other books). In other words, American Protestants read the Bible—often without knowing it—while wearing spectacles colored by consumerism, militarism, and nationalism. Hauerwas agrees, calling for the freeing of the Bible from captivity to America (see his book with that subtitle). This tendency is sometimes more explicit in fundamentalist and evangelical churches, but it is hardly absent from the mainline traditions.

A more recent example than slavery or apartheid will serve to illustrate the concerns of Hauerwas and Brueggemann. On September 14, 2001, three days after "9/11," in the Washington National Cathedral,[2] President George W. Bush (a United Methodist) concluded his address to the American people by quoting an abridged version of Rom 8, which includes the words "nothing can separate us from the love of God in Christ Jesus our Lord." Bush deleted the reference to Christ and implicitly interpreted the word "us" as a reference to the American people. The service concluded with a military color guard marching forward as the congregation sang the "Battle Hymn of the Republic," after the President, the Rev. Billy Graham, and others had assured the American people of God's blessing as the war on terror began. Here was a subtle but sophisticated misreading of a key biblical text: a de-christianizing, universalizing interpretation shaped by pluralism, on the one hand, and by militarism and nationalism on the other.

In some respects, the various methods of biblical interpretation that thrived in the twentieth century were attempts at curbing supposedly "plain-sense" readings and making readers acknowledge their presuppositions and the cultural distance between them and the biblical texts. Attempts at more "scientific" or "historical" readings, and then at more "literary" ones, were ways of addressing the problem. Ultimately, however, these approaches revealed more problems than they solved.

---

[2] Actually, the "Washington National Cathedral" is the Cathedral Church of Saint Peter and Saint Paul and is the seat of two bishops—the Presiding Bishop of the Episcopal Church USA and the Episcopal Bishop of Washington.

The peculiar American Protestant issue we are describing derives from the close relationship between Christianity and American culture since the first Europeans settled in what is now the United States. It is certainly not the only issue. Some, in fact, would claim that the more pressing issue is that of biblical authority, in either theology or ethics or both. But we cannot really discuss biblical authority without having first considered the cultural context of interpreting the Bible as our authoritative text.

Questions of Authority

For many years, most Protestants assumed that biblical authority was the Protestant alternative to the authority of the pope or the authority of tradition. *Sola-Scriptura* slogans like "No creed but the Bible," "God says it, I believe it, that settles it," and "What Scripture says, God says" (the last from Benjamin Warfield, an influential Princeton Seminary professor who died in 1921) may sound trite in certain contexts, but they represent the ethos of much of Protestantism. Indeed, some non-Protestants (and even some Protestants) have accused certain elements in the Protestant tradition of having a "paper pope" or even of "bibliolatry" (Bible "worship").

The acceptance of biblical criticism, the advent of more sophisticated approaches to reading and interpretation, and the "modern" challenges to traditional Christian theology and ethics in the past century generated a widespread crisis in authority within nearly all the Christian churches. The authority of the Bible—both the existence and the nature of that authority—is in dispute. Today the question for Protestants is once again, "What is the primary locus of authority?" Is the primary authority *human experience?* (If so, then do we risk remaking God in our own image?) Is it *the theological tradition?* (If so, which part[s] of the broad Christian tradition?) Is it *the Spirit?* (If so, how do we know what the Spirit is saying? Can the Spirit speak apart from or even against the Scriptures?) Is it *the eternal Word* to which the Scriptures bear witness? (If so, is that Word the living Christ, the Christ of the Gospels, or the historical Jesus? Which version of the historical Jesus?) Is it *the Bible,* the canonical Scriptures, or is it *part of the Bible — a canon within the canon?* (If either of these, does the authority reside in the text itself? Which parts of the text? The text understood by which interpreter or tradition?) Or does the authority reside in *the interpretive community* to which the text speaks and which the text forms? (If so, which "community"?)

Once we recognize the complexity of this question of authority, and admit that even Protestants allow for competing authorities and interpretations of those authorities, then the corollary question is, When there are conflicts within this primary authority itself, or among those who appeal to this authority but interpret it differently, or between this authority and other authorities, what is the church to do?

An obvious example of the crisis of authority is in the question of the permissibility of homosexual relations and the ordination of practicing homosexuals (see the Gagnon and Via book). Protestant Christians differ on every imaginable point:

- What the biblical texts actually say, and why those things are said;

- The ignorance of biblical authors concerning modern discoveries and theories in human genetics and psychology, and whether that ignorance matters;

- The reliability and relevance of those modern discoveries and theories;

- The problem of whether the church's tradition and historical practice is known, or knowable, or just, or relevant;

- The relationship of homosexuality to larger biblical, theological, and ethical topics, such as sexuality, purity, covenant, justice, and even salvation;

- The issue of whether the Spirit can lead the contemporary church along paths that alter the "plain sense," the literal reading, or the "traditional interpretation" of the biblical text; and

- The question of the cultural and ideological contexts (e.g., political liberalism or conservatism) that shape the church's interpretive practices.

Obviously, a general crisis (of authority) that in turn generates a particular crisis like this one is going to take a long time to resolve. It would be misleading to suggest that there is any kind of consensus among Protestants, particularly among mainline Protestants and more "progressive" evangelicals. Similar crises concerning different issues, though perhaps none currently as divisive, remain within the Protestant family of churches.

The challenge of biblical interpretation and authority within the American cultural context has created for Protestant Christians a constellation of persistent issues, but also of emerging trends. To these trends we now turn.

SOME TRENDS IN PROTESTANT BIBLICAL INTERPRETATION

Like any human endeavor, biblical interpretation is not a static but rather an evolving discipline. In the past two decades, several closely interrelated trends in Protestant biblical interpretation have emerged, especially among mainline

Protestants and many evangelicals. Though it would be misleading to suggest that these shifts in emphasis are accepted and practiced by all Protestants, or that the older ways of interpretation have died out, it is nonetheless fair to say that there have been dramatic shifts in emphasis. The following discussion identifies seven of these shifts, even as we stress that there still exists great diversity in Protestant biblical interpretation, and that the evolution we are describing is still "filtering down" from professional biblical interpreters to pastors to lay people.

The shifts have sometimes also occurred outside of Protestantism, but our focus here will of course be on Protestant biblical interpretation. The discussion will necessarily be brief and suggestive rather than definitive.

1. The Focus of Interpretation: From the Nation to the Kingdom of God

Since the founding of the American republic, most Protestants have had some sense that this land and nation have a special place in the divine economy, that it is the "city on a hill" of Matt 5, ordained to give the light (of freedom, democracy, etc.) to all the world. This has resulted in the mission of creating some form of implicit or explicit "Christian America" or Christian culture, however that might be understood. Within such forms of "Christendom," the focus of biblical interpretation (not to mention other theological endeavors, especially ethics) is not merely or even primarily the Christian individual or church. It is the *country*, despite—ironically—the supposed American emphasis on the separation of church and state.

Today, most Protestants recognize that such a Christendom no longer exists in this country, if ever it did. Although some (especially fundamentalists and conservative evangelicals) acknowledge this reality with chagrin and try to "re-Christianize" the country's people and its government, an increasing number of Protestants realize that the experiment was a failure because it was flawed. The focus of the Christian Bible is not the United States, or any other nation-state, but the kingdom of God, which both transcends and incorporates all the world's peoples. The Christian Bible is addressed to a distinct people (the church) called out from the nations, and it is therefore to be interpreted by and for that distinct people as it seeks to spread the good news of the kingdom throughout *all* nations. Living "after Christendom" (see, for example, Hauerwas's book with that title) means reading the Bible with this sort of ecclesial (church) focus, not with an eye on what the Bible means "for our country."

This is not to say, of course, that Protestants now think that nation-states have no accountability to biblical standards. Quite the contrary is the case, in fact, for if *no* nation is the special focus of God's activity, then *no* nation has a claim to special status, but *all* nations are equally answerable, for instance, to the prophetic demands for social justice.

2. The Locus of Interpretation:
From the Individual to the Christian Community

This shift in focus has also entailed a shift in the locus (location, context) of interpretation. Protestant Christians increasingly interpret the Bible in and as the church, rather than merely as individuals. But this shift poses a challenge to the ideal of the Reformation, in which the individual believer is so central. Recently, many Protestants have come to see that this Reformation emphasis was a classic case of the pendulum swinging too far in one direction.

Most of the books of the Bible were written for communities of faith, not for individuals. Moreover, Scripture itself testifies that interpretation is not a private matter (see 2 Pet 1:20–21, a favorite text of many Protestants who, ironically, thrive on the individualistic approach to interpretation). Since NT times, Christian communities have been called to mutual instruction and admonishment, which is to say interpreting Scripture and the ongoing work of the Spirit together, *in communion* (see Fowl and Jones, *Reading in Communion*), not merely in private. For many Protestants, this recovery of community has also meant a renewed appreciation for previous generations of interpreters, both great (like Augustine, Luther, and Calvin) and small (like our parents and grandparents in the faith), and thus also a new respect for tradition. For a growing number of Protestant theologians, this recovery of tradition means also a commitment to biblical interpretation within the framework of the church's core convictions, or *regula fidei* (Rule of Faith; see chs. eight, ten).

To be sure, this new development does not mean the end of the Protestant Christian's private reading of Scripture. Rather, it seeks to situate that experience within a larger, communal context that provides a rationale for personal biblical interpretation, as well as a means of correction for the individual when it is needed. It does mean, however, that it is primarily the church, rather than the individual, that discerns the contours of faithful and appropriate biblical interpretation, spurred on from time to time (paradoxically but necessarily) by a prophetic voice that runs counter to both the community as community and to its many individual voices.

3. The Perspective of Interpretation: From the Powerful to the Powerless

The need for that kind of prophetic voice, in fact, leads to the next recent shift in Protestant biblical interpretation: a shift in perspective from the powerful to the powerless. When American Protestant Christianity as a whole—especially white, middle- and upper-class Protestantism—believed that its perspective on the world and on the faith was the right one (by virtue of its specially blessed location), it was looking out from the perspective of power and privilege. But for several decades now, prophetic voices have been calling Protestants (and others) to see things from the margins, from the perspective of the oppressed: the poor, women and minorities, the socially outcast. There has been a call, and in many circles an affirmative response, to read the Bible with "third-world eyes," to interpret the Bible as the revelation of the God of the oppressed (see the books by Robert McAfee Brown and James Cone).

This shift is still very definitely a work in progress. Some Protestant interpreters feel strongly that now the only legitimate Christian **hermeneutic** (interpretive approach) is a liberationist approach that evaluates all scriptural texts and scriptural interpretations in light of their perceived ability to liberate the oppressed (see the discussion in chapter ten). At the other extreme are those who absolutely reject this approach as wrongheaded. At present, the majority of Protestant interpreters seem to understand the importance of the reader's own social location when he or she interprets the Bible, as well as the need to try to read the Bible from the perspective of the marginalized and oppressed, without necessarily using "liberation" as the filter to determine the value of a biblical text.

4. The Presupposition of Interpretation: From Inerrancy or Suspicion to Polyvalence and Trust

The mention of a text's "value" leads inevitably to the question of the Bible's inspiration. John Calvin talked of Scripture as divine accommodation to human weakness, while Luther compared Scripture to the hay-filled manger that housed the divine Word at its incarnation. But after the eighteenth-century Enlightenment, and especially in the late nineteenth and twentieth centuries, many Protestants increasingly felt the need to defend the Bible's inspiration against the attacks of detractors. Strict defenders of the Bible's inspiration argued that it was free of error even with respect to history and science. The fundamentalist-modernist controversy, exemplified in the famous Scopes trial about evolution, was perhaps the most well-known manifestation of this phenomenon, which split some Protestant denominations and institutions.

The debate about the Bible's **inerrancy** continued, especially among fundamentalists and evangelicals, through the middle and even into the latter part of the twentieth century, often very stridently. These Protestants asked, Is the Bible without error in scientific and historical matters as well as matters of faith (theology and ethics)? Is it better to describe the Bible less strictly as "infallible" (unable to fail in its divine intention)? or simply as "inspired"? Many mainline Protestants, eventually joined by more progressive evangelicals, adopted the "neo-orthodox" approach of theologian Karl Barth, who saw the Bible not as revelation but as *witness* to revelation. They soon began wondering if there were limitations inherent in the Bible, due to its fully human character as a product of ancient (especially patriarchal) times, and even if there were "errors" in its theology and ethics.

Carried to an extreme, this line of reasoning led (and leads) certain interpreters to embrace a **hermeneutic of suspicion** toward the Bible, a kind of "guilty-until-proven-innocent" approach to the text. Having concluded that much of the Scripture is inherently patriarchal, oppressive, or otherwise problematic, these interpreters reject the notion of Scripture's inherent authority. Rather, they argue, its authority is found only in its power to liberate, and texts perceived to be nonliberating carry no authority for them.

The wide Protestant spectrum of opinion about the Bible's inspiration—from theories of complete inerrancy (some even assuming divine dictation) to the hermeneutics of suspicion—will probably never be compressed into one mediating position. Nevertheless, in recent years there has been a more balanced tendency to acknowledge the complex character of the Bible as both human and divine word, an analogy to the incarnation of the eternal Word as fully human and fully divine (see the books by Work and Goldingay). This perspective allows for a certain "weakness" in the Bible, by virtue of its humanity, without denying its power as inspired divine word. Christians (and Jews) throughout the ages have experienced the Bible as such an inspired divine word, living appropriately and faithfully in its light. Today, then, Christians can still trust that God will speak to them through the same Scriptures (see Richard Hays, "Salvation by Trust?").

This approach to inspiration attempts to avoid the pitfalls of the inerrancy position, among which, frequently, is the assumption that all biblical texts have one defined and discernible meaning, rather than an abundance of valid interpretations. Many Protestants today are more comfortable with the idea that all texts, even biblical texts, have (or generate) a **surplus of meaning,** sometimes described as the **polyvalence** of the text. This approach also attempts to avoid the extremes of the hermeneutic of suspicion, which is sometimes too quick to dismiss texts that appear (at the moment) to be oppressive or obsolete. A **hermeneutic of trust** (the term of Richard Hays) invites the text to speak afresh in new situations, in spite of its real or perceived limitations.

5. The Prerequisite of Interpretation: From Knowledge to Character

The notion of a hermeneutic of trust suggests yet another recent shift: the idea that proper interpretation of the Bible is dependent on interpreters' having a certain character that predisposes them toward the biblical message. This is quite a subtle yet radical shift.

For a long time, Protestants have operated on the assumption that the most important thing needed for biblical interpretation is knowledge. Fundamentalists and some evangelical Christians have thought that the more intimately one knew Scripture (through memorization and study of the text's "plain sense"), the better one could interpret it, especially by comparing Scripture with Scripture. Other evangelical Christians, as well as many mainline Protestants, have put their stock in the sort of knowledge one gains from academic study of ancient history and biblical languages.

Both types of knowledge are, of course, valuable. But the recent emphasis in Protestant biblical interpretation has been on the requisite *character* of the interpreter, not on his or her *knowledge.* In other words, interpretation is a function of certain practices that make interpretation both possible and meaningful. This means, for example, that a person or community cannot rightly interpret the teachings of Jesus about forgiveness and nonviolence without already practicing forgiveness and nonviolence. This principle finds an analogy in music and the arts generally. For example, the best interpreter of Bach's music is not simply one who knows a lot about the composer's life and times, or even about the theory of contrapuntal music. Certainly these are valuable, perhaps even necessary, fields of study for the interpreter of Bach—the conductor or organist, for instance. But to really conduct or play Bach, one must *love* Bach, one must *imbibe* Bach. Similarly, many Protestants now say, one must embrace and live the biblical message before one can truly interpret it. And this leads naturally to the very meaning of the word "interpretation."

6. The Goal of Interpretation: From Information to Transformation

For many Protestants, the interpretation of the Bible has been understood as an intellectual endeavor, whether done in a church Bible class or in a meeting of a professional academic guild. Although few would have denied the need for the "application" of biblical principles to personal or church life, they would have seen—and some still see—the goal of interpretation as the accumulation of more accurate "information," or the acquisition of a more biblically rooted theology.

Good information and sound theology are of course not bad per se, but neither do they constitute the true goal of interpretation, according to the most recent interpreters of interpretation. The proper goal of interpretation, they say, is not *information* but *transformation.* (For an early example of this shift, see Wink,

The Bible in Human Transformation). Character, in other words, is not only the *prerequisite* of interpretation but also the very *purpose* of interpretation. In fact, many say (and as the analogy to music from the previous section suggests), the best way to define interpretation is as *performance:* the essence, the goal, of interpretation is a faithful but creative performance of the text in a new setting. This understanding of interpretation makes it inherently a spiritual and ethical task, not merely an intellectual one. It also reinforces the importance of community. If the goal of interpretation is performance, then an orchestra of musicians, or a cast of characters, is needed to bring the text to life and achieve the goal of interpretation.

Corollary Shifts

Closely related to the shift toward transformation has been a movement away from understanding the Bible primarily as a collection of propositions and viewing it more as a library of metaphors and narratives. In some circles this has led to a corresponding movement in preaching away from "expository preaching"— point-by-point analysis that sometimes resembles an academic lecture—to "narrative preaching" that focuses on the narrative character of so much of the biblical text. This is not to say that Scripture itself or that sermons do not reveal truth; it is more a question of the *manner* in which that truth is revealed and the *goal* of that revelation. Focusing on narrative has complemented renewed interest in character, since stories are so readily amenable to character development.

This shift in the goal of interpretation also coalesces with the shift from the nation to the kingdom of God as the focus of interpretation. Many American Protestants are increasingly aware that they must engage the biblical text first of all as Christians, not as Americans. Their goal is growth in *discipleship* rather than *citizenship.* This is nothing less than a seismic shift within American Protestantism, and it is still far from complete or universal. Recent events (since 9/11 in 2001) seem to have accelerated the process in many circles but also reversed or hindered it in others.

The Persistence of Prophecy

One persistent phenomenon, possibly suggesting that this shift from information to transformation has not occurred, is Protestants' fondness for eschatology (the doctrine of the last things), and specifically speculation about Christ's second coming. This phenomenon is as old as Christianity itself, but it has been a major focus of American fundamentalism and evangelicalism (see Paul Boyer's book). In the early twentieth century, the theories of J. N. Darby, a nineteenth-century British leader of the Plymouth Brethren, were incorporated into the notes of the popular Scofield Bible. By the 1970s they had made their way into the writings of Hal Lindsey (e.g., *The Late Great Planet Earth*), and a generation later into the best-selling Left Behind series of apocalyptic novels.

Pastors and Bible teachers influenced by this school of thought have constructed elaborate end-time scenarios and timetables. Critics contend that such interpreters use the Bible as a box of puzzle pieces, without examining the original context and purpose of individual biblical texts, to create a coherent story that would, ironically, be incoherent to any of the biblical writers. They find predictions about contemporary world events (particularly concerning the Middle East) in the ancient biblical texts. Again, critics of these interpreters argue that their perspectives reveal more about the interpreters' own politics and fantasies than about the biblical text.

Nevertheless, there has been a shift even in the meaning of prophecy among some Protestants. Reading biblical apocalyptic literature less literally and more imaginatively, some evangelical, and many mainline, interpreters have moved from the politics of prophetic *prediction* to the politics of prophetic *imagination*. They ask questions about what kind of world apocalyptic literature beckons its readers to perceive, and therefore what kind of church to envision and what kind of future to imagine. This transforms apocalyptic literature from something that mysteriously forecasts future world events into something that challenges the status quo and is therefore truly prophetic.

7. The Means of Interpretation: From Excavation to Engagement

Finally, these new understandings of interpretation raise questions about the means to do biblical interpretation in the twenty-first century. When interpretation is understood primarily as the discovery of knowledge (eschatological or otherwise) about the Bible, or the Bible in its cultural and linguistic worlds, the Bible is treated like an archaeological site—something to be excavated for all the information about the artifacts and their world that it can provide. Archaeology is a noble academic discipline, and the sort of understanding of the biblical text it provides can be useful; but it is not sufficient for biblical interpretation in the church.

Rather, the trend that has emerged in recent discussion and practice is a focus on fully engaging the text as God's word, as divine address to the church. Interpretation understood as biblical excavation—however fascinating and useful—is an abortive process. This means that even the most sophisticated tools of excavation, such as the various methods of historical-critical inquiry and literary analysis discussed in chapter nine, are inherently insufficient for the task because they help us to encounter the text merely in its humanity. Such tools may be helpful and even necessary, though some interpreters—and not just fundamentalists—would argue that they not only fail to engage the holiness and in-spired character of the biblical text, but that they are in some cases inherently alien to the text and thus to its proper engagement (see Braaten and Jenson, *Reclaiming the Bible for the Church*).

Thus these means of biblical analysis must be supplemented (some would even say replaced) by means that allow the church to engage the Bible as sacred text. Some have suggested, for example, that premodern, precritical approaches to the text be recovered for use today. (For additional discussion of this problem and its possible solution, see chapter ten.) Whether or not the future of Protestant biblical interpretation belongs to the past, one thing is clear: if Protestant churches are going to offer a life-giving word to people, and if they are to face the internal and external challenges of the twenty-first century, they will have no choice but to engage the Bible, in their preaching and teaching, as word of God.

CONCLUSION

In many ways, the story of Christianity—and especially of Protestantism—is the story of its interpretation of the Bible. In this chapter we have attempted to look briefly at the complexity of that story as it has been recently told in American Protestantism. The trends that we have examined ought not to obscure the fact that Protestantism remains a richly variegated, complicated, and, in many ways, divided house. Whether the trends identified in this chapter continue, and whether they contribute to further rupture or further healing, we of course cannot know. But the future story of Protestant Christianity will no doubt remain the story of its biblical interpretation. Therefore the current divisions will be healed, or not, and the contemporary crises resolved, or not, through processes of biblical interpretation.

FOR FURTHER READING AND STUDY

Achtemeier, Paul. *The Inspiration and Authority of Scripture: Problems and Proposals*. Philadelphia: Westminster, 1980. Repr., Peabody, Mass.: Hendrickson, 1999. A Presbyterian NT scholar's overview of various theories about the Bible and the issues they raise.

Boyer, Paul. *When Time Shall Be No More: Prophecy Belief in Modern American Culture*. Cambridge, Mass.: Harvard University Press, 1992. A comprehensive scholarly analysis of the sources and expressions of American Christian eschatology and its related politics.

Braaten, Carl E., and Robert W. Jenson, eds. *Reclaiming the Bible for the Church.* Grand Rapids: Eerdmans, 1995. A critique by an ecumenical group of first-rate biblical scholars and theologians of the perils of the use of an unchecked historical-critical method and a response to the crisis of biblical authority in the church, especially mainline Protestantism.

Brown, Robert McAfee. *Unexpected News: Reading the Bible with Third World Eyes.* Philadelphia: Westminster, 1984. A demonstration of liberation themes in the Bible and their importance for the church.

Brueggemann, Walter. *Theology of the Old Testament: Testimony, Dispute, Advocacy.* Minneapolis: Fortress, 1997. A provocative reading of OT theology as a counternarrative to the West's metanarrative ("grand story") of militarism and consumerism.

Burgess, John. *Why Scripture Matters: Reading the Bible in a Time of Church Conflict.* Louisville: Westminster John Knox, 1998. An argument by a Presbyterian theologian for Scripture as a sacramental, poetic, life-giving word for conflicted churches and denominations.

Cone, James H. *God of the Oppressed.* New York: Seabury, 1975. A landmark liberationist reading of Scripture from a distinguished African-American theologian.

Davis, Ellen F., and Richard B. Hays, eds. *The Art of Reading Scripture.* Grand Rapids: Eerdmans, 2003. Essays and sermons by an ecumenical group of eminent scholars who represent a theological approach to interpretation for the church after Christendom.

Fowl, Stephen E., and L. Gregory Jones. *Reading in Communion: Scripture and Ethics in Christian Life.* Grand Rapids: Eerdmans, 1991. Repr., Eugene, Ore.: Wipf & Stock, 1998. A modern classic by an Episcopalian biblical scholar and a Methodist theologian on the role of character and community in understanding interpretation as embodiment.

Gagnon, Robert A. J., and Dan O. Via. *Homosexuality and the Bible: Two Views.* Minneapolis: Fortress, 2003. An exemplary model of the issues surrounding Protestant use of the Bible in considering a moral issue, written by two biblical scholars, a Presbyterian and an Episcopalian.

Goldingay, John. *Models of Scripture.* Grand Rapids: Eerdmans, 1994. Repr., Eugene, Ore.: Wipf & Stock, 2002. A progressive evangelical Anglican theology of Scripture as witnessing tradition, authoritative canon, inspired word, and experienced revelation.

Hauerwas, Stanley. *After Christendom? How the Church Is to Behave If Freedom, Justice, and a Christian Nation Are Bad Ideas.* Nashville: Abingdon, 1991. An accessible manifesto by a leading Protestant theologian on the role of the church as an alternative community.

————. *Unleashing the Scripture: Freeing the Bible from Captivity to America.* Nashville: Abingdon, 1993. A collection of essays and sermons criticizing nationalistic interpretation and promoting communal performance of Scripture.

Haynes, Stephen R. *Noah's Curse: The Biblical Justification of American Slavery.* New York: Oxford University Press, 2002. A history of American (especially Southern) interpretations of Gen 9:25, Noah's curse of his son Ham.

Hays, Richard B. "Salvation by Trust? Reading the Bible Faithfully." *The Christian Century* (February 1997): 218–23. A significant call for the use of a hermeneutic of trust in reading the Bible, by an internationally recognized NT scholar who is a Methodist.

————. "Scripture-Shaped Community: The Problem of Method in New Testament Ethics." *Interpretation* 44 (1990): 42–55. Methodological considerations about how the NT should be used to form the life of the Christian church.

Mitman, F. Russell. *Worship in the Shape of Scripture.* Cleveland: Pilgrim, 2001. A demonstration of the comprehensive role of Scripture in worship, by a United Church of Christ minister.

Wink, Walter. *The Bible in Human Transformation: Towards a New Paradigm for Biblical Study.* Philadelphia: Fortress, 1973. A brief but significant diatribe against the historical-critical method as an end in itself and a proposal for transformative Bible study (may be viewed in full at www.religion-on-line.org/cgi-bin/relsearchd.dll/ showbook?item_id=652).

Work, Telford. *Living and Active: Scripture in the Economy of Salvation.* Grand Rapids: Eerdmans, 2002. An insightful treatise by a progressive evangelical Pentecostal theologian on Scripture's human and divine character and on its role in the life of God and of the church.

Chapter 12

The Interpretation of the Bible in the Roman Catholic Church and the Orthodox Churches

RONALD D. WITHERUP

This chapter is divided into two major sections, one devoted to the interpretation of the Bible in the Roman Catholic Church, and one to its interpretation in Orthodox churches. Each section is followed by a conclusion, and two separate bibliographies appear at the end of the chapter.

THE INTERPRETATION OF THE BIBLE IN THE ROMAN CATHOLIC CHURCH

As noted in chapter one, the Roman Catholic Church has a canon of Scripture that is slightly larger than that of the Protestant churches. This is because the Catholic Church includes the deuterocanonical books—what Protestants call the OT apocrypha—that are not in the Hebrew Bible but come from the Septuagint (LXX), the Bible of the first Christians. These seven extra writings, plus some additions to books in the Jewish (and Protestant) canon, are: Tobit, Judith, 1-2 Maccabees, Wisdom of Solomon, Sirach (Ecclesiasticus), and Baruch (including the Letter of Jeremiah), plus additions to Esther and Daniel.[1] These forty-six books, together with the twenty-seven-book NT canon (exactly the same as the Protestant and Orthodox NT canons), constitute the authoritative Scriptures for Roman Catholics.

---

[1] As we saw briefly in chapter one, and will consider again below, the Orthodox OT canon is similar to, but not exactly the same as, the Roman Catholic OT canon.

The Roman Catholic Church is the only Christian church with a substantial body of official teachings that relate to the Bible and its use in the life of the church. Unlike Protestant traditions that have historically emphasized the principle of *sola Scriptura* (see chapter eleven), the Catholic Church emphasizes that Scripture *and* Tradition inform the life of the Church. Thus any discussion of biblical interpretation within Roman Catholicism must take into account the official documents that have expressed and governed this complex relationship between Scripture and the teachings of the Church (see Béchard, *Scripture Documents*). These began as early as the fourth Christian century, the time of St. Cyril of Jerusalem, and have continued to the present.

Key Documents

For hundreds of years, until the time of the Enlightenment, Catholics—like most everyone else—accepted the Bible literally. The historicity of the text was seldom questioned. However, Catholics had also developed a great sensitivity to deeper, more spiritual meanings of biblical texts, primarily under the influence of many patristic commentators (the early, post-NT Fathers of the church from ca. 100–600). With the onset of significant scientific studies of the Bible in the eighteenth and nineteenth centuries,[2] most of which Protestant scholars were conducting, the Catholic Church became fearful of the skeptical results of such research. Thus the tendency was to avoid promoting Bible study and to rely solely on the Church's interpretation of biblical texts. It is not an exaggeration to say that Catholics viewed the Bible as the sole domain of Protestants, while Catholics concentrated on the sacraments.

Only near the end of the nineteenth century, under Pope Leo XIII, did a glimmer of light shine on the Church's official stance. Leo's **encyclical** (papal letter) *Providentissimus Deus* cautiously urged Catholic scholars to participate in biblical research, but in a way that would not raise questions about the historicity of the Bible and cause skepticism on the part of the faithful. In 1902, Pope Leo XIII also established the Pontifical Biblical Commission, an official body of experts whose job was to help guide Catholics in the appreciation of the Bible, albeit in a cautious and vigilant manner. Thus began a tiny ripple that was felt primarily in monastic settings, where a small number of Catholic scholars were, in fact, already quietly doing biblical research. From then on, however, the Church's official stance grew in stages. While it is not possible to rehearse all the

---

[2] Among Roman Catholics, the term "scientific studies" is often used generically to describe all scholarly approaches to the Bible, including the traditional historical-critical methods and newer methods. The term is meant to be as broad and encompassing as possible and to contrast with simplistic "literal" readings.

official documents, there are certain key texts worth noting. The following table conveniently summarizes them.[3]

Key Catholic Documents				
Document Title	Date	Author	Description	Authority Level
Providentissimus Deus (*Encyclical on the Study of Holy Scripture*)	1893	Pope Leo XIII	Papal encyclical that promoted some scientific study of Scripture but within certain limits, to protect the historicity of the biblical data	B
Divino Afflante Spiritu (*Encyclical on Promoting Biblical Studies*)	1943	Pope Pius XII	Papal encyclical sometimes called the *Magna Carta* of Catholic biblical studies; strongly promoted use of linguistic and scientific means for professional Bible study among Catholic scholars	B
Sancta Mater Ecclesia (*Instruction on the Historical Truth of the Gospels*)	1964	Pontifical Biblical Commission	Instruction that recognizes three embedded levels of history and tradition even in the Gospels: 1) historical life of Jesus; 2) apostolic preaching; 3) time of each evangelist and his community	C
Dei Verbum (*Dogmatic Constitution on Divine Revelation*)	1965	Vatican Council II	As a conciliar document, the highest authoritative text that recognizes Scripture and Tradition as the combined source of revelation and promotes the value of the Bible for Catholics and all Christians	A
The Interpretation of the Bible in the Church	1993	Pontifical Biblical Commission	Instruction that recognizes strengths and weaknesses in virtually all methods of scientific biblical studies and rejects a fundamentalist approach	C
The Jewish People and their Sacred Scriptures in the Christian Bible	2002	Pontifical Biblical Commission	Significant statement that affirms the ongoing validity of the covenant between God and the Jewish people and recognizes the value of the Christian OT on its own terms	C

These six documents are the most important in terms of their promotion of historical-critical methods (and beyond) of studying the Bible. In essence, in the

---

[3] Customarily, many of these documents have Latin titles that become the convenient title for reference. The English titles of the documents are provided here, but they are not translations of the Latin. One should also note that there is a hierarchy of authoritative teachings within Roman Catholicism, even though all of the documents in the chart constitute *official* Church teachings. Constitutions created by ecumenical councils have the highest authority, followed by papal encyclicals, and other papal writings. The table indicates this hierarchy of authority in the last column, with A being the highest.

short span of little more than one hundred years, Roman Catholics came from an underdeveloped and fearful approach to scholarly study of the Bible to a full-fledged participation in it, even to the point of becoming equal dialogue partners with Protestant counterparts (see Harrington, "Catholic Life").

The process was not entirely smooth. As in the case of some Protestant churches, battles have been fought periodically over the results of modern biblical scholarship. At one point (1905–1914), the Pontifical Biblical Commission issued a series of instructions condemning the results of certain OT studies that called into question such positions as the Mosaic authorship of the Pentateuch. This occurred in the midst of the Modernist crisis, a time when the Church felt threatened by "modern influences" out to destroy the Church's authority. These statements no longer inhibit Catholic scholars from pursuing their research freely, and later Church teaching has made it clear that Catholics are free to accept the results of biblical scholarship on such matters (see Collins, "Rome and the Critical Study of the New Testament," and Brown and Collins, "Church Pronouncements" [1990]).

Scripture, Laity, and Church Renewal

The impact of the Second Vatican Council (1962–1965) cannot be exaggerated in terms of its effect on Catholic appreciation of the Bible. Many of the theological experts who advised the world's Catholic bishops attending this groundbreaking event were themselves biblical scholars or theologians familiar with the results of historical-critical study of the Bible. Vatican II brought a breath of fresh air to Catholics who were enthusiastic to learn more about the Bible. It also created rituals shaped by the word of God. The Mass, for instance, now includes many more quotations from and allusions to Scripture (e.g., the Lord's Prayer, and all sorts of liturgical expressions and formulae, such as "The grace of the Lord Jesus Christ and the love of God and the fellowship of the Holy Spirit be with all of you" [2 Cor 13:13]). Vatican II also reformed the celebration of all the sacraments, so that they always incorporate some biblical passage in the ritual. (It should be noted that Catholic bishops, priests, and deacons had routinely been exposed to Scripture through the **Liturgy of the Hours** and the practice of *lectio divina.*)

Furthermore, the entrance of Catholic biblical scholars into the scholarly conversation of biblical studies, the founding of the Catholic Biblical Association (1937; see Fogarty, *American Catholic Biblical Scholarship*), and the publication of many popular programs for Bible study (e.g., the Little Rock Scripture Study series and the Denver Catholic Biblical School Program) have fed the hungers of Catholics for the word of God. Ordinary Catholics have benefited greatly from these developments, especially in the form of countless Bible study groups (some constituted ecumenically) and catechetical instruction that has been shaped largely by biblical themes.

An important factor in the appreciation of the Bible among Catholics was the revision of the liturgy and the reinstitution of a lectionary, a tool that has now become commonplace among many Protestant churches as well, in the form of a "common lectionary."[4] The lectionary, a vast collection of excerpts from the Bible formulated to coincide with the liturgical year and the liturgical seasons (Advent, Lent, etc.), exposed Catholics to most segments of Scripture that had largely been ignored prior to Vatican II. It is designed on a three-year cycle, with each year devoted to one of the Synoptic Gospels, which is read in sequence during much of the year. (John is used *every* year through much of Lent and Easter.) Since Vatican II, the Catholic Sunday Mass includes three readings from Scripture (usually excerpts from one OT book, one NT letter, and always a gospel) plus a psalm response. In addition, priests were instructed to give a homily (a short, liturgically centered sermon) that expounds the biblical readings of the day and applies them to daily life.

Whereas Roman Catholic liturgy had for centuries primarily emphasized in its preaching practice the sacramental dimensions of faith and instruction on moral issues, by the 1960s the Bible had become a centerpiece in Catholic worship, including the Eucharist (communion). Regular exposure to the Scriptures led to further interest. Moreover, the burgeoning publications of Catholic scholars, on both a popular and a scholarly level (e.g., *The Bible Today* and *The Catholic Biblical Quarterly*, respectively), led to further excitement about biblical studies. A landmark publication was *The Jerome Biblical Commentary* (1968), the first one-volume, fully historical-critical commentary produced entirely by Catholic biblical scholars. (Its successor, *The New Jerome Biblical Commentary*, was published in 1990.) The three editors (Raymond E. Brown, Joseph A. Fitzmyer, and Roland E. Murphy) became virtual household names identified with the maturation of Catholic biblical scholarship.

The Bible began to exercise considerable influence on the level of formal teachings as well. Official documents issued from the Vatican or from local episcopal conferences (regions of bishops, such as the bishops of the United States) now usually contain sections that expound the teaching of the Bible on one topic or another. Thus, for example, documents addressing topics like poverty, war and

---

[4] After the Catholic Church revived the lectionary during the Second Vatican Council, several Protestant churches created a "Common Lectionary" modeled on the Catholic version. In 1992, this came out in a new edition as the "Revised Common Lectionary." Thus the current Catholic lectionary and that used by many mainline Protestant churches are very similar.

peace, the arms race, immigration, abortion, medical ethics, and so on begin their reflections with a summary of biblical perspectives on the topic. (Two prominent examples are the U.S. bishops' pastoral letters, *The Challenge of Peace* [1983] and *Economic Justice for All* [1985].) In short, the Bible has become a regular feature in Catholic life and has helped rejuvenate the Catholic Church in multiple ways.

The Distinctiveness of Roman Catholic Biblical Scholarship

Given this rebirth of Roman Catholic interest in the Bible, a vital question has emerged: what is distinctive about a Catholic approach to the Bible? From one perspective, we could say that Catholic biblical scholars are no different from their Protestant or Jewish counterparts. Scholars evaluate research results on the basis of generally accepted, objective scientific criteria. Catholic scholarship is no exception. As is clear from the Pontifical Biblical Commission's instruction on biblical study (1993), Catholic scholars are free to use whatever methods are being developed for Scripture research that might help elucidate the text. Thus, Catholic scholars employ textual criticism, linguistics, all sorts of historical-critical methods, and more recent methods such as rhetorical, canonical, narrative, reader-response, and social-scientific criticism, among others (see chapter nine).

The *Catechism of the Catholic Church* (in sections 112–14), the current official compendium of Catholic teachings, points to three major characteristics of Catholic biblical interpretation, as summarized in the teachings of Vatican II:

- *First, Catholics must pay attention "to the content and unity of the whole of Scripture."* This means that there is a unity even between the OT and the NT that must be recognized and that is part of God's mysterious plan of salvation.

- *Second, Catholics should interpret the Bible within "the living Tradition of the whole Church."* This is an acknowledgement that the Holy Spirit always guides the process of interpretation and that no one period of Church history or any single Church teaching contains all that the Scriptures can teach.

- *Finally, Catholics must pay attention to the "analogy of faith," that is, "the coherence of truths" that are contained in God's revelation.* The Catholic approach, then, is not identified with any particular scientific method but with the interaction of the word of God and the ongoing, living Tradition of the Church.

There are specific implications that flow from these three distinctive principles, summarized in the following seven statements. (See also Witherup, "Is There a Catholic Approach to the Bible?")

- *Catholic biblical interpretation recognizes the complex relationship between the Bible and Tradition.* These are not two sources of divine Revelation but one source through which the Holy Spirit guides the life of the Church. The Spirit helps interpret the Scriptures and their meaning for each generation of the faithful. This principle is exemplary of the Catholic tendency to prefer a "both/and" approach rather than an "either/or" approach (e.g., word and sacrament; human and divine; proclamation and response).

- *Catholic biblical interpretation recognizes deeper senses of Scripture beyond but not contradictory to the literal sense.* These additional senses include, but are not restricted to, the traditional categories of the spiritual, moral, allegorical, and anagogical senses of Scripture (see chapter eight). Some Catholic scholars have used the term ***sensus plenior*** to describe what the 1993 Pontifical Biblical Commission document calls "a deeper meaning of the text, intended by God but not clearly expressed by the human author" (§II.B.3), but the literal sense must always be considered first (see Brown and Collins, "Church Pronouncements" [1990]).

- *Catholic biblical interpretation does not hold to a specific theory of inspiration or doctrine of verbal inerrancy.* Catholics do, however, recognize and honor the Bible as God's inspired word that does not err in the essentials of faith and morals.

- *Catholic biblical interpretation accepts fully the human dimension of the Bible.* For Catholics, the Bible is God's word in human words. Interpreters should explore texts in context and read them critically, recognizing the human conventions employed to express the divine message.

- *Catholic biblical interpretation views the canon of sacred Scripture as the result of a long process directed by the apostolic Tradition and defined by the Church.* Catholics believe that although God is the ultimate author of the Bible, the Church conducted the process of the selection and ordering of the canon under the guidance of the Holy Spirit (see chapter six on the process of canonization).

- *Catholic biblical interpretation gives special but not exclusive precedence to patristic interpretations.* The history of interpretation is important for Catholics, and although the patristic period (the era of the early church fathers) is especially revered, medieval, scholastic, and modern commentators are also important.

- *Catholic biblical interpretation honors the **magisterium*** (the Church's
  teaching authority) *as the official interpreter of biblical texts.* This is true
  mostly in cases where disputed meanings arise that have doctrinal implications (see Brown, *Biblical Exegesis and Church Doctrine*). The Roman
  Catholic Church does not have an "official" interpretation of every biblical text. In fact, the Church *rarely* pronounces a definitive meaning of a
  text, but at times it points out interpretations that are unacceptable, usually for doctrinal reasons. One example would be the classic explanation
  of the texts that speak of Jesus' brothers and sisters.[5] Roman Catholics,
  relying on the explanation of some patristic interpreters, prefer to understand these passages to refer to a wider network of Jesus' relatives rather
  than to blood brothers and sisters. The reason is the Church's doctrine of
  the perpetual virginity of Mary, a doctrine intimately tied to the doctrine
  of the incarnation. In this instance, the Church officially pronounces
  what the text does *not* mean, even though there is no definitive explanation of how to understand the Greek or underlying Semitic terms
  involved.

These seven propositions are crucial to a Catholic approach to the Bible.
Other Christian churches would share some of them, while some might demur
on one or another point. Essentially, the Catholic Church has come to incorporate the Bible much more into the mainstream of Catholic life, and in doing so
has fostered ecumenical relations with other Christians (see chapter sixteen).
For example, such studies have greatly influenced the general Christian understanding of biblical figures like Peter and Mary, which have been explored mutually through the eyes of Catholic and Protestant exegetes (see Brown, et al., *Mary*
and *Peter,* both volumes the product of fruitful Roman Catholic–Lutheran dialogues, and the discussion of them in chapter sixteen).

Catholics and Fundamentalism

Since the nineteenth century, biblical fundamentalism has been a feature of
American life that has had its impact on church and society. Biblical fundamentalism is essentially a loose Protestant movement opposed to modernity and
committed to preserving the "literal" truth of the Bible. Catholics have not been
immune to fundamentalist tendencies. Historically speaking, prior to the twentieth century, the Catholic Church took positions on the Bible that were essentially fundamentalist in perspective. For instance, one section of Pope Leo XIII's
otherwise admirable encyclical *Providentissimus Deus* is essentially a defense of

---

[5] Matt 12:47; Mark 3:31–32; 6:3; Luke 8:19; John 7:3, 5; Gal 1:19.

verbal inerrancy, a position that later changed in Roman Catholic teaching, but one that nonetheless remains current in certain conservative Protestant circles.

Some Catholics are attracted to contemporary biblical fundamentalism because it seems to preserve basic values that are reflected in the Bible and that seem to be under attack in modern society, especially with regard to family life and morality. Moreover, fundamentalism is often allied with certain conservative political movements that some Catholics find appealing. As attractive as biblical fundamentalism is to some people, it is contrary to a Catholic approach to the Bible. In fact, it is the only approach to biblical interpretation that is singled out officially as incompatible with a Catholic approach. A quotation from the 1993 Pontifical Biblical Commission document summarizes why biblical fundamentalism is unacceptable to Roman Catholics:

> The fundamentalist approach is dangerous, for it is attractive to people who look to the Bible for ready answers to the problems of life. It can deceive these people, offering them interpretations that are pious but illusory, instead of telling them that the Bible does not contain an immediate answer to each and every problem. Without saying as much in so many words, fundamentalism actually invites people to a kind of intellectual suicide. It injects into life a false certitude, for it unwittingly confuses the divine substance of the biblical message with what are in fact its human limitations. (*Interpretation of the Bible in the Church,* §I.F)

Essentially, fundamentalism is incompatible with Roman Catholic biblical interpretation because of its opposition to historical-critical methodologies, plus its concomitant overemphasizing of the divine and underplaying of the human dimensions of Scripture. Fundamentalists are concerned that any perceived error in the Bible, even historical or scientific, necessarily erodes the belief in the Bible as God's word. Such is not the case with Catholics. A Catholic approach to the Bible has much more in common with mainline Protestant and more progressive evangelical approaches than with fundamentalism.

On the other hand, rejecting a fundamentalist approach to the Bible does not mean rejecting everything fundamentalists hold. Catholics recognize certain aspects of the faith of fundamentalists that are admirable. Examples include the fervor for their faith and willingness to testify publicly to it, their promotion of the value of human life, their respect for the integrity of the family as a sacred institution, and their love and respect for the Bible as God's word (see Witherup, *Biblical Fundamentalism*).

Current Issues and Trends

The progress that has been made in Catholic appreciation for the Bible, especially since the middle of the last century, is remarkable. Catholics in general have become more enlightened about the Bible. Catholic scholars continue to

participate fully in the exegetical and hermeneutical challenges of biblical scholarship. They are active in the formal academic societies, international symposia,
and so on. From this perspective, they share the challenges facing all biblical
scholars. Yet it is also true that Catholic biblical scholarship has its own concerns. Guessing future directions is always risky, but it is possible to point to at
least six areas that will likely shape future discussions of Catholic interpretation.

- *Where is the historical-critical method going?* There is widespread dissatis-
  faction among scholars, as well as many laypeople, that the results of scientific studies of the Bible have been too negative, too esoteric, and too
  skeptical, and that they have consequently led to an erosion of faith.
  These people point to the severe questioning of the historicity of parts of
  the Bible, including the Gospels. As an antidote, some Catholic scholars
  argue for a rediscovery of patristic and medieval exegetical methods,
  something that is characteristic of and compatible with Catholic scholarship (see Johnson and Kurz, *The Future of Catholic Biblical Scholarship*).
  As noted in chapter eleven, this debate is ongoing in Protestant circles as
  well, including the question of whether earlier methods are actually *superior* to the historical-critical methods.

- *Which modern methods of biblical studies will prove to be the most enduring?*
  Newer methods in biblical studies have been appearing at an astonishing
  rate. As noted above, in addition to the traditional historical-critical methods
  (e.g., form, literary, source, and redaction criticism, among others) Catholic scholars have used narrative, rhetorical, canonical, reader-response, and
  social-scientific methods, as well as other newer methods. Some have also
  used broader approaches that are not exactly methods but are oriented
  toward specific hermeneutical interests, such as feminist, liberationist,
  African, and Asian approaches. At issue is also whether some methods,
  such as semiotics, structuralism, and various postmodern approaches, will
  have any lasting value or are merely passing fads.

- *What is distinctively Catholic about Catholic biblical studies?* This will remain
  a burning question among Catholic exegetes. Some scholars wish to promote more use of the imagination in interpretation, others want to import
  more postmodern interpretive techniques, and still others want to emphasize dogmatic teachings to guide interpretation (see the book by Johnson
  and Kurz). These lead to the obvious question of how one avoids both
  fundamentalist readings and overly imaginative readings imposed on the
  text—the results not of exegesis, but **eisegesis** (reading *into* the text). Catholics seek a balance in biblical studies, one that accepts the necessary scholarly tools for biblical study but also feeds and nourishes people's faith.

- *How do interpreters relate Catholic teachings to the Scriptures in ways that do not violate the integrity of the Bible?* The close relationship in Catholicism between Scripture and Tradition is fundamental to Catholic interpretation. Relating the two concretely with regard to specific teachings is delicate, however, for it is important to avoid eisegesis. Achieving absolute objectivity is impossible, since everyone brings to biblical texts certain biases. One major flaw in historical criticism is its presumed independent objectivity, something that has been shown to be false. A challenge to Catholic scholars in the future will be how to achieve as much objectivity as possible while interrelating the Scriptures with the Church's teachings.

- *What role will the Pontifical Biblical Commission play in Catholic biblical studies?* This time-honored institution has made enormous contributions to Catholic scholarship, but Pope Paul VI redefined its role in 1971 when he reorganized the **Roman Curia** (Vatican departments). The Commission was reduced to the status of a consultative body to the Congregation for the Doctrine of the Faith rather than a teaching arm of the Church. The Commission continues to issue important documents, most recently one addressing the sensitive topic of so-called anti-Jewish parts of the Bible (*The Jewish People and Their Sacred Scriptures in the Christian Bible*, 2002). The level of authority of such studies, however, will likely be questioned, even though they are issued with full papal approbation. (The 2002 document, as indicated in the table, has a level C authority.) This question inevitably goes beyond the domain of biblical scholarship into the field of systematic theology, but will remain of interest to Catholic biblical scholars.

- *What role will biblical studies play in Catholic relations with other Christians and people of other faiths?* Catholic entrance into biblical studies has clearly had a positive impact on ecumenical and interfaith relations. The Bible is one area that touches all in the Judeo-Christian Tradition. The Pontifical Biblical Commission's recent document on the Jewish Scriptures, mentioned above, is one example of the Catholic Church's abiding interest in ongoing discussions with other faiths about issues of mutual concern. Biblical studies will likely be one area where ecumenical and interfaith relations will continue to grow.

Conclusion

The six questions above are merely highlights of the questions that Catholic scholars are likely to pursue in the years ahead. They clearly overlap with the concerns of other Christians with regard to the Bible. As this chapter has shown, Roman Catholics in the last century have grown enormously in their appreciation for and use of the Bible. On both the scholarly and the popular level, the Bible continues to influence Catholics in multiple ways. While there is a distinctive Roman Catholic approach to the Bible, expressed in official Church documents, much that Roman Catholics believe about the Bible is shared with other Christians. In particular, methods of biblical studies are largely exercised in common. There is little reason to doubt that biblical studies will continue to foster ecumenical relations and likely raise new questions that succeeding generations will have to wrestle with in their own creative ways. There will also likely be more battles fought on interpretation, as history has amply demonstrated in the past. Biblical fundamentalism will continue to appeal to certain individuals who remain uncomfortable with scholarly approaches to biblical studies, and the Bible will doubtless be used to justify one position or another, one action or another, one theory or another, which will require an objective reexamination of the biblical data. Roman Catholics will join with other Bible-believing Christians in trying to apply the Bible judiciously to the challenges that await us in the third millennium.

THE INTERPRETATION OF THE BIBLE
IN THE ORTHODOX CHURCHES

Orthodox Christianity is a family of churches with diverse ethnic and cultural backgrounds that are united in doctrinal beliefs and respect for the primacy of the patriarch of Constantinople. Orthodox Christianity encompasses churches in Egypt, Syria, Greece, Turkey, Russia, and Eastern Europe, all of which remain independent in their administration (*autocephalous;* that is, "self-governing"). Since the time of the Reformation, Orthodox Christianity has adopted positions on the Bible that are similar to, but not identical with, those held within Roman Catholicism. After a brief historical overview, we will point out significant Orthodox notions about the Bible, focusing on the main topics of canonicity, methodology, and contemporary and future challenges.

Historical Overview

Orthodox Christians view themselves as the authentic Church rooted in the gospel of Jesus Christ and with a faith defined by the teachings of the first seven ecumenical councils (see the table below).[6] As such, the Orthodox faith relies

---

[6] The relatively recent term "Oriental Orthodox Church" is to be distinguished from the Eastern Orthodox Church (sometimes called the Greek or Greco-Russian Orthodox). The latter accepts all seven ecumenical Councils. The former designates a group of Or-

heavily on these teachings to inform and shape the faith. The early creeds that developed are important summary statements of essential doctrines, many of which depended upon interpretation of key biblical passages or concepts. A common misconception about Orthodoxy, however, is that these teachings and the Traditions of the church take precedence over the Scriptures. That is not entirely accurate. For the Orthodox, the Bible is an essential part of the church's Tradition (see the books by Clendenin and Cronk). They believe that the church itself helped to shape the Scriptures, under the guidance of the Holy Spirit, and that the Bible, in turn, guided church teaching.

The First Seven Ecumenical Councils		
Council	**Date (C.E.)**	**Major Teachings**
Nicaea	325	Defended Christ as of the same substance (*homoousios*) as God the Father by issuing a creed to that effect; condemned Arianism (movement indebted to Arius holding that Christ was not equal to God but a creature)
Constantinople	381	Ratified Nicaea and also defended the full humanity of Christ; condemned Apollinarianism (movement indebted to Apollinarius denying that Christ possessed full humanity and thus that he was a perfect model for human beings)
Ephesus	431	Affirmed the previous two councils and defended the unity of the person of Christ; condemned Nestorianism (movement indebted to Nestorius holding that Christ possessed two distinct natures, one human and one divine)
Chalcedon	451	Affirmed Mary as Mother of God (*theotokos*) and upheld the two distinct natures of Christ in one person; condemned Monophysitism (movement holding that Christ has only one nature); divided the Church into five (ancient) patriarchates: Rome, Constantinople, Alexandria, Antioch, Jerusalem
Second Constantinople	553	Tried to resolve longstanding controversies related to various early heresies; declared Theodore of Mopsuestia and others as heretics
Third Constantinople	680–681	Affirmed earlier councils and declared that Christ's human and divine will could not be collapsed into one; condemned Monothelitism (movement holding that Christ had only one "will" despite being both divine and human)
Second Nicaea	787	Affirmed that icons are to be venerated and treated with respect; condemned Iconoclasm (movement to destroy icons)

---

thodox Churches (Egypt, Armenia, Ethiopia, Syria, and India) that refused to accept the Council of Chalcedon because of its teaching that Jesus Christ was "one person [*hypostasis*] with two natures [*en duo physesin*]." These churches subsequently became known as "monophysites" (an ambiguous term they reject) because of their emphasis on the one nature (Greek *mono* + *physis*) of Christ.

Much of Orthodoxy has been shaped by the divisions that have occurred in Christianity. Indeed, Orthodox Christianity views the schism that developed within the Christian communion over time, and culminated over the controversy of the *filioque* ("and the Son") phrase in the Nicene Creed (1054)[7] as the essential division that remains at the heart of many subsequent divisions within the Christian tradition.

It is a truism to say that the biblical interpretive tradition of Orthodox Christianity is virtually the same as the rest of Christendom. Basically, the hermeneutical tradition of Orthodoxy lacked any distinctive characteristics, at least from the seventh to the seventeenth centuries (Stylianopolous, p. 228). Subsequently, however, the Protestant Reformation awakened the Orthodox to the specific challenges to church authority expressed in the doctrine of *sola Scriptura* promoted by the Protestant reformers. In their rejection of this doctrine, the Orthodox gradually developed an approach to the Bible that became similar to that of the Roman Catholic Church. The last four hundred years of Orthodox interpretive history has reflected some of this development, especially in the area of the relationship between Scripture and Tradition. For instance, in the face of some Protestant charges that the Orthodox rely on human traditions rather than divine ones, the Orthodox maintain that the Traditions of the Orthodox Church developed from the biblical faith and remain expressive of it (Gillquist, *Making America Orthodox,* p. 13). For the Orthodox, there is no dichotomy between Scripture and Tradition, as some might suggest. As one Orthodox writer states: "Scripture and tradition are not two different expressions of the Christian faith. Holy tradition is the *source* of Holy Scripture; holy tradition is the faith of which the Holy Scripture is an expression" (Cronk, *The Message of the Bible: An Orthodox Christian Perspective,* p. 24).

The Orthodox Canon

As with Protestants and Roman Catholics, the Orthodox accept the number and order of the twenty-seven books of the NT as canonical, inspired literature, normative for the life of the church. The book of Revelation, however, requires separate consideration. Although the Orthodox include it in the canon, it is thought to be too problematic, controversial, and obscure to be included among

---

[7]The "Nicene Creed" is actually the longer Nicene-Constantinopolitan Creed, which combined doctrines from the ecumenical councils of First Nicaea (325) and First Constantinople (381). The *filioque* refers to the Latin phrase meaning "and the Son" within a Trinitarian formula that appears in the Nicene Creed. It affirms that the Holy Spirit proceeds from *both* the Father and the Son, not from the Father alone. This controversy, among others, eventually resulted in the split between East and West in the Christian communion, usually dated to 1054.

the lectionary readings for liturgy. It is the only NT book excluded from public reading at Orthodox divine services.

With regard to the OT, however, the situation is much more complex. Even today there is no absolute uniformity in the OT canon among Orthodox churches. Historically, most of the Orthodox churches adopted the larger Alexandrian canon because of its association with the Septuagint. Thus, they included in their canon the seven deuterocanonical or apocryphal books that are also found in the Roman Catholic tradition (see above, plus chapters one and six on the canon). (The Syrian Church was an exception, adopting the shorter Palestinian canon [i.e., the Hebrew Bible] and using Tatian's harmony of the four Gospels, the *Diatessaron* [ca. 150 C.E.], until about the fifth century, when they also adopted the four canonical Gospels in place of the *Diatessaron*.)

To the larger canon of the Septuagint, however, the Orthodox (Greek and Slavonic [Russian]) add 1 Esdras, 3 Maccabees, 4 Maccabees (as an appendix), Psalm 151 (a portion of 1 Samuel 16–17), and the Prayer of Manasseh (as an appendix). The Slavonic Bible of the Russian Orthodox Church also includes 3 Esdras (as an appendix), and the Ethiopian Orthodox include 1 Enoch and Jubilees. So the extent of the OT canon is not uniform in the Orthodox tradition and somewhat depends upon one's national and ethnic heritage.

Methodology: An Orthodox Approach to Scripture

Just as there is no uniformity in every aspect of the canon, so also the Orthodox churches do not have any distinctive methodology for studying the Bible. Orthodox scholars employ all the standard methods of biblical studies currently available, from historical-critical methods to more recent literary, rhetorical, and narrative methods. The Orthodox also have not produced any specific English translation of the Bible characteristic of their tradition. Rather, they use many different modern translations, to which are appended explanatory notes and interpretations (cf. the *Orthodox Study Bible* edited by Allen), often citing from ancient patristic commentaries (see further discussion below).

As with all other mainline Christians, the Orthodox accept the inspiration of the Bible as God's word. Their understanding of inspiration, however, is not connected with any notion of the literal inerrancy of Scripture. Their position on inerrancy is more akin to the Roman Catholic understanding that the Bible may contain historical or scientific inaccuracies, but no errors with regard to the faith. God directed the writing of the Bible under the inspiration of the Holy Spirit, but the human authors utilized common literary means to produce their books. The divine message is contained in the human words that formulate it.

In the interest of promoting wider access to the Bible among Orthodox laity, one author has expressed five essential characteristics of the Bible for

Orthodox Christians (Cronk, *The Message of the Bible,* pp. 13–14). These express the basic stance of the Orthodox toward the Bible:

- The Bible is the divinely inspired record of God's revelation.

- It is also God's Word to humanity about God and God's reign over the universe.

- The Bible is a verbal icon of God that makes God "really present" to those who read it.

- The liturgical life of Orthodoxy is rooted in the Bible; in fact, almost all of the liturgical texts are formulated from biblical readings.

- The Bible expresses the sacred Tradition of the Orthodox Church.

Although these statements sound familiar, two aspects of this list are particularly noteworthy. One, as we have already noted, is that the Orthodox accept an essential connection between the Bible and the Traditions of their church. These are not two distinctive sources of divine revelation. Rather, God's revelation comes from only one source, Jesus Christ, but it is expressed in both the Bible and the church's teachings through the ages. This is also seen in Orthodox liturgical services. Virtually all of the liturgical texts are either direct quotations of the Bible or allusions to biblical texts and themes. Consequently, the Orthodox believe that their liturgy is a lived experience of the sacred Scriptures.

A second important aspect is the distinctive use of the image of the "icon" to describe the Scriptures. Most everyone is familiar with icons—the delicately painted pictures of Christ, the Theotokos (Mary), the saints, and so on that are used in Orthodox services and are crucial to Orthodox spirituality. Icons, however, are not merely paintings of important people and themes, according to Orthodox theology. They are living presentations of the images they portray. To label the Bible a "verbal icon" is thus a very strong statement. It affirms that the Bible communicates the actual presence of God through the word. This understanding, while unique, resonates well with the Roman Catholic teaching in Vatican Council II that in the Scriptures Christ is made truly present (see "Constitution on the Sacred Liturgy [*Sacrosanctum Concilium*]," #7).

Two other factors make an Orthodox approach to Scripture similar to that of Roman Catholics. One is the respect for and frequent use of interpretations from the patristic period for plumbing the depths of biblical passages. The Orthodox claim many early church fathers for their own, especially those from the second to the fifth centuries, such as Justin Martyr, Irenaeus, Origen, Athanasius, Basil of Caesarea, Gregory of Nazianzus, Gregory of Nyssa, Ambrose, John

Chrysostom, Theodore of Mopsuestia, and Cyril of Alexandria. The Orthodox have always had a high regard for patristic biblical interpretations, and they have found many ways to keep these writings alive in contemporary explorations of the Scriptures. Among these patristic figures, John Chrysostom (ca. 347–407) deserves special mention. Chrysostom ("golden mouth") was a renowned preacher and eloquent interpreter of Scripture, being perhaps the best example of the Antiochene school of biblical interpretation. The Antiochene school emphasized rather sober, straightforward, and literal interpretations, as compared with the Alexandrian school that emphasized allegorical and spiritual interpretations (see the discussion in chapter eight). Much of Chrysostom's work survives today and includes the most important patristic interpretations of the Pauline letters. So renowned did Chrysostom become in the Orthodox tradition that the ordinary Orthodox eucharistic liturgy became known as "the divine liturgy of St. Chrysostom."

A second note familiar from Catholic interpretation is sounded in the Orthodox emphasis on the relationship between the two testaments. For the Orthodox, the OT clearly prefigures the New, and the NT is a fulfillment of the Old. The primary rationale for this stance is their strong christocentric approach to the Bible. Jesus Christ is both the primary source and object of the revelation of the sacred word. Indeed, for the Orthodox, Jesus Christ is the only true source of revelation. Both Testaments taken together testify to the unity of the Scriptures. The entire canon taken as a whole thus bears witness to God's revelation, and one part of Scripture must be informed by other parts.

Contemporary and Future Challenges

Orthodox biblical scholars point to three primary issues and challenges that confront their Tradition.

First, while the Orthodox acknowledge the important role of the Bible—God's living word—in their ongoing liturgical and theological lives, there is also an admitted discrepancy between theory and practice. Orthodox scholars certainly study the Bible in ways consonant with mainline Protestantism and Roman Catholicism. But they observe that the average Orthodox Christian remains rather uninformed about the Bible. The progress of scholarship has not sifted down to the pew (perhaps a common observation among other traditions as well!). Some Orthodox Christians limit their faith to liturgical and spiritual formulae, and there has been no systematic promotion of Bible study in Orthodox churches.

A second challenge, which some consider a burning issue, is the hermeneutical question of just what constitutes an Orthodox approach to the Bible. Is there really a distinctive Orthodox approach to the Bible? (See also earlier in this chapter on similar questions among Roman Catholics.) Responses to this question diverge among Orthodox scholars. One author posits the existence of at least three distinct responses to this issue, which really concerns what relationship exists between the Bible and contemporary Orthodox life (see Stylianopoulos, p. 230):

- One group of scholars suggests that the liturgical life of the Orthodox Church is where Bible and modern life are bridged.

- Others believe that the notion of a "charismatic saint," in the model of many Orthodox saintly figures, constitutes the most important locus for putting the teaching of the Bible into action in the world.

- A third group proposes that Orthodox Christians have a combination of beliefs and practices in the contemporary world that will transform the Orthodox Church into a "living Bible."

None of these positions dominates the present scene, but they will likely influence future directions of the conversation among both scholars and laity in the Orthodox tradition.

A third challenge is the recent promotion of the longstanding patristic heritage of Orthodox interpretation for the life of the church. This is not merely a new "traditionalism" among the Orthodox but an authentic desire to revisit ancient interpretations that continue to hold insights for biblical interpretation. Some thus call for a rediscovery of the spiritual vision (*theōria*) of the Greek fathers that has largely been neglected in modern times (see, e.g., Breck, *The Power of the Word in the Worshiping Church*). This is coupled with recent calls by Orthodox scholars to reawaken in the hearts of the faithful the powerful sense that the Bible is a living word that has the power to transform one's life.

An astute observer will note that some of the approaches and issues summarized in this section are similar to those in the Roman Catholic tradition. Furthermore, the issues are not entirely distinct from those faced by Protestants. That should not, however, overlook the special contribution that Orthodox Christianity has made (especially the Orthodox emphasis on Scripture as an icon and on the importance of patristic interpretations), and will doubtless continue to make, to biblical studies in its own fashion. While there is some overlapping of concerns and approaches with Christians from other traditions, the Orthodox remain devoted to their own traditions and will continue to apply them for future generations.

FOR FURTHER READING AND STUDY

The Interpretation of the Bible in the Roman Catholic Church

Béchard, Dean P. *The Scripture Documents: An Anthology of Official Catholic Teachings.* Collegeville, Minn.: Liturgical, 2001. A compendium of the most important Catholic documents on the Bible promulgated throughout history.

Brown, Raymond E. *Biblical Exegesis and Church Doctrine.* New York/Mahwah, N.J.: Paulist, 1985. A fine study of the basic questions about how Catholic exegetes and theologians relate to Church authority and vice versa.

Brown, Raymond E., and Thomas Aquinas Collins. "Church Pronouncements." Pages 624–32 [ch. 72] in *The Jerome Biblical Commentary.* Edited by Raymond E. Brown, et al. Englewood Cliffs, N.J.: Prentice-Hall, 1968; and pages 1166–74 [ch. 72] in *The New Jerome Biblical Commentary.* Edited by Raymond E. Brown, et al. Englewood Cliffs, N.J.: Prentice-Hall, 1990. A good digest of Catholic teaching on the Bible through official documents.

Brown, Raymond E., Karl P. Donfried, and John Reumann, eds. *Peter in the New Testament: A Collaborative Assessment by Protestant and Roman Catholic Scholars.* New York: Paulist; Minneapolis: Augsburg, 1973. An ecumenical study produced by the Lutheran–Catholic dialogue.

Brown, Raymond E., Karl P. Donfried, Joseph A. Fitzmyer, and John Reumann, eds. *Mary in the New Testament: A Collaborative Assessment by Protestant and Roman Catholic Scholars.* New York: Paulist; Philadelphia: Fortress, 1978. An ecumenical study produced by the Lutheran–Catholic dialogue.

Catechism of the Catholic Church. 2d ed. Vatican City: Libreria Editrice, 1997 #101–41. The most current authoritative, brief summary of Catholic teaching on the Bible.

Collins, Raymond F. "Rome and the Critical Study of the New Testament." Pages 356–86 in *Introduction to the New Testament.* Garden City, N.Y.: Doubleday, 1983. A historical survey of how the Roman Catholic Church has dealt officially with scientific study of the Bible.

Fogarty, Gerald P. *American Catholic Biblical Scholarship: A History from the Early Republic to Vatican II.* San Francisco: Harper & Row, 1989. The most thorough history of the Catholic Biblical Association and its antecedents.

Harrington, Daniel J. "The Bible in Catholic Life." Pages RG 16–30 in *The Catholic Study Bible.* Edited by Donald Senior, et al. New York: Oxford University Press, 1990. A brief popular introduction to the most essential issues Catholics should know about studying the Bible.

Johnson, Luke Timothy, and William S. Kurz. *The Future of Catholic Biblical Scholarship: A Constructive Conversation.* Grand Rapids: Eerdmans, 2002.

A scholarly set of essays arguing for the existence of serious flaws in the historical-critical method and the need to rediscover patristic exegesis.

Lysik, David A., ed. *The Bible Documents: A Parish Resource.* Chicago: Liturgy Training Publications, 2001. A useful collection of the most important official Catholic documents on the Bible in the twentieth century, accompanied by explanatory introductions.

Pontifical Biblical Commission. *The Jewish People and Their Sacred Scriptures in the Christian Bible.* Rome: Libreria Editrice Vaticana, 2002. An official instruction on the relationship between the OT and NT and the presentation of Judaism and the Jewish People in the Bible from a Catholic perspective.

Williamson, Peter S. *Catholic Principles for Interpreting Scripture: A Study of the Pontifical Biblical Commission's* The Interpretation of the Bible in the Church. Subsidia biblica 22. Rome: Pontifical Biblical Institute, 2001. A dissertation on the 1993 document that surveys methods used by Catholic scholars for Bible study, proposing twenty principles for Catholic exegesis and discussing an agenda for the future of Catholic biblical studies.

————. "Catholic Principles for Interpreting Scripture." *Catholic Biblical Quarterly* 65 (2003): 327–49. A digest of some of the author's major points from his dissertation (previous entry).

Witherup, Ronald D. *Biblical Fundamentalism: What Every Catholic Should Know.* Collegeville, Minn.: Liturgical, 2001. A brief but thorough overview of biblical fundamentalism, its origins, and how a Catholic approach differs from it.

————. "Is There a Catholic Approach to the Bible?" *The Priest* 51 (1995): 29–35. A succinct proposal for basic elements of a Catholic approach to biblical interpretation.

FOR FURTHER READING AND STUDY

The Interpretation of the Bible in the Orthodox Churches

Allen, Joseph et al., eds. *The Orthodox Study Bible: New Testament and Psalms.* Nashville: Thomas Nelson, 1993. A handy edition of the King James Version with introductions to the biblical books and comments tied to the Orthodox liturgical cycle. A new edition, with the OT (LXX), is scheduled for publication in 2005.

Breck, John. *The Power of the Word in the Worshiping Church.* Crestwood, N.Y.: St. Vladimir's Seminary Press, 1986. A scholarly work showing the advantage of patristic biblical interpretation and the power of God's Word.

Clendenin, Daniel B. *Eastern Orthodox Christianity: A Western Perspective.* Grand Rapids: Baker, 1994. A balanced and informed analysis of Orthodox Christianity from a Protestant perspective.

Cronk, George. *The Message of the Bible: An Orthodox Christian Perspective.* Crestwood, N.Y.: St. Vladimir's Seminary Press, 1982. A thorough introduction.

Gillquist, Peter E. *Making America Orthodox.* Brookline, Mass.: Holy Cross Orthodox Press, 1984. A brief question-and-answer booklet on basic Orthodox teachings.

Stylianopoulos, Theodore. "Orthodox Biblical Interpretation." Pages 227–30 in *Dictionary of Biblical Interpretation, K-Z.* Edited by John H. Hayes. Nashville: Abingdon, 1999. The best succinct summary of the topic currently available.

Chapter 13

The Interpretation of the Bible in African-American Churches

C. ANTHONY HUNT

For African-American Christians, the Bible has invariably been the foundational source for comprehending and appropriating faith in God. To discuss the Bible is to engage in conversation about the church's book. In this respect, the Bible—with its stories, personalities, and places—has taken on life. It is a living document. Its stories are not mere historical episodes but narratives that have taken on existential reality for persons over the course of a number of generations.

The Bible has been the primary source of knowledge and experience of God, guidance for the expression of the Christian faith in personal life, and unquestionable strength and wisdom in the development of social values. According to Cain Hope Felder, the Bible has come to occupy a central place in the religions of the black diaspora (dispersion from the African homeland). The biblical narrative has inspired and captivated those in the black churches. The Bible has given meaning amidst conditions that have often been oppressive, and it has served as a basis of hope for a liberated and enhanced material life (Felder, *Troubling Biblical Waters: Race, Class and Family,* p. 6).

After providing a brief description of the African-American churches, this chapter will address the matter of the interpretation of the Bible in African-American churches from an historical as well as a contemporary perspective, with some considerations about the future.

THE AFRICAN-AMERICAN (BLACK) CHURCHES

As a way of beginning a discussion of the Bible's role in the African-American Christian experience, it seems helpful to provide a brief description of the

African-American (or black) churches. It is important first to point out that although the terms "African-American" and "black" are not completely synonymous relative to socio-cultural context, for the purposes of this chapter they will be used interchangeably.

To speak of black churches is to speak of a multifaceted set of realities. They are essentially comprised of black persons who have arrived in America under various circumstances and who exist today amidst a variety of conditions. This is to say that black churches include people who have been born in America; persons who have arrived in America directly from various countries on the African continent; and black persons from the Caribbean, Latin America, and—to a lesser degree—Asia and Europe. Black churches reside in urban, rural, and suburban communities. They are comprised of people with various levels of education—from the illiterate to persons with graduate degrees. These churches encompass the economically poor, the middle class, and the prosperous. Socially, politically, and theologically, black Christians are conservatives, liberals, and moderates. Over the course of history, it has not been uncommon for persons from many of these divergent categories to worship, exist, and intermingle within the same local congregational or parish setting.

The African-American Christian community is also diverse in the sense of being multidenominational. Most black Christians have been (and continue to be) Baptist and Methodist, but many are also Catholic, Episcopalian, and Presbyterian. Today, many African-American churches are evangelical, Pentecostal, or nondenominational. In fact, over the last decade, the fastest-growing black churches and denominations are among these latter three groups.

THE BIBLE AND THE BLACK CHURCH IN HISTORICAL PERSPECTIVE

Amidst this diversity, three common features have historically shaped the identity of African-American churches.

First, African-American churches were formed out of the lived reality of slavery in America and its concomitant dehumanization, racism, subjugation, and oppression. From the time the first blacks in America encountered Christianity in the seventeenth century until today, the songs, prayers, and preaching of the black churches have served as sources of community solidarity, strength, and hope for people who have been otherwise disintegrated, disenfranchised, segregated, separated, and alienated.

Second, the life and character of African-American churches, while linked in some respects to the Christianity of the churches of white Americans, is organically and inherently derived from the experiences of African traditional religions. This is seen today in the rituals, mores, customs, traditions, and values that continue to be extant in much of the African-American religious experience. For example, the importance of preaching in the black church tradition can be directly traced to the role of narrative and narrator (the storyteller or jali/fundi/griot) in African tribal culture. The African storyteller typically held a central role, similar to the role that the black preacher has assumed in African-American churches. The preacher—as the central figure in the black religious experience—has been viewed as the person "called by God" who is appointed to "tell the story," thus offering hope found in the gospel of Christ who could "make a way out of no way."

The third common feature in shaping the African-American churches has been the central role of the Bible. Catholic theologian Cyprian Davis states that

> American blacks, both Protestant and Catholic, found their roots in the Old Testament and the New, and most particularly in the many references to Ethiopia in the Psalms and the Prophets. (*The History of Black Catholics in the United States*, p. 1).

Davis points out that the suffering of the children of Israel has been likened to the suffering of black people. Many blacks grew up with stories of Abraham, Moses, Jonah, Daniel, Ezekiel, Ruth, and Esther. Identification with suffering, as experienced by the people of Israel, has been considered to be a key to understanding the kingdom of God for black Christians.

Along with the ongoing identification with these biblical stories, themes, and personalities, there has emerged a growing awareness in African-American churches that truly understanding the role and the interpretation of the Bible requires careful analysis.

THE DEVELOPMENT OF AFRICAN-AMERICAN BIBLICAL SCHOLARSHIP

In the mid-twentieth century, with the groundbreaking research of African-American biblical scholars such as Charles Copher, there began a movement to engage in critical analysis of the biblical text from the perspective of black persons. Many questions began to surface about the presence of blacks in the Bible. Who were the Cushites, the Nabateans, the Egyptians, and other African peoples in the Bible? Where were Cyrene, Niger, Sheba, and other locations that are mentioned? Who was the Queen of Sheba (1 Kgs 10:1–3), Zipporah (Exod 2:21; Num 21:1), Ebed-melech (Jer 38:7–13), and Hagar (Gen 16:1–3)?

Today, there is considerable consensus among many scholars of a prominent African presence in Scripture, as evidenced in numerous biblical references to African lands, nations, and people whose ancestral roots were African. It has been proposed that the Eden of the biblical tradition included mainland Africa to the Tigris/Euphrates valley (see the books by Copher and Felder) and that the location of the garden of Eden would have been totally or partially situated in what has come to be known as Africa. Of the four rivers named in the biblical account of the garden, two of these can be associated with regions in Africa where Hamitic people were significant early developers of civilization.

For African-American churches, considering the role of Africans in Scripture has helped to facilitate the ongoing appropriation of the God of Israel as the God of black Christians, and an appreciation of the notion that black persons are indeed created in the image of God (*imago dei*). The contemporary research of scholars such as Renita Weems (Old Testament, Vanderbilt), Brian Blount (New Testament, Princeton), Randall Bailey (Old Testament, Interdenominational Theological Center), and Brad Braxton (New Testament, Wake Forest), continues to build upon the foundational work of Charles Copher, Cain Hope Felder, Vincent Wimbush, and others by addressing issues relative to how the Bible is read, interpreted, and appropriated given the issues facing black churches and communities. Some of these issues involve the place and role of black women within the framework of the biblical text, along with issues of class, politics, justice, health care, and other matters relative to the plight of African-Americans today.

A great deal has been learned by black biblical interpreters from recent developments in black liberation theology as put forth by James H. Cone, Jacqueline Grant, J. Deotis Roberts, and others. Liberation theologians generally agree that the experience of one's own group is a legitimate context for establishing categories and criteria for theological discourse. That experience is also a means of identifying with biblical texts and extracting meaning from the theological processes evident in those texts.

THE ROLE OF THE BIBLE IN SHAPING AFRICAN-AMERICAN IDENTITY

Over time, African-American churches have engaged in the ongoing process of discerning what the Bible, as a foundational document of the church, says and means in light of its ancient context. This hermeneutical (interpretive) process has been critical in shaping the identity of blacks, both individually and communally, providing a framework for meaning and relevance in black life.

Many African-American biblical scholars and theologians have pointed out that there is clear evidence that, through the biblical text, God has continued to speak to the plight of African-American Christians. The Bible has been (and continues to be) a source of common story and shared vision—speaking to all of the tragedy and triumph of the community. Furthermore, it has been (and continues to be) a means of educating the untutored, inspiring the weak, consecrating the secular, motivating the tired, and transforming the misdirected.

Vincent Wimbush points to the significance of the biblical witness as a critical component in shaping black identity. He states:

> In their sermons and testimonies, African Americans interpreted the Bible in light of their experiences. Faith became identification with the heroes and heroines of the Hebrew Bible, and the long-suffering but ultimately successful Jesus. As the people of God in the Hebrew Bible were once delivered from enslavement, so, in the future, the Africans sang and shouted, would they. As Jesus suffered unjustly but was raised from the dead to new life, so, they sang, would they be "raised" from their "social death" to new life. (Wimbush, *The Bible and African Americans: A Brief History,* p. 24)

The Bible has also served specifically as a point of reference for appropriating and rationalizing the notion of the African-American family as critical to black existence. Cain Hope Felder points out that the NT has a distinct concern for quality relationships in the household (Greek *oikos*), which emerges as a theological paradigm for membership in the household of God (the church). Felder sees a particular theological challenge and opportunity to make the biblical story relevant, given the contemporary realities of the black family (Felder, *Troubling Biblical Waters,* p. 150).

This interpretive process of shaping African-American identity is connected to several central biblical themes—what Marcus Borg refers to as "macro-stories" (*Meeting Jesus Again for the First Time,* in pp. 121–27). These macro-stories are the story of exodus; the story of exile; and the priestly story of sin, guilt, sacrifice, and forgiveness.

The Exodus Story

The first macro-story is the *exodus* story, which shaped the identity of the people of Israel. It is a journey from *bondage* to *freedom.* Humanity's great need here is not for forgiveness or reconciliation, but freedom. The religious life is a journey to *liberation* as God moves us out of captivity, through the wilderness, and into the land of promise. From this perspective, the problem facing the children of Israel in Egypt was not that they were *sinful;* it was that they were *slaves.*

It is the story of the exodus of Israel from Egyptian bondage (Exod 14) that continues to serve as the primary liberation motif for black Christians and is thus the foundational biblical paradigm for communal solidarity and hope. God's saving activity in the exodus events resulted in liberation of the Hebrews from enslavement to an oppressive power. This also established a relationship between Israel and God, the Liberator. The exodus motif is reinforced by the famous Lukan text in which Jesus announces his own ministry of liberation (Luke 4:18–19):

The Spirit of the Lord is upon me, because he has anointed me to bring good news to the poor. He has sent me to proclaim release to the captives and recovery of sight to the blind.

The image of God's deliverance continues to engender a powerful spirituality within the life of African-American churches and helps to form a theological framework for the struggles of African-Americans against systems of oppression that have often stripped persons of their human dignity and left them without hope. The exodus drama of God's intervention against hostile forces to effect deliverance has provided the basis for hope.

Swing Low, Sweet Chariot	
Refrain: Swing low, sweet chariot, Comin' for to carry me home! Swing low, sweet chariot, Comin' for to carry me home!	*Elijah's chariot ride to heaven (2 Kgs 2:1–12) refers to going home to heaven, but also to escaping to the North or Canada via the Underground Railroad.*
I looked over Jordan and what did I see, Comin' for to carry me home! A band of angels comin' after me, Comin' for to carry me home!	*The slaves hoped not only for angels to take them to heaven, but also for angelic workers in the Underground Railroad to take them to safety.*
Refrain	
If you get there before I do, Comin' for to carry me home, Jess tell my friends that I'm acomin' too, Comin' for to carry me home.	*The expectation of a great reunion in heaven, or in the North, kept hope alive among the slaves.*
Refrain	
I'm sometimes up and sometimes down, Comin' for to carry me home, But still my soul feels heavenly bound Comin' for to carry me home!	*Sorrows and setbacks did not quench hope, either for heaven or for freedom.*
Refrain	
The brightest day that I can say, Comin' for to carry me home, When Jesus washed my sins away, Comin' for to carry me home.	*No matter what the slaves' human fate, salvation, forgiveness, and the assurance of heaven was their greatest joy.*
Refrain	

Swing Low, Sweet Chariot is a traditional spiritual that is classified as a coded song because its biblical allusions and other aspects of the lyrics refer, not only to heavenly freedom, but also to earthly freedom (probably via the Underground Railroad). This coded language demonstrates the close connection between spiritual and political realities in African-American experience and biblical interpretation.

The Story of Exile

The second theme is that of *exile,* epitomized by the Babylonian captivity. Humanity is *separated* and *alienated* from the place it truly belongs, rendering people sad, lonely, and desperate. According to the exile story, people are estranged from the center of their being and yearning.

The two interchangeable Hebrew terms for exile are *gola* and *galut.* These terms speak to "captivity" and "deportation" and for black Christians continue to conjure up images of removal from the African continent and transplantation in the western hemisphere. This exile has dimensions that are physical, psychological, social, emotional, spiritual, and relational. Through the Middle Passage,[1] slavery, and related experiences over four centuries, blacks have experienced separation, not only from their native land, but also from family members, language, and culture, as well as religious and spiritual traditions and customs.

The solution is a journey of *return* to where persons truly belong, and the image is that of a joyful reunion or homecoming. The writer of Ephesians shares a NT vision of belonging:

> So then you are no longer strangers and aliens, but you are citizens with the saints and also members of the household of God, built upon the foundation of the apostles and the prophets, with Christ Jesus himself as the cornerstone. In him the whole structure is joined together and grows into a holy temple in the Lord; in whom you also are built together spiritually into a dwelling place for God. (Eph 2:19–22)

For persons of the black diaspora, the Bible and its use in the black churches has been a critical source where this return from separation, estrangement, and alienation is seen as a possibility. Amidst exile, the Bible has offered hope and provided a framework for the actualization of community through worship, service, advocacy, and fellowship.

The Priestly Story

The third theme is that of *sin, guilt, sacrifice, and forgiveness.* Borg calls this the *Priestly* story because it is grounded in the institution of temple sacrifice. Humanity is depicted primarily as sinful with good reason to be ashamed. Borg sees a problem in that for many people this third story has dominated the understanding of Jesus and the Christian life.

---

[1] The "Middle Passage" is the term used to refer to the voyage from Africa to the Americas of persons who would be sold into slavery. Ships were characteristically overcrowded because more slaves meant greater profits. These conditions resulted in much disease and death.

Today, the *Priestly* story—and concern with matters such as individual sin, guilt, sacrifice, and forgiveness—tends to be a primary focus of many African-American Pentecostal and evangelical churches. But the theme also affects social ethics. For instance, black evangelicals tend to focus on reconciliation—with Christ as reconciling agent. The focus here is on the biblical mandate for the church to work toward overcoming cultural and racial barriers that divide the church and society. Three of the proponents of this perspective are William Pannell, John Perkins, and Tony Evans. In *Let's Get to Know Each Other: What White Christians Should Know About Black Christians,* Evans states:

> Racism, whether based on skin color or ethnicity, has always been a terrible sin in the eyes of God, and worthy of His severest judgment. Both white and black people who allow race to determine social and political structure in America need to remember that. (pp. 25–26)

Evans also emphasizes that the Bible is a multiracial book. He further states:

> When a person understands the glorious presence of African people in God's drama of redemptive history, Scripture is clearly the primary source for legitimate black pride. Scripture allows us to take pride in who we are and what God has made us, without feeling we have to become something other than what God has created us to be. (p. 25)

For African-American Christians, the *Priestly* story has usually been connected with the stories of the *exodus* and *exile,* and has therefore often played a less dominant role than among some other Christians. But as each of these themes speaks to some dimension of the reality of the African-American socioreligious experience, they have all been interwoven to play an integral role in shaping black identity, depicting the ongoing drama and journey of African-American Christians.

FUTURE PROSPECTS

For African-American Christians, preaching, teaching, singing, praying, and living the hope that is found in Scripture has continued to provide the primary means of survival amidst oppressive structures and realities. Jesus' sense of mission, as noted above, is embodied in his striving for the "liberation" of humanity. This notion of liberation beckons the Christian community to deal faithfully with the difficult, perennial problems that separate and segregate persons in the church and society. From both black liberation and black evangelical perspectives, today's churches are called to faithfully interpret what the biblical text says about the treatment of women, persons of color, the poor, and those who are otherwise denigrated, marginalized, and ostracized.

If African-American churches persist in taking the Bible seriously, the Scriptures will continue to serve as a source of inspiration, consecration, motivation, and transformation. In the future, African-American churches will face the significant challenge of reappropriating ancient biblical stories and themes in ways that are relevant to contemporary realities. This reappropriation must be accomplished within the context of what philosopher Cornel West refers to as the prevailing condition of the "nihilism of black America." According to West, this nihilism is characterized by a certain lovelessness, hopelessness, meaninglessness, and nothingness that pervades and permeates much of African-American life today (West, *Race Matters*, p. 14).

It is amidst such despair that the reality of the Bible—as the living word of God—must continue to offer the possibility of spiritual, communal, and political transformation. This will involve tapping into the deep streams of past African-American engagement with the biblical text, while building upon these encounters in ways that facilitate the development of a hermeneutic that intentionally promotes the wholistic preservation and perpetual progress of African-American churches in the contemporary society.

It is within the context of the cross—and the concomitant suffering and rejection that Jesus experienced—that African-Americans can continue to identify a critical means of comprehending their own suffering. The notion that Jesus is passionately concerned with the condition of all people is central to black faith. Jesus demonstrated his concern by associating with despised and rejected persons of his own time. For black Christians, there is a clear and indelible connection with the notion of the suffering and rejected Christ. Today, Christ continues to take the pain of suffering persons upon himself.

The resurrection of Christ must remain the basis of realized and future hope for African-American Christians. The resurrection must continue to speak not merely about immortality, but about life amidst death and despair. Without ongoing faith in the resurrection, there will be no good news to preach and no faith to sustain humanity.

For African-American Christians, resurrection symbolizes the promise of new possibilities for meaning amidst the existential sense of dread and despair. It means that the oppressed can be set free to struggle against injustice, and humanity can be liberated to move toward an appropriation of hope. The resurrection is God's breaking into history to transform suffering into wholeness—to move persons from being victims to being liberated agents of change. The gospel message of Christ's resurrection given to us in Scripture continues to call for personal, communal, and systemic transformation. If the contemporary African-American churches persist in taking the Bible seriously and cling to the hope that is found in the resurrected Christ, such transformation will continue to be realized in the church and in society.

FOR FURTHER READING AND STUDY

Blount, Brian K. *Then the Whisper Put on Flesh: New Testament Ethics in an African American Context.* Nashville: Abingdon, 2001. An approach to the NT from the perspective of oppressed African peoples in America, demonstrating how interpreting NT writings from the point of view of African-American slaves reveals its underlying message of liberation.

Borg, Marcus. *Meeting Jesus Again for the First Time: The Historical Jesus and the Heart of Contemporary Faith.* San Francisco: Harper, 1994. An account of contemporary scholarship on the historical Jesus, offering an imaginative image of Jesus with important implications for today's church.

Braxton, Brad. *No Longer Slaves: Galatians and African American Experience.* Collegeville, Minn.: Liturgical, 2002. An exploration of Galatians in light of African-American culture, stressing liberation as a foundational construct within the context of African-American religious and sociocultural experience.

Cone, James H. *A Black Theology of Liberation.* Maryknoll, N.Y.: Orbis, 1970. A groundbreaking analysis of the African-American Christian experience from the perspective of liberation theology.

Copher, Charles B. *Black Biblical Studies: An Anthology of Charles Copher.* Chicago, Ill: Black Light Fellowship, 1993. A compilation of Copher's foundational research in biblical, theological, hermeneutical, historical, and cultural perspectives on the Black and African presence in the biblical world.

Davis, Cyprian. *The History of Black Catholics in the United States.* New York: Crossroads, 1990. A full-length analysis of the African-American Catholic experience, tracing the African roots of the Bible, OT and NT personalities, and the church, and documenting the contributions of African Americans.

Evans, Tony. *Let's Get to Know Each Other.* Nashville: Thomas Nelson, 1995. Evangelical perspectives on efforts to foster understanding in order to help break the bonds of racial separation in the church and society.

Felder, Cain Hope. *Troubling Biblical Waters: Race, Class and Family.* Maryknoll, N.Y.: Orbis, 1989. A comprehensive look at the significance of the Bible for Blacks and the importance of Blacks in the Bible, especially in relation to black religion and the contemporary church.

Weems, Renita J. *Just a Sister Away. A Womanist Vision of Women's Relationships in the Bible.* San Diego, Calif.: LuraMedia, 1988. An approach to biblical interpretation from a black Christian, feminist (womanist) perspective, focusing on the women of the Bible, with particular attention given to relationships, race, and class.

West, Cornel. *Race Matters*. Boston: Beacon, 1993. A classic examination of the most urgent issues confronting African-Americans: from discrimination to despair, and from leadership to the legacy of figures like Malcolm X and Martin Luther King Jr.

Wimbush, Vincent L. *The Bible and African Americans: A Brief History*. Minneapolis: Fortress, 2003. An examination of five phases of African-American biblical reading, showing how the language of the Bible has enabled African-Americans to negotiate the realities of the church and society in America.

————, ed. *African Americans and the Bible: Sacred Texts and Social Textures*. New York: Continuum, 2001. A comprehensive anthology addressing textual and social issues confronted in the interpretation of the Bible from the perspective of African-Americans.

Chapter 14

The Bible and Spiritual Growth

PATRICIA D. FOSARELLI AND MICHAEL J. GORMAN

Throughout the ages, the words of Scripture have encouraged believers to grow in their knowledge and love of God. It is appropriate, therefore, that the ecumenical Christian community in Taizé, France, points those who visit its web site to two early Christian theologians who knew that the Bible is "the inexhaustible wellspring by which God gives himself to thirsting human beings" (Origen, third century) and that it is a "letter from God to creatures" that enables them "to discover God's heart in God's words" (Gregory the Great, sixth century).[1] In this chapter we explore the relationship between Scripture and spiritual growth, beginning with a brief definition of the latter before considering how Scripture can promote it.

It may surprise some readers that a chapter about spirituality even appears in this book. This is because there are two common, but misguided, sentiments in some quarters of the Christian church regarding the relationship between spirituality and the academic or intellectual life. One is the belief that intellectual pursuits do not benefit the spiritual life and may even be dangerous to it. The other is the belief that spirituality is somehow "beneath" those who are intellectually serious about Christianity and specifically about the literary and historical study of the Bible.

Unfortunately, at times professional theologians and biblical scholars have perpetuated these notions, particularly the second one. However, as practicing Christians and as professors of spirituality and of biblical studies, one Catholic and one Protestant, we have found neither of these sentiments to be true for us or for the majority of our colleagues and mentors—or our students.

WHAT IS SPIRITUAL GROWTH?

In his letter to the Romans, the Apostle Paul writes:

---

[1] See www.taize.fr, under "Prayer and Song."

I appeal to you, therefore, brothers and sisters, by the mercies of God, to present your bodies as a living sacrifice, holy and acceptable to God, which is your spiritual worship. Do not be conformed to this world, but be transformed by the renewing of your minds, so that you may discern what is the will of God—what is good and acceptable and perfect. (Rom 12:1–2)

Earlier in the same letter (Rom 8:29), and elsewhere (e.g., 2 Cor 3:18), Paul reveals that this process of transformation is the work of God's Spirit and is transformation into the image of Christ. For Christians, to grow spiritually is to become more like Jesus Christ. Since Jesus was a Jew who lived and taught the basic covenantal requirements of his Scriptures, to become more like him is to become more loving and loyal toward God. It is also to become more loving and just toward our fellow human beings. Putting this in Trinitarian terms, Stephen Fowl has defined the meaning of the church's existence—and thus the goal of engaging Scripture—as the process of entering into ever-deeper communion with the Triune God and with one another (see Fowl, *Engaging Scripture,* and chapter ten in this book).

Spiritual growth, therefore, is a deeply *personal* but not a *private* experience. It is the deepening of one's relationship with God, with others, and, indeed, with all creation because of this all-encompassing relationship with God. For this reason the present chapter needs to be seen as integrally related to the next, which deals with the Bible and social justice.

Because of its outward movement, growth in the spiritual life *must* translate into a deeper fellowship or communion, not only with God, but also with others, whom God also loves. If any practice fails to do this, it does not foster true spiritual growth. Spiritual growth is not, therefore, primarily an intellectual exercise, though it involves the mind, as Paul clearly notes in the Romans text quoted above. That is to say, spiritual growth is not so much about gaining *information,* as it is about experiencing *transformation.* It means listening to Scripture, not merely with the head, but primarily with the heart, as great spiritual writers have said.

Hence, Bible study that *only* results in a greater fund of knowledge without making an impact on the way a person relates to God and others is more of an academic exercise than a spiritual one. It is tempting to think that because we "know" the Bible we are growing spiritually, but that is not the case unless greater devotion to God and greater love for others is the result.

APPROACHING THE SCRIPTURES IN TRUST

The transformation we have been describing can occur when we read and reflect on Scripture, because encountering Scripture can be a discipline, a grace, an icon, and perhaps even a sacrament that permits us to encounter God and

God's transforming love. For many centuries, believers have found that they meet God in Scripture.

For several generations now, however, much reading of the Bible, even in churches, has been done with what theologians call a "hermeneutic of suspicion" (see discussion in ch. eleven). Rather than approaching the Bible as the source of divine revelation and the locus of an encounter with God, many people have found it necessary to approach the Bible warily or even skeptically. This approach began during the Enlightenment with a distrust of the "miraculous" dimension of biblical narratives, continued during the rise and heyday of modern biblical criticism with a general distrust of the historical reliability of the Bible, and took on a new form in the late twentieth century as liberation movements accused the Bible of being patriarchal and otherwise oppressive.

This is not the place to examine or critique the "hermeneutic of suspicion" in detail. To be sure, faithful Christians should not deny or gloss over the difficulties in Scripture; that would be either dishonest or naive. Nor should believers be afraid to "wrestle with God" by wrestling with such texts. However, contemporary believers can learn from the examples of their Jewish and Christian forebears that, despite these difficulties, Scripture has been and still is a "revelatory text" (to borrow from the title of Sandra Schneiders' book) that we can approach with a basic "hermeneutic of trust" (the words of Richard Hays, in his important article "Salvation by Trust"). A hermeneutic of trust, however, need not be an anti-intellectual stance.

Readers of Scripture who have come to grips with its difficult dimensions and/or the questions raised by critical study of the Bible may need to embrace what some have called a **second naïveté**. We may define this as a decision to approach the text, not with the (first) naïveté of an uninformed novice, but with the informed freedom of one who knows the intellectual challenges but nonetheless chooses to open oneself fully to the text as a place for encountering God.[2]

SPIRITUALITY, INTELLECTUAL LIFE, AND THE BIBLE

There is, therefore, no ultimate conflict between intellectual and spiritual approaches to Scripture. To be sure, doing academic biblical studies and reading Scripture for spiritual growth are different activities, with distinct means and goals. In academic studies we are primarily interested in the worlds "behind"

---

[2] The great philosopher-theologian Paul Ricoeur explained the process of interpretation as moving from an innocent, uninformed "first naïveté" through the "critical distance" created by analytical, rational study to the "second naïveté" that is *informed* by criticism but not *enslaved* by it, and through which we can "hear again."

and "within" the text. This knowledge can guide and assist us as we read the Bible for spiritual growth, but encountering Scripture for spiritual growth is less concerned about the world behind or within the text than it is about the reader—the person and the world "in front of" the text. In academic biblical studies, we are seeking to make an exegesis of the text; in reading Scripture for spiritual growth, we are seeking to allow the Holy Spirit to make us into a living exegesis of the texts we read.

Although overall knowledge of the scholarship surrounding a scriptural text might enable the reader to better understand the *what* and *why* of the passage in its original contexts, knowledge of such scholarship is not necessary for, and may or may not play a role in, an individual's own spiritual growth in reading that passage. Yet reading Scripture for spiritual growth does not mean that "anything goes." All interpretations of a passage are not equally meritorious; some have actually been dangerous, even deadly. It is possible to fool ourselves into thinking that we have "discovered" the meaning of a text. Certainly, a particular text might speak to one person eloquently while it fails to touch another person, or that same text may say different things to different people, or different things to the same person on different occasions. While academic knowledge about the text cannot *force* the meaning of a passage for us, it can *guide* our understanding of it, and it can deter us from pursuing interpretations that do violence to the original sense of the text or to the Christian tradition.

This points us to another aspect of the role of the intellect in reading the Bible for spiritual growth: the importance of the Christian tradition. Although few Bible readers will ever be experts in the history of biblical interpretation or of Christian theology, even the most basic knowledge can be helpful in guiding our reading. For example, if our private interpretation of a passage runs contrary to the main contours of the Christian tradition, we might very well have to reevaluate that interpretation (e.g., if "love your neighbor as yourself" were understood to mean loving only members of one's own race, or "zeal for God" were interpreted as a license for violence).

The Jewish and Christian traditions call us to love God with our entire being: heart, soul, mind, and strength. One way to grow in this holistic love of God is through encountering the words and images of Scripture.

NECESSARY DISPOSITIONS AND PRACTICES FOR SPIRITUAL GROWTH THROUGH ENCOUNTERING SCRIPTURE

Spiritual growth through reading the Bible does not happen automatically. In addition to adopting a basic hermeneutic of trust and appropriately using our God-given minds, certain dispositions and corollary practices are required.

The first disposition in permitting Scripture to foster our spiritual growth is *openness*—to God, to others, and to change itself. If we approach Scripture firmly believing that we already know its meaning, spiritual growth will be impeded, for inherent in any growth is change. Thus, we must approach Scripture with both humility (admitting that we do not yet have all the answers) and patience (knowing that we will not receive all the answers immediately).

Being open to change means that we must not only read Scripture, but that we must also engage in the practice of *permitting Scripture to read us*—to question and challenge us, even as we read and question Scripture itself. All too often, people think that reading Scripture is like reading any other book. It is not. Reading a novel might be for enjoyment; reading a textbook might be for education. Reading Scripture is for relationship, relationship with God. In all relationships, there is give and take, and frequently a bit of a struggle. For any relationship to succeed, there must be a commitment to the relationship and honesty in dialoging with the other, in this case with God. There must also be a willingness to invest time and energy in the relationship.

Practically speaking, that means *persistence* in reading Scripture, a second necessary disposition. We cannot expect to have a unique encounter with God or receive a profound spiritual insight every time we read Scripture. For some people, failure to have such an experience makes them weary of daily Scripture reading and even leads them to abandon the habit. "It says nothing to me," they will moan. Yet, common human experience tells us that the ability to receive something depends as much on the receiver as it does on the giver. Our mood—how tired, distracted, bored, uncomfortable, preoccupied we are—certainly plays a role in our receptivity to what is being offered. Furthermore, we must recognize that growing in the knowledge of God, as with any person, is a gradual process—not a series of successive mountaintop experiences.

A good way to facilitate this persistence in reading Scripture is to adopt the practice of having a set time (and, perhaps, a set place) allotted to it each day. A commitment to *regularity* is thus another required disposition for spiritual growth. Having a regular time and place does not leave the practice to chance (though if circumstances dictate, the time or the setting can of course be changed). If drawing closer to God through Scripture is a priority, then we must treat it as any other priority and make time for it even in the midst of a busy life.

Finally, the only way that spiritual growth with the Bible can come about is through an attitude of *prayer:* prayer for the grace to allow God to work with us through Scripture; prayer for the grace to be patient, persistent, humble, and open; prayer to be able to move forward after discernment and to be transformed by what we have read. When we struggle with Scripture, or when we feel like we are "learning nothing new" or "coming up dry," we must remember that the process of spiritual growth is often an unconscious one, invisible to ourselves, and that God is the one who gives the growth.

The practice that is corollary to a prayerful attitude is not simply the act of prayer itself (though that is needed), but the *living of a Christian life.* Growth, in other words, only comes to those who are growing. To read Scripture rightly, we must practice the virtues (such as compassion, hospitality, and forgiveness) to which Scripture calls us. Otherwise, we will likely find the God and the call of God attested in Scripture to be so counterintuitive that we may want to reject them or (worse yet) to re-form them in our own image.

READING PRIVATELY AND READING IN COMMUNION

Many Western Christians are accustomed to reading their own Bibles on their own schedules in the privacy of their own homes. They may refer to this time as their "devotions" or "quiet time." Initially, however, Christians did not encounter Scripture by privately reading and meditating on it, but by hearing it read aloud and then interpreted at community gatherings. This occurred both because there may have been only one copy of the inspired text available and because ancient and even medieval societies were fundamentally oral cultures. After the invention of the printing press, the increased translation and dispersion of the Bible, and the sixteenth-century reformations, individual believers (especially Protestants) began to "read, mark, learn, and inwardly digest" the Scriptures, as the Anglican Book of Common Prayer elegantly put it in 1662.

Each approach to reading Scripture—private and communal—has its advantages and disadvantages, so it is important for believers to practice both kinds of reading. As early as the fourth century, the Eastern Christian writer Evagrius expressed his conviction that every Christian should awake in the morning with a Bible in hand. Nevertheless, in our individualistic Western culture, it is especially important for Christians to regain the sense of Scripture as a word addressed to *us,* not just to *me.* Reading Scripture in a community of fellow believers—what is sometimes called a covenant discipleship group, small Christian community, house church, Bible study, or fellowship group—can provide structure, wisdom, and accountability. Returning to Rom 12:1–2, we note that Paul says that the Romans' transformation will come through the power of God's grace as they discern God's will *in community* and as together they become a living exegesis of the gospel. Thus it is spiritually important to understand that Romans, like most of the Bible, was written to a *community of believers* and not as a special message to an individual or a select few. As noted elsewhere in this book (especially chapter eleven), contemporary Christians are increasingly recognizing the necessity of "reading in communion" (the title of a landmark book by Stephen Fowl and L. Gregory Jones).

SOME WAYS OF GROWING SPIRITUALLY WITH SCRIPTURE

Over the years, various ways of using Scripture for spiritual growth have been recommended. Three will be described here: meditation, *lectio divina,* and structured questioning. All three can be used privately or in groups.

Meditation

Meditation with a Scripture passage occurs when we read a portion of Scripture and contemplate it or enter into the text imaginatively. For example, we may choose a narrative text and imagine what it might have been like to have been a person in the story. This is much more than idle daydreaming; it is an exercise in *disciplined* imagination. We normally identify with a figure in a story for a particular reason. Who was the person chosen, and why? What is his or her relationship with God like? What kind of moral and spiritual character does this person seem to have? What might we have done differently if we were that person in the story? What does this imaginative process teach us about our own vocation, gifts, flaws, questions, and concerns?

For example, the story of Jonah is a tale about an unwilling prophet who tries to escape God's call. When that is unsuccessful, Jonah reluctantly goes to Nineveh, as commanded by God, to urge the people to repent. When they do so, Jonah is angered, because he believes them to be an evil people who deserve punishment.

Meditating on this story, we might consider how we would have acted in Jonah's place. Would we have possessed a greater willingness to live out the prophetic call? Why or why not? How would we have responded to the Ninevites' repentance? Having asked ourselves such questions, we might then reflect on times we have felt God's promptings in our own life and either ignored them, tried to escape them, or accepted them. Why did we do what we did? What was the impact of our action, or inaction, on our relationship with God?

Lectio Divina

Another method of encountering Scripture for spiritual growth is *lectio divina* (Latin for sacred or holy reading). This method developed among Christians in the monastic period and reached its height during the Middle Ages. Today, Christians from many traditions are rediscovering its spiritual benefits.

Originally, *lectio* involved reading (aloud) and memorizing Scripture as a means to integrate body and mind, a practice that was adopted from the Jewish tradition. The person then meditated on the text by repeating it inwardly and prayerfully dwelling on it in order to evoke personal prayer. In other words, the reader rested in the words, letting them "soak in," so that he or she might grasp their meaning for him- or herself. Many people have compared this kind of contemplative reading to chewing—a completely unhurried, even prolonged process rather than an act of "gulping down" a few morsels. This process may last for a few minutes or for an hour or more. Sometimes in *lectio divina* nothing seems to come to mind, while at other times a great deal is revealed.

Building on the tradition and stressing that "living out" the text is the ultimate goal of lectio, M. Robert Mulholland (*Invitation to a Journey,* 112–15) outlines six steps for contemporary lectio divina:

- *Silencio*—silent preparation

- *Lectio*—receptive reading

- *Meditatio*—processing

- *Oratio*—heartfelt, responsive prayer

- *Contemplatio*—self-abandonment to God and God's will

- *Incarnatio*—living the text

The goal in *lectio* is not to read (much less "study") a whole chapter at a time; in fact, one might ponder one verse or even one part of a verse, letting it resonate in one's heart and soul. Some people deliberately read, not with a terminus in mind, but until they find a word, phrase, or image that strikes them. Take, for example, the experience of reading Luke's story of the crucifixion and encountering Jesus' prayer from the cross: "Father, forgive them; for they do not know what they are doing" (Luke 23:34). What feelings and other responses to God does Jesus' word of love and compassion generate in me? How many times have I been forgiven by God (or by others) because I didn't really know what I was doing? How often have *I* forgiven another because it seemed that the other person didn't know the enormity of his or her actions? If I have never forgiven someone this generously, why not? What does my honest encounter with this text mean in terms of my relationship with God and others?

Structured Questioning

Yet another method of reading Scripture involves *structured questioning* of the text in order to discern how God might be speaking to us through it. In effect, as noted earlier, this means that our questioning the text is a means of allowing the text to question *us*. Several different question formats have proven beneficial. A very simple approach is to ask the text three questions:

- What does this text say?

- What does it mean?

- What does it mean to and for me/us?

Another set of questions, based on the fourfold medieval approach to Scripture discussed in chapter eight, is:

- What did this text say in its original context?

- What does this text urge us to believe (faith)?

- What does this text urge us to anticipate (hope)?

- What does this text urge us to do (love)?

Yet again, we may pose the following three-part question:

- What convictions does God offer us in this text?

- What comfort does God offer us in this text?

- What challenge does God offer us in this text?

CONCLUSION: PRAYING WITH SCRIPTURE

Whether we use meditation, *lectio divina,* or structured questioning, we can join our forbears in faith, encountering God in Scripture and responding to God in prayer and commitment. For this reason, many people refer to all of the approaches to the Bible described in the preceding section as "praying with Scripture" or just "praying Scripture." Such phrases neatly summarize the trust, openness, and transformation necessary for spiritual growth through Bible reading.

FOR FURTHER READING AND STUDY

Casey, Michael. *Sacred Reading: The Ancient Art of* Lectio Divina. Liguori, Mo.: Triumph, 1996. A modern classic.

Harrington, Wilfrid J. *Seeking Spiritual Growth through the Bible.* New York: Paulist, 2002. Not a "how-to" book, but a discussion of major spiritual themes in both the OT and the NT.

Hays, Richard B. "Salvation by Trust: Reading the Bible Faithfully." *The Christian Century* (February 1997): 218–23. A significant call for the use of a hermeneutic of trust in reading the Bible.

Johnson, Luke Timothy. *Living Jesus: Learning the Heart of the Gospel.* San Francisco: HarperSanFrancisco, 1999. A delightful interpretation of the NT as a means to knowing the living Jesus, by one of the foremost NT scholars of our time.

Mulholland, M. Robert, Jr. *Invitation to a Journey: A Road Map for Spiritual Formation.* Downers Grove, Ill.: InterVarsity, 1993. A guide to various means of spiritual growth, including *lectio divina,* by a Protestant biblical scholar.

———. *Shaped by the Word: The Power of Scripture in Spiritual Formation.* Rev. ed. Nashville: Upper Room Books, 2000. A study of the nature of the Bible and of its role in personal spiritual development.

Pennington, M. Basil. *Lectio Divina: Renewing the Ancient Practice of Praying the Scriptures.* New York: Crossroad/Herder & Herder, 1998. A modern classic from a Roman Catholic who is one of the great contemporary contemplative Christians.

Schneiders, Sandra M. *The Revelatory Text: Interpreting the New Testament as Sacred Scripture.* 2d ed. Collegeville, Minn.: Liturgical, 1999. A sophisticated analysis of the interpretation of the NT as human and divine word.

Chapter 15

The Bible and Social Justice: "Learn to Do Right! Seek Justice" *(Isa 1:17 NIV)*

JOHN R. DONAHUE

In this chapter we consider biblical resources for social justice, understood as concern for a community where all people can experience equal dignity as sons and daughters of God, with a special attention to the sufferings of powerless and vulnerable people. We will look at both Testaments, but with emphasis on the OT. Within each Testament we will look at some of the most important writings and themes.

Our exploration begins with a discussion of the vocabulary of justice in the Bible, for the Bible is indeed full of such language—though it does not necessarily correspond to our own justice vocabulary.

SPEAKING OF JUSTICE

A major problem confronting initial reflection on justice in the Bible is the existence of multiple Hebrew terms for justice, and injustice, that do not yield to a one-to-one correspondence in English. The principal biblical terms are *tsedaqah* (used 523 times, along with *tsedeq,* 119 times) and *mishpat* (422 times), which are very often used together. In most contemporary English versions, *tsedaqah* is translated "righteousness," while *mishpat* is rendered "justice" or "judgment." The terms for justice are closely allied to other fundamental biblical concepts, as in the famous covenant renewal text of Hos 2:19–20[1]:

> I will take you for my wife forever; I will take you for my wife in righteousness and in justice (*be tsedeq we be mishpat*), in steadfast love (*be hesed*), and in mercy

---

[1] NRSV; NAB = 2:21–22.

(*be raḥamîm*). I will take you for my wife in faithfulness (*b 'emunah*); and you shall know the LORD. (see also Isa 32:16–17)

That English translations of the Bible generally renders *tsedaqah* as "righteousness" and *mishpat* as "justice" can be deceptive for contemporary readers. The *Oxford English Dictionary* defines righteousness as "justice, uprightness, rectitude, conformity of life to the requirements of the divine moral law, virtue, and integrity." In most people's minds, however, "righteousness" evokes primarily *personal* rectitude, virtue, or holiness, and the *social* dimension of the original Hebrew is lost. This has resulted in a virtual "biblical dialect" where "righteousness" is relegated to the sphere of religion and personal piety. Imagine, for instance, people's reaction if the United States had a "Department of Righteousness" (rather than the "Department of Justice"), or we talked about "social righteousness" (instead of "social justice").

Recent commentators, however, have stressed the social dimension of *tsedaqah* and *mishpat*. For example, Walter Brueggemann, arguably the premier OT theologian today, describes *tsedaqah* as "equitable, generative social relations" (in his book *Isaiah 1–39*, p. 48). In commenting on Amos 5:24, Barbara Johnson, author of two foundational studies of these terms, writes, "Here *tsedeq* is understood as the normative principle and *mishpat* as the standard of conduct which must conform to *tsedeq* (cf. Ps. 119:160)." Especially significant is the joining of *tsedaqah* and *mishpat* to convey a single meaning, which many recent scholars render as "social justice" (e.g., Isa 1:27; 5:16; 9:7; 32:16; 56:1; Pss 72:2; 89:14).

In general terms, the biblical idea of justice can be described as *fidelity to the demands of a relationship.* God is just when he acts as a God should, defending or vindicating his people or punishing violations of the covenant. People are just when they are in right relationship to God and to other humans. In contrast to modern individualism, "to live" in ancient Israel was to be united with others in a social context, either by bonds of family or by covenant relationships. This web of relationships—king with people, judge with those pleading a cause, family with tribe and kinfolk, the community with the resident alien and those suffering in their midst, and all with the covenant God—constitutes the world in which life is played out. The demands of the differing relationships cannot be specified in advance but must be seen in the different settings of Israel's history. "Biblical justice" is concerned not so much with recognizing rights but with creating right relationships with God and within the human family.

TORAH AND SOCIAL JUSTICE

In contrast to a philosophical foundation for justice, biblical justice is mediated by God's self-disclosure and human response. Paradigmatic for this is the covenant between God and the people. When Israel is freed from the slavery of Egypt, this freedom is to be a *bonded* freedom; it is not simply freedom from external oppression, but a freedom expressed in commitments to God and others.

The Decalogue

Foundational to the bonded freedom of the Sinai Covenant are the Ten Commandments, the Decalogue (found in two versions: Exod 20:1–17 and Deut 5:6–21), which represent early covenant law. As Walter Harrelson has carefully shown (in *The Ten Commandments and Human Rights*), these "ten words" have a similar structure—a prologue that roots the observance of the commands in what God has done for the people, and then four elements:

- God's exclusive claim on humanity (the initial three commandments);

- God's basic institutions (Sabbath observance and reverence for parents);

- Basic human obligations (respect for life; sexual fidelity); and

- Basic social obligations (respecting the goods of others).

Though the word "justice" is not mentioned here, Harrelson notes how the Decalogue reverberates through history as a foundation for human rights and equitable social relationships.

The Law Codes

The distinctive understandings of justice are revealed in the law codes of Israel and particularly in their concern for the powerless in the community. The codes themselves comprise:

- *The Covenant Code* (Exod 20:22–23:33), parts of which date from northern Israel in the ninth century B.C.E., and which reflect premonarchic rural life (though, like the rest of the Pentateuch, the Code receives its final shape after the exile);

- *The Deuteronomic Code* (Deut 12–26), which embodies traditions from the seventh century B.C.E., and perhaps from Josiah's reform, but which was incorporated into the full-blown "Deuteronomic history" only after the exile; and

- *The Holiness Code* (Lev 17–26), put together after the exile, often attributed to priestly circles, and similar to the thought of Ezekiel.

Especially significant are the sections of the codes that deal with those who are without power (often made concrete as the poor, the widow, the orphan, and the stranger in the land). In Israel, care for such persons was part of the "contrast society" that is created through the exodus, so that responsibility for the well-being of such people rests on the covenant community as a whole and not simply on the king.

The Covenant Code

Concern for the powerless emerges as part of the Covenant Code (Exod 20:22–23:33). The first important section is Exod 22:21–27. Here God says, "You shall not wrong or oppress a resident alien, for you were aliens in the land of Egypt" (v. 21; note the motivation of a contrast society). The following verse forbids abuse of the widow and the orphan, with the promise that God will heed their cry and "kill . . . with the sword" their oppressors. The section concludes with the prohibition of lending to the poor at interest and the duty of restoring a neighbor's coat taken in surety for a loan. The motivation is God in his role as the protector of the poor: "And if your neighbor cries out to me, I will listen, for I am compassionate" (Exod 22:27).

The next section of the Covenant Code contains a series of laws on the proper administration of justice. For example, one text says, "you shall not side with the majority so as to pervert justice; nor shall you be partial to the poor in a lawsuit" (Exod 23:2b–3). The prohibition of "partiality" to the poor in the specific context of a lawsuit does not contradict the concern for the marginal, since Exod 23:6 immediately says that "[y]ou shall not pervert the justice due to the poor in their lawsuits" (with no corresponding statement on the rich or powerful), and 23:9 repeats the protection of the alien.

The Deuteronomic Code

The second major block of legal material that deals with the poor comes from the Deuteronomic legislation of Deut 12–26. While retaining an ideal that there will be "no one in need among you, because the Lord is sure to bless you" (Deut 15:4; cf. Acts 4:34), Deuteronomy realistically states that "there will never cease to be some in need on the earth," and it therefore issues a command: "Open your hand to the poor and needy neighbor in the land" (Deut 15:11). More strongly than the other codes, Deuteronomy commands justice and compassion for the powerless (Deut 15:1–18; 24:10–15; 26:11–12).

The historical significance of Deuteronomy is as evidence for a continuing concern in Israel's law for the *personae miserae* (Latin for "afflicted people") that attempts to institutionalize the covenant ideal through law and practice. Deuteronomy in its present canonical location is cast in the form of farewell speeches from Moses to the people on the brink of the promised land. The land is God's gift on condition of fidelity to the covenant (see Deut 12:1: "These are the statutes and ordinances that you must diligently observe in the land that the Lord, the God of your ancestors, has given you to occupy"). When read *after the exile,* it can be seen as a warning against an infidelity that allows the kind of society to develop that is in opposition to the exodus event and the Sinai covenant.

The Holiness Code

The Holiness Code (Lev 17–26) contains provisions similar to Deuteronomy. According to Lev 19:9–10 and 23:22, gleanings from the harvest are to be left for "the poor and the alien." The Holiness Code has other provisions for the poor that spell out in detail responsibilities to the poor, very often those who have come suddenly upon hard times (Lev 25:35–42, 47–52). Leviticus is also more concerned with the details of repayment of debts and cultic offerings made by the poor (e.g., Lev 12:8 = Luke 2:24).

Summary

The events of salvation history, especially the leading out from Egypt and the covenant at Sinai, are thus the foundations in Israel of a society that seeks justice and manifests concern for the marginal. This concern is incorporated in law and custom, which take different shapes in different historical circumstances, stretching over five centuries. As founding documents not only of the historical people of Israel, but also of the Christian church, they offer a vision of life in society before God that is to inform religious belief and social practice.

The laws of Israel have two great values. First, they show that religious belief must be translated into law and custom that guide life in community and protect the vulnerable. Second, while not offering concrete directives for our complex socioeconomic world, they offer a vision of a "contrast society," not ruled by power and greed, where the treatment of the marginal becomes the touchstone of "right relationship" to God. Christians today must ask soberly how our lives provide a contrast society, and whether, when we think of our "right relation" to God, the concerns of the marginal in our own time have been really made concrete in our attitudes and style of life.

BIBLICAL JUSTICE, THE POOR, AND THE PROPHETIC CRITIQUE OF WEALTH

Concern for the poor and the marginal is a pervasive biblical motif in both Testaments. The biblical vocabulary for the poor is rich and diverse, but all the terms suggest a sense of oppression or lack of the necessities of life: for example, the Hebrew terms *'anî* (plural *'aniyyîm*), from the root to be "bent down"; *'ebyon,* suggesting "miserable or wretched"; and *dal,* also from a root suggesting "bent over." The NT uses predominantly *ptōchos,* literally "beggar." The importance of the terminology is twofold. First, it shows that "poverty" in itself is not a value. Even word origins reveal that the Bible views the poor as bent down, wretched, and beggars. While the Bible has great concern for "the poor," poverty itself is an evil.

Second, the terminology (as well as actual use) is a caution against misunderstanding or misuse of the phrase "spiritually poor." Though later literature (the Psalms and the Qumran scrolls) often equates the poor with the humble or meek, and though the poor are those people open to God (in contrast to idolatrous or blind rich people), the primary meaning of the term is an economic condition. When the "poor in spirit" are praised, as in Matt 5:3, it is because in addition to their material poverty they are open to God's presence and love. Certain contemporary usages of the notion of "spiritual poverty," which allow it to be used of extremely wealthy people who are unhappy even amid prosperity, are not faithful to the biblical tradition.

Nor is an idea of "spiritual poverty" as indifference to riches amid wealth faithful to the Bible. The "poor" in the Bible are almost without exception *powerless people* who experience economic and social deprivation. In both Isaiah and the Psalms, the poor are often victims of the injustice of the rich and powerful. Isaiah tells us that the elders and princes "devour" the poor and grind their faces in the dust (Isa 3:14–15); they turn aside the needy from injustice to rob the poor of their rights (Isa 10:2); wicked people "ruin" the poor with lying words (Isa 32:7). In the Psalms, the poor, often called "the downtrodden," are contrasted not simply to the rich but to the wicked and the powerful (e.g., Ps 10:2–10; Ps 72: 4, 12–14). Even today, poverty is most often not simply an economic issue but arises when one group can exploit or oppress another.

When a people forgets its origins or loses sight of its ideals, figures arise who often speak a strident message to summon them to return to God. In Israel's history the prophetic movement represents such a phenomenon. The prophet, as the Greek origin of the name suggests (*pro-phēmi,* "speak for"), speaks on behalf of another, in a dual sense. The prophet speaks on behalf of God (he or she is a "forth-teller"), who also speaks on behalf of those who have no one to speak for them, specifically the powerless and poor in the land.

Those concerned for social justice among Catholics, Protestants, Orthodox, and Jews have continually drawn on the powerful language of the great prophets of Israel, who castigate the abuse of justice by the powerful and give a voice to the voiceless poor. Though there is no substitute for deep engagement with the biblical texts, a few "snapshots" of this preaching can lead hopefully to a deeper engagement.

Amos, one of the earliest prophets, laments the sins of Israel: "You who turn *justice* into bitterness and cast *righteousness* to the ground" (Amos 5:7 NIV; emphasis added). This is manifest when "they . . . trample the head of the poor into the dust of the earth" (2:7) and engage in deceptive business practices, "buying the poor for silver and the needy for a pair of sandals" (8:5–6). For Amos, the root cause of these sins is the lavish lifestyle of the upper classes of the northern kingdom (3:15–4:3; 6:4–7).

A generation later, Isaiah of Jerusalem, himself from the upper classes and one who has easy access to the king, utters some of the harshest criticisms of injustice, calling the city once known for its justice and righteousness a "whore" (Isa 1:21). He castigates the leaders because God looked for justice, but found bloodshed, and for righteousness but heard rather a cry (5:7). In capsule form, Isaiah captures the cause of the city's infidelity: they "deprive the poor of their rights and withhold justice from the oppressed of my people, making widows their prey and robbing the fatherless" (10:2, NIV). Also, like Amos, Isaiah avers that the desire for ostentatious wealth drives the oppression of the poor by the rich (1:23; 5:8).

A century after Isaiah, beginning during the reign of the reforming king Josiah, Jeremiah repeats in vivid imagery the attack on the self-satisfied wealthy:

> Like a cage full of birds, their houses are full of treachery; therefore they have become great and rich, they have grown fat and sleek. They know no limits in deeds of wickedness; they do not judge with justice the cause of the orphan [or "fatherless," NAB], to make it prosper, and they do not defend the rights of the needy. (Jer 5:27–29)

More strongly than his predecessors, Jeremiah roots the quest for justice in the very nature of God: " 'I am the LORD, who exercises kindness, justice and righteousness on earth, for in these I delight,' declares the LORD" (9:24 NIV). Jeremiah therefore describes the "good king" Josiah in these words: " 'He judged the cause of the poor and needy; then it was well. Is not this to know me?' says the Lord" (Jer 22:16).

The most significant shift in Israel's religious history occurs with the Babylonian exile (587–539 B.C.E.) and then the long years of occupation by foreign powers (Persia, Greece, and Rome). Prophetic activity virtually ceases, and this period witnesses the rise of apocalyptic thought where the hope for a just society is transferred to the end-time, when a new heaven and new earth will appear with peace and justice. During this period, as Ezekiel testified, there is a rise in a sense of individual responsibility, so that justice takes on the nuance of an individual's right relation to God—which is most significant for the debate about Paul's understanding of justification by faith.

OTHER OLD TESTAMENT VOICES

Space does not permit a full discussion of social justice in the entire Hebrew Bible, though it does appear not only in the legal and prophetic materials discussed above but also in wisdom literature, the psalms, and narrative literature. Examples from these texts include:

- *Wisdom literature*—Prov. 14:21, 31; 19:1; 21:13; Sir 4:1–8;

- *Psalms*—Pss. 10; 11:7; 37; 72; and

- *Narrative literature*—Gen. 38; 1 Kgs 21 (Naboth's vineyard); 2 Sam 12:1–4 (Nathan's parable); and the entire book of Ruth.

NEW TESTAMENT PERSPECTIVES

It is not only the OT that contains a call for social justice. We find it also in the NT.

The Teaching and Ministry of Jesus

While it is axiomatic to say that Jesus was not a social reformer, his teachings and actions had strong social implications during his lifetime, and they continue to shape the consciences of his followers today. A key to his life is his proclamation of the imminence of God's reign or kingdom, both through direct proclamation and in parable (e.g., Mark 1:14–15; 4:26–32). Jesus also brings about the kingdom through acts of power (exorcisms and healings: e.g., Luke 10:9; 11:20; 17:21) and by his association with, and offer of God's love to, "the marginal" of his day, especially tax collectors and sinners.

Continuing the Prophetic Voice

Many scholars today locate Jesus' teaching in the wider context of different "restorationist" movements alive in Palestine. Jesus, like the prophets of old, summoned people to a renewed dedication to the primacy of God in their lives and to a renewed concern for their neighbor (i.e., the dual command of love, Mark 12:28–34). This command of love is made perfect in love and forgiveness of enemies (Matt 5:43–48). The God disclosed by Jesus makes his sun shine on the good and the bad. Jesus' teaching breaks down the penchant that people have for dividing the world into clearly identifiable friends and enemies, outsiders and insiders.

Like many of his contemporaries, Jesus hoped for the intervention of God in history in the near future (imminent eschatology), yet he proclaimed that the reign of God has *already* begun in his teaching and action, and that people are to live in response to it (eschatology in the process of realization, or inaugurated eschatology). The eschatological thrust of Jesus' teaching (and later of Paul's) should not be invoked to undermine its effective impact (as if the nearness of the end makes ethical behavior superfluous), but is rather "a view from the future" of what life should be *in the present.* The fact that God's definitive reign is still in the future does not dispense us from living according to its norms and values in our everyday lives.

Jesus' teaching is a summons to conversion that will affect the way people live in the world. In the Lord's Prayer (in the Matthean version, Matt 6:9–10), Jesus prays that God's will be done and God's kingdom come *on earth.* In the Beatitudes, which (like the Lord's Prayer) are in the Q source and thus have high claims to being authentic sayings of the historical Jesus, Jesus calls the poor and the oppressed "blessed." He does so, not because their actual condition is such, but because the kingdom he proclaims and enacts will confront those values and conditions that have made them marginal. When Jesus says that "the kingdom of God is theirs" (referring to the poor), he is not simply promising future blessings, but rather claiming that the reigning of God is on the side of the poor and other suffering people mentioned in the Beatitudes (Matt 5:3–11).

Proclaiming in Parables

The kingdom as proclaimed by Jesus challenged deep-seated expectations of his hearers. This is especially true in his parables, which contain frequent reversals: those who worked only one hour received the same wage as those who had worked all day (Matt 20:1–16); Jesus says that one should invite, not friends, but unknown strangers gathered from the highways to a banquet (Luke 14:12–14); the hated outsider, a Samaritan, teaches the true meaning of love of neighbor (Luke 10:25–37); the prodigal is accepted as readily as the dutiful (Luke 15:11–32). These reversals challenge deeply held values and invite people to enter imaginatively into a different world, providing a paradigm for the manner in which a new vision of social justice can be presented to people today.

The most profound reversal in the teaching of Jesus is in the "parable" of the sheep and the goats, where those who are called "just"[2] are people who care for the hungry, the thirsty, the stranger, the naked, the sick, and the imprisoned, and who, at the end of history, will be revealed as the brothers and sisters of Jesus (Matt 25:31–46).

---

[2] Greek *dikaioi,* usually translated (as in the case of parallel OT terms) as "righteous."

Suffering the Cost

Jesus' acceptance of marginal groups countered the evaluation of people by class and social status that was characteristic of first-century society. Also, by associating with those seen as ritually unclean, and by his willingness to break the law on their behalf, Jesus alienated the religious establishment of his day in such a way that he was both a political and a religious threat. By taking the side of these people, Jesus—like the OT prophets—gave a voice to the voiceless. Ultimately, Jesus died by a mode of execution, crucifixion, reserved for those who were threats to the "public order," due to collusion between certain Jerusalem temple authorities (whose power rested on proper subservience to Rome) and the Roman prefect, Pontius Pilate. Jesus' life is a paradigm of the cost of discipleship for those who take the side of the poor and the marginal.

The Gospel of Luke

The presentation of Jesus in Luke has long sustained people committed to social justice. Jesus is clearly a prophet in Luke, and his inaugural sermon repeats Isaiah's good news for the poor: release to captives, sight to the blind, and freedom to the oppressed (4:18–19; Isa 61:1–9). As a prophet, Jesus speaks on behalf of God (6:7, 20–49) and shows concern for the widow (7:11–17) and for the stranger in the land (e.g., the Samaritan, 10:29–36; 17:11–19).

Allied to this is the strong prophetic critique of wealth that only the Lukan Jesus expresses so fervently. The Lukan Beatitudes are followed by woes on the rich (6:20–26); the rich man is a fool because of his covetousness and because he did not leave the gleanings of his harvest for the poor (12:15–21; see Lev 19:9–10; Deut 24:19–22). The rich man is condemned because he does not even see the poor Lazarus at his gate (16:14–31). The true disciple of Jesus is one who can leave all things to follow him (5:28; 12:33), and the banquets of the community are to be celebrated with the poor, the maimed, the blind, and the lame (14:13–22).

Other aspects of Luke are important to a NT foundation for social justice. *Compassion* is an important motif in Luke and is listed as a motive for the incarnation (1:78). When Jesus "sees" and "has compassion," he restores to life the widow's son (7:13), and when the Samaritan "sees" and "has compassion" he enters the world of the dying man as a healer (10:34). Compassion is the bridge over which men and women must cross if they are to enter the world of the suffering neighbor. Biblical social justice must involve a renewed vision before it can move to saving action.

Noteworthy also is the inclusive character of Luke's vision. In Acts, the early communities include people of different races (e.g., the Ethiopian official of Acts 8:27) and transcend ethnic origin (Acts 10:14, 27 and 15:51, where the Gentiles are incorporated). By constantly juxtaposing stories of men and women in the Gospel, Luke affirms the complimentarity of both in salvation history:

- Annunciation to Zechariah and to Mary (1:8–23);

- Hymn of praise of Mary (1:46–55) and of Zechariah (1:67–79);

- Miracle on behalf of the centurion at Capernaum and the widow at Nain (7:1–17);

- Good Samaritan and Martha and Mary (10:25–42);

- Twin parables:

  - man with mustard seed, woman with leaven (13:18–21);

  - lost sheep, lost coin (15:4–10);

  - widow and judge, Pharisee and tax collector (18:1–14).

Furthermore, in Luke both men and women follow Jesus to the cross (23:49), and the resurrection proclamation/appearance involves both women and men (24:1–35). This motif is continued in Acts (2:12–14; 5:1–11; 9:32–42; 16:13–34; 17:34).

Paul

Rather paradoxically, Paul, the author who most uses the term "justice" (Greek *dikaiosynē*, often translated "righteousness"), has unfortunately not been a major resource for those interested in social justice. This may arise from the individualism inherent in the traditional "justification by faith debate" and from the rejection of "works righteousness" by large segments of Christianity. Yet those sections of his letters where Paul spells out the *effects* of justification by grace through faith mirror the kind of covenant community envisioned in the OT.

Theologically, Paul states that the Christ event frees the Christian from sin, law, and death. Equally important as this "freedom *from*" is the Pauline notion of "freedom *for*." Paul states this succinctly: "For freedom Christ has set us free" (Gal 5:1a). Freedom for Paul is liberation from the self-serving and self-destructive aspects of "striving" and "boasting" in human achievements in order to direct one's attention to the needs of others.

In Galatians (which, along with Romans, is his major theological statement on justification), after somewhat polemically rejecting those opponents who want to reimpose Jewish practices on Gentile Christians, Paul says: "For you were called to freedom, brothers and sisters; only do not use your freedom as an opportunity for self-indulgence [NAB: 'the flesh'; Greek *sarx*], but through love become slaves [or 'servants'] to one another" (Gal 5:13). In the same context, Paul alludes to the dual covenantal requirements toward God and neighbor in highlighting the essence of the Christian experience: "faith [toward God] working through love [toward others]" (Gal 5:6). Paul then goes on to describe "walking" according to the Spirit and "walking" according to the flesh (Gal 5:16–21).[3] The virtues ("the fruit of the Spirit") and vices listed here for the most part either foster or destroy life in community. Paul then concludes this whole section with the statement, "Bear one another's burdens, and so you will fulfill the law of Christ" (Gal 6:2 NAB). Therefore, the justified and graced Christian is a person who seeks not a community of isolated individuals but one in which concern for the weak and suffering is the touchstone of living according to the law of Christ. Such concern includes economic justice (e.g., 2 Cor 8:13–15).[4]

CONCLUSION

Any theology or practice of social justice must attend to the whole Bible and especially to the rich resources of the OT. The stress on law there reminds us that any vision of care and concern for neighbor must be translated into binding practice. The prophetic heritage is a constant warning that practice can be corrupted and that people must be summoned to renewal and reform. The prophetic edge of the teaching of Jesus must not be submerged by pietism and individualism. Also, the Bible is not impartial in a philosophical sense, but on the side of the powerless and those most in need. True knowledge of God and actions on behalf of justice are complementary, not in opposition.

Karl Barth, arguably the greatest Christian theologian of the last century, once wrote that to ask what the Bible teaches

> . . . is a dangerous question. We might do better not to come too near this burning bush. For we are sure to betray what is—behind *us*. The Bible gives to every man [and woman] and to every era such answers to their questions as they deserve. (*The Word of God and the Word of Man*, p. 32)

Issues of social justice—of the gap between the rich and the poor, and of respect for the dignity of others—are paramount in our world today. Can we approach the burning bush?

---

[3] Paul's vivid language about "walking" is frequently translated in terms of "living."

[4] Space does not permit discussion of other NT writings, such as James, but see the brief summary of James in chapter four.

FOR FURTHER READING AND STUDY

Barth, Karl. *The Word of God and the Word of Man.* New York and Evanston: Harper and Row, 1957. A theological classic.

Birch, Bruce C. *Let Justice Roll: The Old Testament, Ethics and the Christian Life.* Louisville: Westminster John Knox, 1991. An excellent survey of the OT material.

Brueggemann, Walter. *The Prophetic Imagination.* Rev. ed. Minneapolis: Fortress, 2001. A very influential and challenging interpretation of the prophets.

Donahue, John R. *What Does the Lord Require: A Bibliographical Essay on the Bible and Social Justice.* St Louis: Institute of Jesuit Sources, 2000. An extensive bibliography with introductory comments.

Grassi, Joseph A. *Informing the Future: Social Justice in the New Testament.* Mahwah, N.J.: Paulist, 2004. A fine discussion of texts with suggestions about their relevance for today.

Harrelson, Walter. *The Ten Commandments and Human Rights.* Philadelphia: Fortress, 1980. Repr. Macon, Ga.: Mercer University Press, 1997. A foundational work on the Decalogue.

Herzog II, William R. *Jesus, Justice and the Reign of God: A Ministry of Liberation.* Louisville: Westminster John Knox, 1999. An original and powerful study of the social dimension of Jesus' teaching.

Howard-Brook, Wes, and Sharon H. Ringe, eds. *The New Testament: Introducing the Way of Discipleship.* Maryknoll, N.Y.: Orbis, 2002. A fine collection of essays relating the NT books to themes of social justice.

Johnson, Barbara. "*mishpat.*" Pages 86–98 of *Theological Dictionary of the Old Testament.* Vol. IX. Edited by G. Johannes Botterweck, H. Ringgren, and H.-J. Fabry. Grand Rapids: Eerdmans, 2003. The best scholarly study of one of the key terms related to social justice available.

———. "*tsedaqah.*" Pages 239–64 of *Theological Dictionary of the Old Testament.* Vol. XII. Edited by G. Johannes Botterweck, H. Ringgren and H.-J. Fabry. Grand Rapids: Eerdmans, 2003. The best scholarly study of another of the key terms related to social justice available.

Pleins, John David, *The Social Visions of the Hebrew Bible: A Theological Introduction.* Louisville: Westminster John Knox, 2000. The most important work on this topic of the past decade.

Stegemann, W. *The Gospel and the Poor.* Philadelphia: Fortress, 1984. An excellent, short overview of NT themes.

Weinfeld, Moshe. *Social Justice in Ancient Israel and in the Ancient Near East.* Minneapolis: Fortress, 1995. A comparison of early Israelite concepts of justice with those of surrounding cultures, showing how concern for justice and liberation shaped Israelite society.

Chapter 16

The Bible and Ecumenism: "That They May All Be One" *(John 17:21)*

JANYCE C. JORGENSEN

Formative to ecumenical efforts among divided Christians is the prayer of Jesus from John's gospel:

> ... that they may all be one. As you, Father, are in me and I am in you, may they also be in us, so that the world may believe that you have sent me. The glory that you have given me I have given them, so that they may be one, as we are one. (John 17:21–22)

Jesus' words assert that the unity sought by Christians throughout the ages is not something humanly created, but rather is given in Christ. Thus, efforts at unity are our becoming what we already are—one in Christ—and are reflective of the unity among the Father, Son, and Holy Spirit. Jesus' prayer for the unity of his followers has guided **ecumenism** throughout the centuries.

The Bible as a whole and the NT in particular have played a varied role in the promotion of the unity of the church. In one sense, each Christian group has used the NT as the foundation of its distinct tenets and practices, sometimes suggesting that it has the true faith while others have deviated from the teachings of Jesus and his apostles. Such efforts at self-identification and understanding, while important within each Christian tradition, have more often been divisive rather than unifying. In another sense, however, various Christian traditions can talk about the Bible as a common source of divine revelation, where Christians of various shapes and sizes hear of the good news of Jesus Christ. Scripture, then, serves as the primary source for Christians to speak and learn about their Christ-given unity.

This brief chapter on the Bible and ecumenism will trace the role of the Bible in the ecumenical efforts of the last century. It will note the global nature of Christian ecumenism yet also give a more detailed analysis of the significant and distinct contributions of ecumenism in North America. It will consider ecumenism among the Catholic, Protestant, and Orthodox traditions, but it will focus on the rich ecumenical conversations between Catholics and Lutherans (in part because I am a Lutheran minister). It will recognize significant accomplishments in the areas of biblical translations and ecumenical Bible societies and will study in more depth the well-documented and voluminous genre known as ecumenical dialogue. Finally, it will chart a course for the future relationship of the Bible and ecumenism, as directed by certain new initiatives.

CHARACTERISTICS OF ECUMENICAL STUDY OF THE BIBLE

First, a few observations about the nature of ecumenical biblical study are in order. We begin by noting what many others have discovered: that ecumenical biblical study has been overwhelmingly historical-critical, as scientific methods are applied to the biblical text to determine its meaning in its historical setting and to its original audience. While it is accepted that the biblical writings are infused with the faith-perspective of their authors and their communities, efforts at excavating historical words and deeds within the narrative proclamation figure prominently in historical-critical and ecumenical study.

Also, we note the tension in ecumenical biblical study in the relationship between Scripture and Tradition. While the Christian churches have a common understanding and definition of what constitutes the canonical NT, different denominations have points of commonality as well as points of divergence in their traditional elements. For example, while the ancient creeds of the church (the Nicene Creed and the Apostles' Creed) are common elements of tradition for many Christian churches, other traditions—such as Lutheranism's "canon within a canon" or Catholicism's role of the magisterium as an interpreter of Scripture—are distinctive of their respective denominations. While it is often said that the role of Tradition in biblical interpretation is exclusively a Roman Catholic or Orthodox phenomenon, it should be remembered that all Christian churches and traditions, in varying degrees and ways, bring considerations out of their respective traditions to the task of biblical interpretation. As noted in chapter eleven, Protestants are now recognizing this reality.

Finally, Scripture is the starting point, the bridge, and the ending point in ecumenical discourse. To say that Scripture is the starting point is to assert that in ecumenical dialogue the Bible has the highest authority in matters of faith; the Bible is the first and foremost source when discussing theological issues. To say that Scripture is the bridge in ecumenical discourse is to maintain that Scripture is the ultimate norm for all Christians, whether every point of interpretation is agreed upon or not. To say that Scripture is the ending point in ecumenical discourse is to ensure that subsequent church teaching from the time of the early church to the present be evaluated in light of its faithfulness to the biblical witness. (On these points, see Tavard, "The Bible in Ecumenism," pp. 321–22, as well as the important book by the prominent Catholic biblical scholar Joseph Fitzmyer, *Scripture: The Soul of Theology,* p. 96.)

MODEST BEGINNINGS: THE BIBLE AND ECUMENISM IN STUDENT MOVEMENTS, MISSIONARY CONFERENCES, AND THE WORLD COUNCIL OF CHURCHES

The relationship between the Bible and ecumenism can be traced to the modest beginnings in the international youth student movements of the late nineteenth and early twentieth centuries. Traveling youth staying in Christian student hostels in different parts of the world would gather for Bible study and prayer. Although from different churches and cultures, these students shared a sense of purpose in the unity they realized in Jesus Christ.

The movement was formalized in 1895 in the creation of the World Christian Student Federation (WCSF), which in many ways served as a training ground for the future leaders of the ecumenical movement. Much credit is given to the efforts of Suzanne de Dietrich of the WSCF (and later of the Ecumenical Institute in Bossey, Switzerland). She devoted decades to enabling youth to share in the ecumenical study of Scripture.

Missionary efforts in the early twentieth century also brought to light ecumenical concerns. In particular, Christian missionaries of different churches and traditions often found themselves to be rivals in the same mission land. The World Missionary Conference at Edinburgh in 1910 brought back the urgency and the importance of Jesus' prayer that his followers be one. Speaking at Edinburgh for the biblical principles of the unity of the church in mission was Bishop Charles Brent, an Anglican Missionary in the Philippines, and American Episcopal student John Mott, two early ecumenical leaders. The WCSF, as well as missionary efforts, continued to shape and inform ecumenical Bible study throughout the first half of the twentieth century.

An "Ecumenical Institute" was established in 1946 in Bossey, Switzerland, for study, dialogue, and prayer, with one of the subjects of ecumenical study being "The Bible, the World, and the Universal Church." That same year, a predecessor study group of the World Council of Churches (see further below) gathered to study its first chosen topic: "From the Bible to the Modern World." Both studies demonstrate how the Bible served as the starting point of ecumenical study.

In 1948, the World Council of Churches (WCC) was formed. From its inception, the study of Scripture was foundational to this organization of Protestant churches throughout the world. Biblical topics and new directions in biblical studies were integral to the work of the WCC, which considered and received many studies related to the Bible and ecumenism at its gatherings. A few of these studies and topics were:

- "Scripture, Tradition, and traditions" (Montreal, 1963);

- "The Significance of the Hermeneutical Problem for the Ecumenical Movement" (Bristol, 1967); and

- "Authority of the Bible" (Louvain, 1971).

(For further discussion of the WCSF, the Ecumenical Institute, and the WCC, see Weber, "The Bible: Its Role in the Ecumenical Movement" and Dietrich, *God's Unfolding Purpose*).

The WCC's commitment to ecumenical study of the Bible was fortified by its cooperative efforts with the United Bible Societies (UBS). The UBS was formed in 1946 as a federation of Protestant Bible Societies from around the world that previously had existed and worked independently of one another. The primary mission of the individual societies, as well as that of the new federation, was ecumenical cooperation in the translation and dissemination of the Scriptures. A longstanding joint committee of the WCC and the UBS (1951–1968) developed a study and eventually a joint statement on the "Bible and the Ecumenical Movement" (Uppsala, 1968).

In its own right, the UBS has served to coordinate the efforts of member societies throughout the world. Since 1946, the UBS has provided technical assistance to, and financial coordination of, efforts in translation. UBS-affiliated and independent societies have produced translations of the Bible, in portion or in whole, in more than 2,000 languages and dialects. (For further discussion of the UBS, see Weber, "The Bible" and Cann, "Bible Societies.")[1]

ROMAN CATHOLICS, THE BIBLE, AND ECUMENISM

The Roman Catholic Church was a relative latecomer to the ecumenical scene. While the Second Vatican Council (Vatican II, 1962–1965) is often regarded as the impetus for biblical renewal among Roman Catholics, seeds for re-

---

[1] The UBS has also gathered groups of international scholars to produce a series of critical editions of the Greek NT, the first of which appeared in 1966.

newal had been planted two decades earlier in the writings of Pope Pius XII. In 1943, he issued the papal encyclical *Divino Afflante Spiritu*, which promoted the use of modern methods in Catholic biblical study (see chapter twelve). Thus, Roman Catholic scholars began to make use of the historical-critical method, and by the time of the Second Vatican Council, these efforts were noticed, celebrated, and further encouraged.

Within the documents of Vatican II, two documents hold special significance for the topic of the Bible and ecumenism: *Dei Verbum* (the *Dogmatic Constitution on Divine Revelation*) charts the use of Scripture in the Church's life in regard to its formal teaching, theology, and spiritual life; and *Unitas Redintegratio* (the Decree on Ecumenism) maintains that Scripture is of prime importance in ecumenical dialogues.

Both *Dei Verbum* and *Unitas Redintegratio* recognize the ecumenical sticking point that the role of the magisterium (the Church's official teaching authority) creates in the interpretation of Scripture, though that role is strongly reaffirmed:

> The authentic magisterium has a particular place in the explanation and proclamation of the word of God. (*Unitas Redintegratio*, 21)

> The task of providing an authentic interpretation of God's word in Scripture has been entrusted only to the Church's living magisterium, the authority of which is wielded in the name of Jesus Christ. (*Dei Verbum*, 10)

With a renewed interest in the place of Scripture in its teaching and theology, a clear understanding of the role of the magisterium, and a deep and abiding concern for the "separated brethren" (as the Council documents sometimes call non-Catholic Christians), the Roman Catholic Church was ready to enter into the realm of serious and thoughtful ecumenical dialogue.

BILATERAL DIALOGUES

The Bible and ecumenism are uniquely intertwined in the Christian church's recent flurry of **bilateral** (two-party) **dialogues.** The latter half of the twentieth century for the church can aptly be characterized as "ecumenical" because of the tremendous efforts and results in this specialized format of ecumenical discussion. Bilateral dialogues have taken place between different Protestant denominations, as well as between Roman Catholics and Protestants. The Orthodox Church has also participated in bilateral dialogues with Catholics and with Protestants.

In bilateral dialogues, particularly between Protestant denominations, **full communion** (mutual recognition of sacraments) is generally the goal, and it has been realized between several Protestant bodies. In other dialogue efforts, where full communion is not stated as an intended or imminent goal, the purpose of the dialogue is to create a closer fellowship between the churches. A still more modest goal is a deeper appreciation of each other's tradition and beliefs.

While Scripture is at the heart of bilateral dialogues, ecumenical biblical study is not the stated purpose for coming together for dialogue. Most often, dialogue team members gather around what have been identified as "church-dividing" or "neuralgic" issues. Biblical, theological, confessional, historical, and sometimes also liturgical studies shed new light on an ancient problem, in an attempt to determine whether the issue must continue to divide the churches.

As George Tavard points out in an important article ("The Bible in Ecumenism"), there have not been any formal statements by churches involved in ecumenical dialogue regarding the place of Scripture in ecumenical methodology. Some dialogues, however, have treated the issue of the "fundamental problem" of the place of Scripture in theology. In the 1978 document *Teaching Authority and Infallibility: Lutherans and Catholics in Dialogue VI*, the dialogue team speaks of the primacy of the gospel, and of Scripture, Tradition, and Church as means of transmission in service to the gospel. Scripture is the primary witness to the gospel, and is normative for all later Tradition (p. 13). This shared understanding of the place of Scripture in theology comes very close to the Reformation principle of *sola Scriptura* (Scripture alone).

A Case Study in Bilateral Dialogues: Lutherans and Catholics

In the North American dialogue between Lutherans and Roman Catholics, which commenced shortly after Vatican II and spanned nearly three decades, the study of Scripture has been given its most important place in ecumenical discussions. For this reason, and because Lutheran perspectives on Scripture bring into sharp focus the concerns of Protestantism generally, we will consider this particular dialogue at some length.

Lutherans brought their principle of *sola Scriptura* to the dialogue. Historically, Luther and the Reformers sought to reemphasize the truths of Scripture over and against aspects of church life and teaching that they believed were not in accord with the biblical witness (e.g., the practice of selling indulgences). Roman Catholic thought and teaching at the time of the Reformation saw Scripture to be under and judged by the teaching office of the Church. Thus, Lutherans relied on Scripture alone as the sole norm and rule for all faith.

In the centuries following the Reformation, these differing attitudes on the authority of Scripture continued to divide Lutherans and Catholics. But beginning in the late 1960s, with a renewed sense of the role of Scripture in theology, and following the ecumenical directives of Vatican II, Catholics were prepared to enter into dialogue with Lutherans, as Lutherans were also eager to engage in ecumenical conversation with Catholics. There was great hope that a common emphasis on Scripture would allow for an exploration of faith in new and exciting ways.

The joint study of Scripture has taken a prominent role as Catholics and Lutherans have tackled church-divisive issues. The results of shared biblical studies have made their way into all of the joint Lutheran–Catholic statements, usually appearing first in the statement, followed by perspectives from patristic, medieval, Reformation, and post-Reformation studies. In order and in content, as Tavard emphasizes, the Bible serves as a starting point as well as a continual point of reference for the conclusions that have been reached.

Biblical study in the Lutheran–Catholic dialogue is also prominent in the background papers that accompany the study, and uniquely in the work of a subsidiary task force that produced volumes providing the biblical foundations for the issues under study. The first of these volumes was *Peter in the New Testament* (1973), a collaborative study by Protestant and Roman Catholic biblical scholars on every passage in the NT related to Peter. *Peter in the New Testament* was utilized and summarized in *Papal Primacy and the Universal Church: Lutherans and Catholics in Dialogue V*. This critical assessment of the NT data allowed the dialogue team to see an orientation to a "Petrine function" in the NT (*Peter in the New Testament*, pp. 157–68). Such recognition of a Petrine function in the Christian Church, as Fitzmyer observes (in *Scripture: The Soul of Theology*, p. 109), is a worthy advance in ecumenism, especially in light of the debate about the role and function of the papacy in the church.

A second joint study, *Mary in the New Testament* (1978), was similar in format, treating all passages related to Mary in the NT. It provided the biblical data for *The One Mediator, the Saints, and Mary: Lutherans and Catholics in Dialogue VIII*. Once again, the results of the task force were summarized in the proceedings of the dialogue itself. At issue in the dialogue was the practice of intercession to Mary and the saints in relation to the One Mediator, Jesus Christ. Building upon the foundation of the biblical data, the dialogue emphasized Mary's role as a disciple of Jesus Christ, as well as the conviction that any mediation she provides is derived, originating from that of her Son, who is the one true mediator between God and humanity. Another important contribution of *Mary in the New Testament* to the ecumenical study of Mary was to determine that official Catholic teachings on Mary as well as popular devotion to her do not find their basis in the witness of Scripture (pp. 293–94).

Central in the relationship between Lutherans and Catholics has been the issue of justification by faith. For Lutherans, this biblical principle, based mainly in the Pauline writings, is the article of faith "by which the church stands or falls." Biblical material, then, played a major role in the discussions that led to

Justification by Faith: Lutherans and Catholics in Dialogue VII (1985). Unlike *Peter in the New Testament* and *Mary in the New Testament*, the biblical study was provided not by an ecumenical group of biblical scholars, but rather by one Lutheran biblical scholar on the dialogue team, John Reumann. In his book *Righteousness in the New Testament* (1982), Reumann had laid the groundwork for a common understanding of God's righteousness as God's gracious acquittal of the sinner, ascribing to him or her an effect of the passion and death of Jesus Christ. (See also Reumann and Fitzmyer, "Scripture as a Norm for Our Common Faith," p. 101.)

Justification by Faith: Lutherans and Catholics in Dialogue VII maintains that

> [r]ecent biblical scholarship sees the righteousness of which Paul speaks both as a gift from God, and, in some passages, as an attribute or quality of God, a power exercised on behalf of sinful humanity to save and justify (*heilsetzende macht*). This widespread consensus in the modern understanding of *dikaiosynē theou* ["the righteousness of God"], according to which it is an attribute, but also his power present to his gift, should help us go beyond the divisive issues of the sixteenth century. (p. 131)

This dialogue between Catholics and Lutherans on justification by faith shows remarkable consensus on a principle that has divided the church for centuries. The new methods and insights of biblical scholarship shed new light on the biblical understanding of justification and served in many ways as a starting point, a bridge, and an ending point in this important ecumenical dialogue. Furthermore, this *national* dialogue laid the groundwork for an *international* Catholic–Lutheran *Joint Declaration on the Doctrine of Justification* in 1999. That document reports on the substantive common understanding of a biblically informed doctrine of justification, as well as the distinctives of both and Lutherans and Catholics.

NEW DIRECTIONS

Ecumenical study of the Bible has been fruitful, particularly over the last century, and we can safely say that Jesus' followers from various traditions have made great strides toward the unity for which he prayed. There are, however, continued challenges, projects, and directions for the future of the Bible and ecumenism.

First, in the area of *biblical translation,* as Fitzmyer points out in his book, we are just beginning to work together as Catholics, Protestants, and Orthodox for the purpose of providing truly ecumenical translations of the Bible, particularly in the English language. The UBS has cooperated with the Roman Catholic Church, producing "Guiding Principles for Interconfessional Cooperation of the Bible" (rev. 1987), and joint translations continue to progress. Remarkable accomplishments include earlier translations coming from the joint efforts of Protestants and Catholics, such as *Traduction Oecumenique de la Bible* (French, 1988) and *Die Bible: Einheitsubersetzung der Heiligen Schrift, Altes und Neus Testament* (German, 1994).

The process of *ecumenical formation* is a new direction in the area of ecumenism in which the Bible plays a formative role. In *Ecumenical Formation: Ecumenical Reflections and Suggestions,* a study document produced in 1993 by the Joint Working Group between the Roman Catholic Church and the World Council of Churches, ecumenical formation is defined as "an ongoing process of learning within the various local churches and world communions, aimed at informing and guiding people in the movement which—inspired by the Holy Spirit—seeks the visible unity of Christians" (p. 6). For its part, the Roman Catholic Church developed a *Directory for Ecumenism* (originally in two parts: 1967 and 1970) and then a new directory (1993) that chronicled ecumenical achievements since the publication of the first. The text of 1993 is both descriptive and prescriptive, describing the work that has been done since Vatican II and prescribing how that work should continue. The *Directory* calls for continued cooperation in areas such as Bible study, spiritual formation, the creation of liturgical documents, and social and ethical action.

Even the new wealth of *feminist studies* has shown concern for the questions and issues related to the Bible and ecumenism. As early as 1980, in Amsterdam, the WCC took up the topic of "The Authority of Scripture in Light of the New Experiences of Women." Feminist scholars Melanie May and Lauree Hersch Meyer offer a poignant challenge to the subject in "The Unity of the Bible, Unity of the Church: Confessionalism, Ecumenism and Feminist Hermeneutics," in which they emphasize the confines of the written canonical text. They call for diversity in the word of God by looking and listening beyond what is written to a new "orality among all peoples whose voices have been silenced or stifled by our focus on written forms of the word of God" (p. 149). True to the feminist critique of Scripture, May and Hersch Meyer challenge their readers to look for God's word beyond the written, canonical text.

Finally, the *relationship between Scripture and Tradition* needs our continued attention in ecumenical discussions. *Sola Scriptura* will continue to serve as a Protestant contribution to ecumenical discourse, while sacred Tradition will continue to inform Catholic conversations. At the same time, Protestants may need to affirm more explicitly the value of Tradition (such as the early church fathers), as both Calvin and even Luther did, while Catholics may need to work at maintaining the renewed commitment to Scripture gained since Vatican II.

Perhaps Vatican II's designation of Scripture as the "*anima sacrae Theologiae*" (the "soul of sacred theology," *Dei Verbum,* 24) would be helpful for Protestants and Catholics alike to keep before them. Picking up on the importance of this designation of Scripture as the soul of theology, Fitzmyer, in his book with that phrase as the subtitle (pp. 56–72), suggests that Scripture serves as the soul in its literal and spiritual senses, as well as in its normative role in theology and church life.

CONCLUSION

In this overview of the Bible and ecumenism, we have noted and celebrated many instances in which the Bible has served as a starting point, a bridge, and an ending point in ecumenical discussion. We have taken a closer look at the Lutheran-Catholid dialogues of the past three decades, as an example of recent ecumenical endeavors. In reviewing the accomplishments of the past century, we have also begun to chart a course for the future of ecumenical biblical study. While it is an eschatological reality that the complete unity of Christ's followers is allusive on this side of the kingdom of God, Christians will be blessed for having traveled the road toward its fulfillment.

FOR FURTHER READING AND STUDY

Abott, Walter M., ed. *The Documents of Vatican II.* New York: Herder and Herder, 1966. A collection that includes *Dei Verbum* as well as the earlier *Divino Afflante Spiritu,* both promoting ecumenically sensitive Scripture study.

Anderson, H. George, T. Austin Murphy, and Joseph A. Burgess, eds. *Justification by Faith: Lutherans and Catholics in Dialogue VII.* Minneapolis: Augsburg, 1985. Report on dialogues dealing with one of the most neuralgic issues between Catholics and Protestants.

Anderson, H. George, J. Francis Stafford, and Joseph A. Burgess. *The One Mediator, the Saints, and Mary: Lutherans and Catholics in Dialogue VIII.* Minneapolis: Augsburg, 1992. Report on dialogues on the roles of Christ, Mary, and the saints.

Brown, Raymond E., Karl P. Donfried, and John Reumann, eds. *Peter in the New Testament: A Collaborative Assessment by Protestant and Roman Catholic Scholars.* New York: Paulist; Minneapolis: Augsburg, 1973. A joint study that sought to discover how the NT lays the background for the Petrine function within the life of the church.

Brown, Raymond E., Karl P. Donfried, Joseph A. Fitzmyer, and John Reumann, eds. *Mary in the New Testament: A Collaborative Assessment by Protestant and Roman Catholic Scholars.* New York: Paulist; Philadelphia: Fortress,

1978. A joint study of all passages of Marian import in the NT that laid the biblical foundation for *The One Mediator, the Saints, and Mary.*

Cann, Kathleen. "Bible Societies." Pages 112–14 in *Dictionary of the Ecumenical Movement.* Edited by N. Losseley et al. Geneva: WCC Publications, 2002. A survey of the development of Bible societies and their mission as their work became ecumenical.

Dietrich, Suzanne de. *God's Unfolding Purpose: A Guide to the Study of the Bible.* Philadelphia: Westminster, 1960. A classic work on the approaches and emphases of early ecumenical Bible study.

Dutton, Marsha. "One Faith, One Hope, One Baptism: Comments on the 1993 Roman Catholic Directory for Ecumenism." *Ecumenical Trends* 24 (October 1995): 139–48. A celebration and evaluation of the ecumenical efforts of Roman Catholics as they are chronicled in the *Directory for Ecumenism.*

Empie, Paul C., T. Austin Murphy, and Joseph A. Burgess, eds. *Teaching Authority and Infallibility in the Church: Lutherans and Catholics in Dialogue V.* Minneapolis: Augsburg, 1978. Reports on dialogue that dealt extensively with the role of the magisterium in church teaching.

Fitzmyer, Joseph A. *Scripture: The Soul of Theology.* New York: Paulist, 1994. A development of Vatican II's contention that Scripture serves as the soul of theology in its literal and spiritual senses, and a treatment of its normative role in theology and church life.

Joint Working Group between the Roman Catholic Church and the World Council of Churches. *Ecumenical Formation: Ecumenical Reflections and Suggestions.* Geneva: WCC Publications, 1993. A document defining ecumenical formation as an ongoing process of learning that seeks the visible unity of Christians.

Lutheran World Federation. *Joint Declaration on the Doctrine of Justification.* Grand Rapids: Eerdmans, 2000. A recent declaration between Lutherans and Roman Catholics worldwide that enumerates and celebrates common understandings of justification.

May, Melanie A., and Lauree Hersch Meyer. "The Unity of the Bible, Unity of the Church: Confessionalism, Ecumenism, and Feminist Hermeneutics." Pages 140–53 in *Searching the Scriptures: A Feminist Introduction;* vol. 1. E. Schüssler Fiorenza, ed. New York: Crossroad, 1993. A rare feminist critique of the church's ecumenical efforts at joint Bible study.

Reumann, John. *Righteousness in the New Testament: Justification in the United States Lutheran–Roman Catholic Dialogue.* Philadelphia: Fortress, 1982. The biblical groundwork for the dialogue team that produced the document *Justification by Faith: Lutherans and Catholics in Dialogue VII.*

Reumann, John, and Joseph A. Fitzmyer. "Scripture as a Norm for Our Common Faith." *Journal of Ecumenical Studies* 30 (1993): 81–107. Reflections upon the authors' ecumenical experiences of the role of Scripture in ecumenical dialogue.

Rusch, William G. ed. *A Commentary on "Ecumenism: The Vision of the ELCA."* Minneapolis: Augsburg, 1990. An outline of ecumenical goals for the Evangelical Lutheran Church in America.

Tavard, George. "The Bible in Ecumenism." *One In Christ* 32 (1996): 310–22. Reflections on the importance of Scripture as a starting point, a bridge, and an ending point in ecumenical discussion.

Weber, Hans-Ruedi. "The Bible: Its Role in the Ecumenical Movement." Pages 108–12 in *Dictionary of the Ecumenical Movement.* Edited by N. Losseley et al. Geneva: WCC Publications, 2002. A brief overview of how the Bible has functioned throughout the ecumenical movement.

Glossary

Chapters in parentheses indicate the principal chapter(s) in which the term is considered, thus making this glossary a sort of general index, with links to chapters rather than pages. A full subject index begins on page 281.

Alexandrian school an early Christian school of biblical interpretation emphasizing allegorical exegesis (ch. 8)

allegorical interpretation a method of interpreting texts in which characters and events are assigned a symbolic significance in addition to, or instead of, their literal meaning (ch. 8)

allegory a text deemed to have symbolic meaning expressed in its characters and events (ch. 8)

anagogical sense see **senses of Scripture**

Ancestral Period also known as the Patriarchal Period, the time from Abraham and Sarah to Moses (chs. 2, 3)

Ancient Near East ancient Mesopotamia (the land between the Tigris and Euphrates Rivers), Egypt, and Israel (ch. 2)

Antiochene school an early Christian school of biblical interpretation emphasizing literal exegesis (ch. 8)

apocalypse Greek for "revelation," referring to a genre of Jewish and Christian literature filled with symbolism and records of revelations about unseen realities and/or the future (chs. 1, 3, 4, 5)

apocalyptic shorthand term for a world view ("apocalypticism") and its literature ("apocalyptic literature") that reflect a dualistic belief in good and evil cosmic powers as well as successive chronological ages of evil/sin and justice/peace (chs. 3, 4, 15) *apocrypha* from the Greek adjective meaning "hidden," a term applied since 1520 (sometimes also "OT Apocrypha"), especially by non-Catholics, to the books of the Greek OT (Septuagint) not included in the Hebrew canon or the Protestant canon but included in the Catholic and/or Orthodox canons; see also *deuterocanonical;* also refers to certain early Christian writings not included in the NT (usually "NT Apocrypha") (chs. 1, 3, 5, 6)

apology an account of or defense for one's religious convictions and/or practices (chs. 5, 8)

Aramaic the language that gradually replaced spoken Hebrew after the Babylonian exile (587/6–539 B.C.E.) and was thus the language of some later parts of the OT and of Jesus (chs. 1, 6)

Authorized Version (AV) the English translation of the Bible published in 1611 in England during the reign of King James I, known popularly as the King James Version (KJV) or King James Bible (ch. 7)

AV abbreviation for the Authorized Version (ch. 7)

Babylonian exile the period (587/6–539 B.C.E.) in which many of the people of Judah were deported to Babylon and lived there as exiles, also known as the Babylonian captivity (chs. 2, 3, 13)

Bible from the Greek word for book, *biblion* (pl. *biblia*), referring to the sacred writings of Judaism and Christianity; see also *Scripture* (chs. 1, 6, 7)

B.C.E. "before the Common Era," a scholarly alternative to the traditional "B.C." ("Before Christ"); see also *C.E.* (ch. 1)

biblical criticism the application to biblical texts of the standard methods of investigation and norms for truth used with other historical documents (ch. 9)

bilateral dialogues ecumenical discussion between two, rather than among three or more, Christian traditions (e.g., Catholics and Lutherans) (ch. 16)

Book of the Twelve see *Minor Prophets*

canon an official list of "Scriptures" (authoritative writings) that the Jewish and/or Christian communities consider inspired and authoritative for their faith and practice (chs. 1, 3, 4, 5, 6)

canon within the canon the concept of the existence of books that play a more central role within the formal canon, or of a central, governing theme or principle (such as "justification by faith" or "liberation) that functions as a means of determining the value, meaning, or authority of the biblical canon as a whole or its various parts (chs. 6, 8, 11)

Catholic Epistles (Letters) the non-Pauline letters of the NT, so-called because of their alleged universal or "catholic" audience, sometimes excluding Hebrews and/or 1–3 John; also called the General Letters/Epistles (ch. 4)

C.E. "Common Era" (i.e., the shared Christian and Jewish era), a scholarly alternative to the traditional "A.D." (*Anno Domini,* "in the year of our Lord"); see also ***Common Era*** and *B.C.E.* (ch. 1)

codex (pl. ***codices***) originally, writing tablets framed in wood (Latin *caudex*); later, a set of individual sheets of papyrus or parchment joined at one side and protected by a leather or wooden cover (chs. 1, 6, 7)

Common Era the common period and calendar Jews and Christians share beginning with the appearance of Jesus and the early church; see also *B.C.E.* and *C.E.* (chap 1)

concordance an alphabetical list of words in a corpus of literature (esp. the Bible), with their reference, or textual location (e.g., Gen 1:1) (ch. 1)

Conquest, the see ***Settlement, the***

covenant originally, a contract specifying mutual benefits and obligations between the contracting parties; one of the major theological terms for describing the relationship of God with Israel and all humankind (ch. 1)

critical apparatus a series of footnotes in the critical Greek or Hebrew text of the Bible giving evidence from manuscripts and other ancient sources that (a) both supports and challenges parts of the biblical text printed above and (b) provides alternative readings for disputed texts (ch. 7)

critical text a scholarly reconstruction of the biblical text based on textual-critical evidence indicating the most original reading of the text (for the OT: the uncorrected Masoretic Text, with critical notes; for the NT: a reconstruction based on numerous manuscripts) (ch. 7)

D abbreviation for the book of Deuteronomy, understood as one of the four written sources of the Pentateuch and representing the style and theology that existed in the reign and reform of King Josiah during the latter part of the seventh century B.C.E. (chs. 3, 9)

Dead Sea Scrolls (***DSS***) a series of more than 800 ancient Hebrew and Aramaic manuscripts (and some Greek fragments) of biblical and extrabiblical writings, dating from the third century B.C.E. to the first century C.E., and discovered in eleven caves near the Dead Sea between 1947 and 1956 (ch. 5)

Decalogue from the Greek for "ten words," referring to the Ten Commandments (chs. 3, 15)

Deism a belief system in which God is understood as involved in the initial creation of the universe but not in its ongoing existence (ch. 10)

deuterocanonical referring to a "second canon," a Roman Catholic designation for the seven books (plus additional portions of Esther and Daniel) from the Septuagint, not found in the Hebrew canon or in Jerome's Latin Vulgate but included in the Catholic (and Orthodox) canon; see also **apocrypha** (chs. 1, 3, 5, 6, 7)

Deutero-Isaiah see **Second Isaiah** (ch. 3)

Deuteronomist Historian the author or authors of the Deuteronomistic History (ch. 3)

Deuteronomistic History the historical account of ancient Israel recorded in Joshua–2 Kings (ch. 3)

deuteropauline letters a term (abbreviated as "the deuteropaulines") used for a group of six letters (2 Thessalonians, Colossians, Ephesians, 1–2 Timothy, Titus) by those who deem the letters' claims to authorship by Paul to be inauthentic; known more neutrally as the "disputed" or "contested" letters" (ch. 4)

Diaspora literally "dispersion," referring to Jewish communities living outside Palestine and also to Africans living outside Africa (chs. 2, 6, 13)

Divided Monarchy the period of Israel's history (922–721 B.C.E.) following Solomon in which a unified nation became two entities, Israel in the north and Judah in the south (ch. 2)

Documentary Hypothesis the theory first espoused by Julius Wellhausen that advocated that the Pentateuch was comprised of four distinct written sources; see **J, E, D,** and **P** (chs. 3, 9)

E abbreviation for the Elohist source, named for its use of the Hebrew word *Elohim* for God, and understood as one of the four written sources of the Pentateuch, reflecting a period somewhere around the eighth century B.C.E. when the Israelite monarchy was well established and still united (chs. 3, 9)

early Judaism see **Second Temple Judaism**

ecumenism the search for and practice of Christian unity (ch. 16)

eisegesis the act of "reading into" the text a meaning that is imposed upon it, in contrast to **exegesis** (ch. 12)

encyclical a circular letter that popes of the Roman Catholic Church write to address matters of faith and morals (ch. 12)

Enlightenment, the the period of European intellectual history (also known as "The Age of Reason") in the late seventeenth and the eighteenth centuries when human reason was cultivated and applied to traditional teachings, including religious claims, texts, and authoritative teaching (chs. 9, 10)

eschatology the doctrine or study of the "last things" (ch. 4)

etiology a narrative that explains the origin of something (ch. 3)

evangelical referring to Christian (usually Protestant) individuals and bodies characterized over the last century by (1) gradual and cautious acceptance of biblical criticism; (2) moderate to conservative theological, social, and political agendas; and (3) interdenominational cooperation primarily with Christians of similar conviction (ch. 11)

evangelist from the Greek word for "good news," *euangelion,* referring generally to a Christian preacher or missionary, or more specifically to a writer of a canonical gospel (Matthew, Mark, etc.) (ch. 4)

exegesis the careful literary, historical, and/or theological analysis and interpretation of a text; contrast ***eisegesis*** (ch. 8)

exile see ***Babylonian exile***

exodus the foundational event of the people Israel (probably ca. 1250–1240 B.C.E.) in which, according to the biblical accounts, Moses led the people out of Egypt (chs. 2, 13)

extracanonical see ***noncanonical***

feminist interpretation a term descriptive of two different but related interpretive strategies: (1) through rigorous historical investigations, documenting and describing the lives of women in the biblical period; and (2) bringing various contemporary feminist concerns to bear on the practice of biblical interpretation (chs. 9, 10, 16)

Fertile Crescent the area of arable land stretching from the Nile Valley at the southeast coast of the Mediterranean Sea to the Persian Gulf (ch. 2)

figural interpretation the use of a variety of techniques (including but not limited to ***allegory, typology,*** and mystical interpretation), to advance and extend the literal or conventional interpretations of biblical texts (ch. 10)

First Isaiah a designation for Isa 1–39, the book of the eighth-century prophet Isaiah of Jerusalem (ch. 3)

First Testament an alternative name for the Christian ***Old Testament*** (ch. 1)

form criticism the study of different forms of (especially preliterary) communication, their setting and function, and the stages in the evolution and transmission of various forms (ch. 9)

Former Prophets the historical books in the **Nevi'im** ("Prophets"), including Joshua, Judges, 1–2 Samuel, and 1–2 Kings; see **Prophets** (ch. 3)

fourfold exegesis see **senses of Scripture**

Four-Source Theory the scholarly theory that Matthew and Luke each used two main sources, Mark and Q, to which each added unique material, labeled M (Matthew's special material) and L (Luke's special material) (chs. 4, 9)

full communion generally, mutual recognition of sacraments (with emphasis on "communion"/the Eucharist) and ministerial offices by two or more Christian traditions (e.g., Lutheran and Episcopalian)

fundamentalist referring to individuals and churches (usually Protestant) characterized by (1) adherence to the so-called fundamentals of Christian doctrine (virgin birth, verbal inspiration and inerrancy of the Bible, etc.); (2) general rejection of biblical criticism and adherence to very "literal" interpretations; (3) support for very conservative theological, social, and political agendas; and (4) a separatist approach to much intra-church cooperation (chs. 11, 12)

Gemara Jewish rabbinic commentary on the **Mishna** produced from ca. 200 until the publication of the combined Mishna and Gemara in the two versions of the **Talmud** (ch. 8)

General Epistles see **Catholic Epistles (Letters)**

genre literary type or classification, such as historical narrative or apocalypse (chs. 1, 9)

gloss an interpretive comment, written between the lines or in the margins of biblical texts and sometimes, in the early medieval period, extracted and compiled into books (ch. 8)

gospel/Gospel "good news," referring both to the salvific message about Jesus preached by his followers ("gospel") and to interpretive narratives of his appearance, ministry, death, and resurrection (the "Gospels") (chap. 4)

Greek the lingua franca (common tongue) of the Mediterranean Basin following the conquests of Alexander the Great, and hence the language of both the Septuagint and the New Testament (ch. 1)

haggadah a Jewish method of detailed interpretation of Biblical narratives, usually drawing a moral from the story (ch. 8) *halakah* a Jewish interpretive practice of deriving concrete regulations governing individual behavior and social practices from Scripture (ch. 8)

Hasmonean referring to the second-century B.C.E. family of the Jewish priest Mattathias and the subsequent dynasty and period of independence in Jewish history (ch. 2)

Hebrew the primary language of the Tanakh or Old Testament (ch. 1)

Hebrew Bible an alternative designation for the Tanakh or Old Testament (chs. 1, 3)

Hebrews The ancestors of the Israelite nation (Abraham and Sarah to Moses) (chs. 2, 3)

Hellenism Greek culture, especially as it was spread beyond Greece by Alexander the Great and his heirs (ch. 2)

Hellenistic Period the period of Greek cultural influence throughout the Mediterranean basin, beginning with Alexander the Great ca. 333 B.C.E. (ch. 2)

heresy religious belief understood to be outside the pale of acceptable ideas (chs. 4, 6)

hermeneutic (sing.) a general interpretive theory, approach, or strategy; *hermeneutics* (pl.) the art and principles of interpretation (ch. 11)

hermeneutic of suspicion a sort of "guilty-until-proven-innocent" approach to the biblical text because of its alleged patriarchal, oppressive, or otherwise problematic nature and/or influence (chs. 11, 14)

hermeneutic of trust in contrast to a *hermeneutic of suspicion,* an approach to the Bible characterized by trust in its ability to be a place of encountering God and the divine word (chs. 11, 14)

Herodian period the period 37 B.C.E.–66 C.E., a kind of "sub-era" of the Roman Period in Palestine, when the Herodian rulers from Herod the Great to his great-grandson (Herod) Agrippa II reigned (ch. 2)

heterodoxy "different belief," in contrast to "orthodoxy" (right belief) and normally meaning *heresy* (ch. 4)

Hexateuch "six scrolls"; the first six books of the Bible, Genesis–Joshua (ch. 3)

historical-critical method the modern approach to biblical texts that attempts to trace their historical origins, development, and meaning (ch. 9)

historical criticism judgments about texts based on their historical setting and the meanings possible in that setting (ch. 9) *homily* a short, liturgically centered sermon (chs. 4, 12)

hypostatic union the union of the divine and human natures in the one *hypostasis*, or "person," of Jesus Christ, formulated by Cyril of Alexandria (d. 444) and accepted by the Church at the Council of Chalcedon in 451 (ch. 8)

ideological interpretation sometimes also known as political interpretation, a term descriptive of two different interpretive practices: (1) uncovering the ideological interests of those who composed and edited biblical materials; and (2) bringing one's own ideological interests and agendas to the task of biblical interpretation (ch. 10)

inerrancy the quality of being without error, usually used to mean Scripture's alleged lack of any sort of error, including historical and scientific (sometimes called "verbal inerrancy"), or (less often) its lack of religious/theological error (chs. 11, 12)

Israel the "promised land" of the Hebrew Bible, referring in biblical texts to both a geographical region and the nation/people residing there (the precise contours varying from era to era) (chs. 2, 3)

Israelites the people of God from Moses to the exile (chs. 2, 3)

J abbreviation for the Yahwist (German "Jahwist") source, named for its use of the Hebrew word *YHWH* (*Yahweh*), and understood as one of the four written sources of the Pentateuch, reflecting the early period of the ancient Israelite monarchy, perhaps sometime during the tenth or ninth century B.C.E. (chs. 3, 9)

Jews a word derived from the Hebrew term for Judeans, referring to the descendents of the Israelites after the exile, in distinction from the *Israelites* (chs. 2, 3, 5, 6, 8)

Judaism the beliefs and practices of Jews ("Judahites," or people of Judah) during and after the period of the Second Temple; see also *Second Temple Judaism* (ch. 2)

Kethuvim Hebrew for "Writings," the third major division of the Jewish Scriptures (chs. 1, 3, 6)

Latter Prophets the three major Old Testament writing prophets (Isaiah, Jeremiah, Ezekiel), plus the *Book of the Twelve (Minor Prophets)* (ch. 3)

lectio divina prayerful meditation on Scripture, usually consisting of several steps, including at least: reading of a passage, meditation on it, a prayer in response to it, and resolution to some action because of it (chs. 12, 14)

lectionary a collection of excerpts from all parts of the Bible, organized around a liturgical calendar for use in public liturgy/worship (chs. 6, 11, 12)

liberationist interpretation (or **hermeneutics**) approaches to biblical interpretation that focus on themes of liberation in the Bible (e.g., the exodus) and their contemporary significance; see also **feminist interpretation** (chs. 9, 10)

literal sense see **senses of Scripture**

literary criticism the analysis of a text with respect to its literary aspects, including characterization, plot, etc. (ch. 9)

Liturgy of the Hours an ancient monastic practice, now required of all Catholic bishops, priests, and deacons, of daily recitation of psalms and readings from Scripture, supplemented by other spiritual readings, throughout each day in accord with the liturgical seasons of the church year (ch. 12)

LXX abbreviation for **Septuagint**

magisterium the teaching office of the Roman Catholic Church, charged with the official interpretation of both Scripture and Tradition in matters of faith and morals (chs. 12, 16)

mainline churches Protestant churches and traditions characterized by (1) general acceptance of biblical criticism; (2) moderate to liberal theological, social, and political agendas; and (3) ecumenical dialogue and cooperation with similar bodies and with mainstream Roman Catholicism and Orthodoxy (ch. 11)

Marxist interpretation a term descriptive of two different interpretive practices: (1) uncovering the material interests and social location of those who composed and edited biblical materials; and (2) taking into consideration the material conditions of modern biblical interpretation and the social location of modern interpreters, often mixed with a Marxist/materialist interpretive agenda (ch. 10)

Masoretic (or **Massoretic**) **Text** (abbr. **MT**) the standard edition of the Hebrew text of the OT, referring to the "Masoretes," Jewish scholars in the first millennium C.E. who handed on the consonantal Hebrew text and inserted vowel marks (chs. 5, 6, 8)

Mediterranean Basin the lands surrounding the Mediterranean Sea—Asia, Africa and Europe—where Greco-Roman cultures thrived in antiquity (ch. 2)

Megilloth Hebrew for "scrolls," referring to a collection of five scrolls in the **Writings:** Ruth, the Song of Songs, Ecclesiastes, Lamentations, and Esther (ch. 3) *midrash* from the Hebrew for "search, inquire," referring to the interpretation of texts, especially by the Rabbis, of which there were two main types, *halakah* and *haggadah* (ch. 8)

millennialism belief in a literal, future time of peace on earth lasting 1,000 years, as suggested by Rev 20 (ch. 5)

Minor Prophets also called the *Book of the Twelve,* including Hosea, Joel, Amos, Obadiah, Jonah, Micah, Nahum, Habakkuk, Zephaniah, Haggai, Zechariah, Malachi; see also *Prophets* (ch. 3)

Mishna the written compilation of oral Jewish rabbinical teachings prepared near the end of the *Tannaitic* period, ca. 200 C.E. (ch. 8)

moral sense see *senses of Scripture*

MT   abbreviation for *Masoretic Text*

Nevi'im Hebrew for "Prophets," the second major division of the Jewish Scriptures (chs. 1, 3)

New Testament (NT) the second part of the Christian Bible, presenting the new testament (covenant) in Christ (chs. 1, 4)

noncanonical referring to important religious texts in early Judaism and Christianity that are not included in their canons; also called *parabiblical,* literally, "surrounding the Bible," or *extracanonical* (ch. 5)

Old Testament (OT) the first part of the Christian Bible, corresponding (more or less) to the Jewish Scriptures, or *Tanakh* (chs. 1, 3)

P the Priestly source for the Pentateuch, considered to be its latest strand, reflecting a postexilic period in the fifth century B.C.E. or later and attentive to matters such as liturgy, ritual, and sacrifice (chs. 3, 9)

Palestine the name of the territory from the Mediterranean Sea to the Jordan Valley and from Galilee to the Negev, deriving from the Hebrew word for "land of the Philistines" and dating from the fifth century B.C.E. (ch. 2)

papyrus a marshland plant found predominantly in Egypt that could be dried and matted to form a writing surface, then glued together to form a scroll (ch. 1)

parabiblical see *noncanonical*

parallelism the "thought rhyme" typical of ancient Hebrew and Jewish poetry (ch. 1) *parchment* writing material prepared from animal skins, which could be used to provide more durable manuscripts than those made from papyrus (ch. 1)

Parousia Greek for "coming" or "appearance," used in the NT and in theological discourse to refer to the eschatological appearance, or "second coming," of Jesus (ch. 4)

Pastoral Epistles three of the Pauline letters, 1–2 Timothy and Titus, ostensibly written by the apostle to his younger colleagues Timothy and Titus (ch. 4)

Pentateuch "five scrolls," the first five books of the Bible (Genesis–Deuteronomy), also referred to as *Torah* (ch. 3)

pericope a passage or short unit of the biblical text, usually of a gospel (ch. 9)

pesher an ancient Jewish method of interpretation with the goal of commenting on the contemporary age by means of a line-by-line exposition of Scripture (ch. 8)

polyvalence the quality of possessing multiple meanings or possible interpretations (ch. 11)

postmodernism the intellectual ethos of contemporary culture that questions objectivity, universal values, and "master narratives" while stressing participatory knowledge (chs. 9, 10)

Prophets designated *Nevi'im* in Hebrew, the second division of the Jewish Scriptures that includes the *Former Prophets* and the *Latter* (writing) *Prophets* (ch. 3)

protocanonical referring to the "first" canon, a designation for the thirty-nine (twenty-four as enumerated in the Jewish tradition) books of the OT or Jewish canon recognized by all Christian traditions; see also *deuterocanonical* (ch. 3)

pseudepigrapha (sing. *pseudepigraphon*) writings with falsely attributed (historically inaccurate) titles or superscriptions; ancient Jewish books purporting to emanate from a biblical character (chs. 1, 5)

pseudonymous descriptive term for writings attributed to writers (usually of an earlier era) who are not the actual authors (chs. 4, 5)

Q abbreviation of the German word *Quelle*, "source," used to designate the material (which may or may not have been an actual document) common to Matthew and Luke but absent from Mark (chs. 4, 9)

reader-response criticism the analysis of texts with respect to their real or anticipated impact on readers (ch. 9)

redaction criticism analysis of the interests of an author or text seen in the collecting, arranging, and editing of sources and in the composing of new material, esp. in the Synoptic gospels (ch. 9)

regula fidei Latin for ***Rule of Faith*** (chs. 6, 8, 10)

rhetoric the art of persuasive speech (chs. 4, 9)

rhetorical criticism the analysis of rhetorical forms and strategies in texts (ch. 9)

Roman Curia the administrative structure of the Vatican, divided into congregations (technically called "dicasteries") that oversee various departmental areas of responsibility (ch. 12)

Roman Empire the military, political, and legislative entity that grew out of the Roman Republic and began with the establishment of the first emperor, Octavian, in 27 B.C.E. (ch. 2)

Rule of Faith (sometimes also referred to as the "Rule of Truth"; Latin ***regula fidei***) a summary account of the whole of the apostolic faith, formally represented in the Apostles Creed (and similar texts) and serving as a theological framework or standard of orthodoxy (chs. 6, 8, 10)

saga a literary genre commonly found in the book of Genesis: a lengthy narrative that consists of shorter episodic stories (ch. 3)

Scripture from the Latin for "writings" (*scriptura*), referring to sacred writings, especially those of Judaism and Christianity; see also ***Bible*** (ch. 1)

scroll a roll of ***papyrus*** sheets glued together, or of ***parchment*** sewn together to form a roll containing (especially sacred) texts (ch. 1)

Second Isaiah also known as Deutero-Isaiah, a designation for Isa 40–55, generally believed to be written during the exile, rather than by the eighth-century prophet Isaiah of Jerusalem (ch. 3)

second naïveté the openness to a text characteristic of those who have moved from an innocent, uninformed "first naïveté" through the "critical distance" created by analytical, rational study to a place from which one can "hear again" (ch. 14)

Second Temple Judaism the (richly varied) Judaism of the Second Temple period, ca. 536 B.C.E.–70 C.E., also known as early Judaism (chs. 2, 5, 6)

Second Testament an alternative name for the ***New Testament*** (ch. 1)

senses of Scripture the levels or aspects of meaning in a biblical text first posited by early Christian writers and incorporated into an interpretive approach called fourfold exegesis: (1) the historical (or literal) sense; (2) the tropological (or moral) sense; (3) the spiritual or *allegorical* (doctrinal) sense; and (4) the anagogical sense (referring to the afterlife) (ch. 8)

sensus plenior Latin for "fuller sense" or "deeper sense," a modern term used especially by some Catholic scholars to describe the multiple meanings of the words of Scripture beyond the literal and spiritual senses; see also *surplus of meaning* (ch. 12)

Septuagint (*LXX*) the traditional name for the oldest Greek translation of the OT (probably originating at Alexandria in Egypt in the third century B.C.E.), originally applied only to the first five books of the Bible (the Greek Pentateuch), but ordinarily designating the entire OT (chs. 1, 3, 6, 7)

Settlement, the the arrival of Israelites in Palestine toward the end of the thirteenth century B.C.E.; based on the book of Joshua, also known as the *Conquest* (chs. 2, 3)

Sitz im Leben German for "life setting"; a technical term for the kind of social setting in which a specific passage or literary genre took shape (chs. 3, 9)

social-scientific criticism the application of methods of social analysis to the study of biblical texts and the communities that produced and received them (ch. 9)

sola Scriptura the Protestant Reformation principle of "Scripture alone" as the authority for Christian faith and practice (chs. 6, 8, 11, 12, 16)

source criticism the analysis of possible written sources in existing texts (ch. 9)

spiritual sense see *senses of Scripture*

surplus of meaning the quality of a text's having a multiplicity of meanings even beyond that intended by the author or understood by the original audience (ch. 11)

Synoptic Gospels also called the "Synoptics," the three canonical gospels (Matthew, Mark, and Luke) that share a similar perspective (synoptic: "seeing together") on the life and teaching of Jesus (ch. 4)

Synoptic Problem the scholarly conundrum of accounting for the similarities and differences among the *Synoptic Gospels,* including which gospel was written first and how the gospels and their supposed sources are interrelated (chs. 4, 9)

Talmud the compilation of the Jewish *Mishna* and the *Gemara,* which appeared in two editions, the Palestinian (ca. 450 C.E.) and the Babylonian (ca. 550 C.E.), constituting the authoritative version of the "Oral Torah" (chs. 6, 8)

Tanakh (also **Tanak**) a word meaning the Jewish Scriptures, originating from the first Hebrew letter (T, N, K) of each of the three divisions (chs. 1, 3, 6)

Tanna'im (adj. **Tannaitic**) the Jewish rabbinical scholars active before about 200 C.E. (ch. 8)

Targum (pl. **Targumim**) an Aramaic translation/interpretation of Scripture (chs. 6, 8)

testament the term from a Latin word (*testamentum*) that can mean "covenant" and referring to the two divisions (Old Testament, New Testament) of the Christian Bible (ch. 1)

Tetrateuch "four scrolls," the first four books of the Bible, Genesis–Numbers (ch. 3)

textual criticism the scholarly discipline that seeks to reconstruct the earliest form of a text and to trace its subsequent evolution and transmission (chs. 7, 9)

theocracy literally, "rule by God," a religiously based government (ch. 8)

theological interpretation the practice of bringing theological concerns to bear on the interpretation of Scripture with the goal of enhancing faithful living and worshipping before God (ch. 10)

Third Isaiah also "Trito-Isaiah," a designation for Isa 56–66, generally believed to be written after the exile, rather than by the eighth-century prophet Isaiah of Jerusalem (ch. 3)

Torah Hebrew for "law" or (better) "tradition," the Jewish designation for the first five books of the Bible (Christian OT), Genesis–Deuteronomy; see also **Pentateuch** (chs. 1, 3)

tradition criticism the application of **redaction criticism** to OT studies (ch. 9)

Trito-Isaiah see **Third Isaiah**

tropological sense see **senses of Scripture**

Two-Source Theory the scholarly theory that Matthew and Luke each used two main sources, Mark and Q; see also **Four-Source Theory** (chs. 4, 9)

typological exegesis; typology an interpretive approach that sees later or contemporary events and figures (the "antitype") foreshadowed in ancient events and figures (the "type") (ch. 8)

United Monarchy the period of a unified Israel under the kings Saul, David, and Solomon (1020–922 B.C.E.) (ch. 2)

verbal inerrancy see **inerrancy**

version a translation of the Bible (ch. 7)

Vulgate the Latin translation of the whole Bible prepared from 382 to 405 by Jerome of Bethlehem (d. 420), drawing on Hebrew and Greek manuscripts and following the Hebrew canon, with the addition of Tobit and Judith from the wider list present in the Septuagint (chs. 1, 7)

Writings designated *Kethuvim* in Hebrew, the third division of the Jewish canon, including Psalms, Proverbs, Job, Song of Songs, Ruth, Lamentations, Ecclesiastes, Esther, Daniel, Ezra, Nehemiah, and 1–2 Chronicles (chs. 1, 3)

Yahweh/YHWH the name of Israel's God, related to the Hebrew verb "to be" (chs. 2, 3)

Subject Index

letters, New Testament, 71, 79–87, 199.
See also under Paul (apostle)
liberationist interpretation, 148, 159–60,
167–68, 185–86, 187, 204, 217, 220,
221–22, 224, 225, 231
African-American, 204, 217, 220,
221–22, 224, 225
feminist (see feminist interpretation)
Lindsey, Hal, 190
literal sense, 136, 139, 141, 171–72, 174,
201
literary criticism, 148, 155, 157, 158, 190,
211
liturgy
Orthodox, 210, 211, 212
Roman Catholic, 8n.6, 198, 199
Liturgy of the Hours, 198
Luther, Martin, 114, 127, 143, 177, 179,
185, 186, 258
Lutheran churches, and Roman Catholic
Church, 254, 258–60
LXX. See Septuagint

M, 74, 76, 150
Maccabean period, 35, 41, 44, 66, 67–68,
104, 108
macro-stories, 221–24
magisterium, Roman Catholic, 202, 254,
257
Maimonides, 142
mainline churches, 154, 177–78, 181, 183,
186, 188, 190, 199n.4, 203, 209, 211
manuscripts, biblical, 5, 17, 46, 47, 55n.6,
68, 75n.4, 85n.7, 105, 108, 109, 111,
112, 113, 120–24, 148, 159
Marcion, 112, 115, 135
Marxist interpretation, 167–68, 174
Mary (mother of Jesus), 259
Masoretic Text, 106, 121–22, 123, 124,
129, 142
Mass, Roman Catholic, 8n.6, 198, 199
medieval biblical interpretation, 138–42,
201, 204, 235
meditation, 235
Mediterranean Basin, 23, 25–27, 29, 168
megachurches, 178n.1
Megilloth. See under scrolls
Melanchthon, Philipp, 81, 127
Middle Passage, 223
midrash, 133–34
militarism, 181
millennialism, 99
Minor Prophets. See Book of the Twelve

Mishna, 134
modern biblical interpretation, 147–55,
163–67
Modernist crisis, 198
modernity, 147, 165, 178n.1, 202
Monarchy, 6n.2, 32–33, 49n.5, 50, 52, 53,
66
Divided, 33, 54, 59, 172–73
United, 32–33, 40, 52, 53
moral sense, 136, 139
Mulholland, M. Robert, 236
Muratorian canon, 97, 113
Murphy, Roland E., 199
music, as biblical interpretation, 218, 221,
222

narrative, biblical, 19, 47–48, 60, 62–63,
134, 135, 136, 150, 151, 152, 153, 154,
158, 164, 165, 189, 217, 219, 231, 235,
246
narrative criticism, 158, 200, 204, 209
nationalism, 181, 184, 189
Nevi'im. See Prophets
New Testament, 7
books of, 71–89
canon of, 71, 97, 98–99, 109–14
names for, 7, 9–10
unity in diversity of, 88–89
Nicholas of Lyra, 141, 143
noncanonical books, 92–100, 109, 166

Old Testament, 7, 45–68
books of, 45–68
canon of, 11–15, 46–47, 104–109
names for, 7, 8–10, 45n.1
New Testament interpretation of, 9–10,
68, 72, 77, 80, 89, 135n.1, 171
oral tradition, 46, 50, 73, 119–21, 133, 234
Origen, 85, 113, 136–37, 138, 139, 210,
229
Orthodox churches, 178n.1, 206–12
and historical-critical method, 209
biblical interpretation in, 195, 206–12
and Protestantism, 208, 211, 212
and Roman Catholicism, 209–11,
212
challenges, 211–12
distinctives, 209–10
canon of, 11n.9, 14, 46, 67, 71n.1,
87n.8, 92n.2, 113, 208–9
Tradition and Scripture in, 207, 208,
210